AIN'T IT COOL?

AIN'T IT COOL?

Kicking Hollywood's Butt

Harry Knowles

with Paul Cullum and Mark Ebner
Foreword by Quentin Tarantino

B◼XTREE

First published as *Ain't It Cool? Hollywood's Redheaded Stepchild Speaks Out* 2002
in the USA by Warner Books, Inc., New York

This edition published 2002 by
Boxtree
an imprint of Pan Macmillan Ltd
Pan Macmillan, 20 New Wharf Road, London N1 9RR
Basingstoke and Oxford
Associated companies throughout the world
www.panmacmillan.com

ISBN 0 7522 6497 4

1 3 5 7 9 10 8 6 4 2

A CIP catalogue record for this book is available from the British Library

Printed and bound in Great Britain by Mackays of Chatham plc, Kent

Book design by H. Roberts Design

To Father Geek, Mother Time, and Forry

ACKNOWLEDGMENTS

L et's see...

Rebecca Rivkin and Eric Vespe for their tireless transcribing duties. Drew McWeeny, Paul Alvarado-Dykstra, David Alvarado, Kevin Biegel, and Jay Knowles for their wonderful help in keeping AICN running smoothly while the process of creating this book came to pass. D. Campbell MacKinlay for turning me into a cartoon. Jay and Mildred Knowles for being the best grandparents in the world. My sister, Dannie Knowles, for making me a big brother. Hollywood for being the wonderful complicated headache and continual orgasm that continues to enthrall and enrage me. Forrest J. Ackerman for being everything I would hope to one day be. Roger Ebert for taking a punk kid like me under his wing and pushing me into the center ring. Robert Rodriguez, Guillermo del Toro, and Paul Dini for sharing a bit of their world with mine and helping me to understand in a greater sense how it gets from one mind to all the rest. Quentin Tarantino for making unabashed love for film cool. Ray Harryhausen for my imagination. Betty Boop for my perception of reality. Willie May for making me realize that food was great and being fat was the price you pay for taste. Rylan Bosher, Roland Dirk Denoie, and Josh O'Quinn for being the best childhood friends around. Robert Vasquez, Edward Shelton, and Paul Hart for being those best friends in the high school years. Mrs. Brister for being my high school English teacher who pushed me to find my own voice in writing. Ms. Brown for teaching me about theater and extemporaneous thought. Robert Magnussan, Bobby Morehead, Walter S. Falk III, Randy Eckels, Roland Denoie Sr., Randy Alamon, David Johnson, Roy Banario, Willie Patterson, Charlie Rose, and Gail Barchus for opening and contributing to my mind. Bill Palmer for making me a Sorceror's Apprentice for real. William Gaines, Jack Kirby, Stan Lee, Tex Avery, Max Fleischer, Willis O'Brien, Roger Corman, Michael Curtiz, Stanley Donen, James Whale, Alfred Hitchcock, Preston Sturges, Stanley Kubrick, Howard Hawks, John Ford, Steven Spielberg, George Lucas, Roger Vadim, Gilbert Shelton, Robert Crumb, Jack Jaxon, Robert Clampett, Chuck Jones, Ray Bradbury, William Burroughs, Edgar Rice Burroughs, Jules Verne, H. G. Wells, Orson Welles, Frank Capra, Jack Pierce, Rick Baker, Tom Savini, Phil Tippett, Douglas Trumbull, Stan Winston, Paul Blaisdell, George Pal, Wah Chang, Walt Disney, Richard Matheson, P. T. Barnum, Gene Kelly, Errol Flynn, Bruce Lee, Jimmy Stewart, Ruby Keeler, Cab Calloway, the Beatles, Bob Wills and the Texas Playboys, and the endless other contributors to my dreams. Again, my father, Jay Knowles. He has been my very best friend, teacher, and enabler in my journey to become the best geek that I can be. He made me believe in ghosts, goblins, zombies, vampires, and an endless realm of possibilities. My editor, Amy Einhorn, for being the nicest, most pleasant editorial experience I've had. Alex Smithline for calling me up and asking if I had an agent and ever wanted to work on a book. Finally . . . Mark Ebner and Paul Cullum. I simply cannot say enough about the tireless work these two have suffered through to make this book half of what it is. They endured hours and hours of close proximity to me as we hammered and pounded and tossed ideas about for this tome. They have been more than co-conspirators, they have become friends. Bless you all!

CONTENTS

FOREWORD

I met Harry Knowles six years ago at my very first Austin QT Film Festival, or, as it is referred to now, "QT Uno." And if you don't know about the film festival I do in Austin with my own personal 35 and 16mm film prints, I can't tell you here. Now when we do the festival, it's at the Alamo Draft House, where you can drink beer and eat blue cheeseburgers as you watch Henry Silva kill a dozen mafiosi in a porno theater with a rocket launcher. But back in the day, it was at the Dobie—a cool art house theater located in a mall right next to a food court. And that's where I noticed redheaded Harry, sitting at a table in the food court (in the Taco Bell section), typing furiously on his laptop. I was told Harry had his own Web site and that he was covering the festival for it. Little did I know that the coverage was day by day, and in such detail that it made the *New York Times* coverage of the Cannes Film Festival look puny by comparison. That Sunday after the Saturday all-night horror marathon, Harry gave me his coverage. And I did what I have always done ever since when Harry gives me his coverage: Go to the bathroom, lock myself in a stall, sit on the can, and read it in private.

I was floored.

The fact that he covered my admittedly cool film festival (if you're a film geek, that is) with the passion, intensity, and dedication of Raymond Burr telling it like it is as Godzilla pulverizes Tokyo was so impressive that I dubbed him the Wolf Blitzer of the Internet. I have met many film reporters and film critics in my day. And for the most part, they are film reporters and film critics. Harry, on the other hand, writes about film the way a war correspondent writes about war on the front lines. But the front lines isn't Hollywood, nor is it academia either. The front lines are the film geeks standing in line to get into the movie.

I attended the Seattle International Film Festival last year, and I found myself on a panel discussing the state of film criticism with some of the most respected critics in America. When asked to list some of my favorite critics, I included Harry on that list. One of the critics on the panel balked at Harry's inclusion. I defended my choice. They shot back with, "You don't see Knowles championing obscure foreign films on his site, do you?" I said, "If he likes them, you do." Where that critic had a bias against something like, say, *Charlie's Angels*, Harry's only bias is against bullshit movies. And if Harry likes or loves a film, no fair lady ever had a stronger defender.

Way, way, way before I ever made a film, I bamboozled my way into director Joe Dante's office under the guise of writing a book. During the interview, Dante—a film geek's film geek—described to me, at the age of eighteen, how there are two kinds of film lovers: (1) the kind who love film, and (2) the kind who love the films that *they* love. The distance between these two camps is so huge that Robbie Knievel on a two-wheel rocket couldn't jump it.

By and large, film critics—even though they're as right as they can be—are paid to be the latter. Harry has dedicated his life so far to being the former. And his love is true.

—Quentin Tarantino
November 20, 2001

AIN'T IT COOL?

INTRODUCTION

Twelve hundred pounds. Three-fifths of a ton. Six baby elephants. Four of me.

Think of the thing you want more than anything else in life. Maybe you don't even know what it is yet. Maybe it's just short breaths and longing; maybe it's a ring above your head or a fire under your feet. Maybe it doesn't matter; it's all in the wanting—like love is all in the loving. But fix it in your mind.

Now what would you go through to get it?

Maybe it's a golden idol deep in the jungles of the Peruvian Andes, guarded by shrouded caverns and feckless subterfuge and warring Hovitos tribesmen. Maybe it's world annihilation, your finger on the trigger of a tactical nuclear device in a speeding boxcar on the radiating shoals of the Mojave Desert. Whatever.

Savor it. Taste it. This is the crucible by which we are tested.

Twelve hundred pounds. I know this because I put it there myself. Neat, orderly piles of posters and one-sheets and lobby cards and miscellaneous collectibles—flat, stacked paper, stamped with the stuff of dreams. Which we sold back to a clamoring public at once-around-the-block prices. People much like us, who were steered here by impulse or secret initiative to try and amass some of the magic—the stardust and wonder—that those posters reminded them of.

We were Sineaters—my father and sister and me. Gypsy vagabonds, carrying spices and delicacies from the Far East. Artifacts that we could offload onto people whose daydreams outweighed their daily lives, and who would pay the going price to be swept up at will into the light and swirl that two hours in a darkened theater could afford them. In return, we would cart away the petty indulgences and indignities and recriminations their own lives required of them, the trivial sump. Truth be told, this was probably the source of most of that weight to begin with.

I remember I had a firm hold on things—my life, my sanity, the metal crossbar on the old four-wheel wooden dolly I was steering. I was in a great mood. It was my third trip of the day, so it was automatic by that point. We were filling up the last of the two vans we always traveled in, heading home after a solid weekend's work at a local collectors' memorabilia fair. All I had to do was get down a 45-degree concrete incline, out some metal emergency doors, and into the City Coliseum parking lot where the vans were parked. Plus I had a system: I would rest the weight of the dolly against my body and skip backward, so it would carry me back ten, twelve feet at a time, then plant both feet solid and check the forward momentum. I mean, I'd done this. It was easy.

God takes the thing—the thing that you want, that you don't know you want—and he holds it out just beyond your reach. To where it shimmers in the fading light. And the closer you get to it, the harder it is to make out, so the faster you run for it. And sometimes, since he's a cheeky fucker with a wicked sense of irony, he'll place it on the other side of a lake of fire or a slough of despond, past dragons and lumbering minotaurs and calculating trolls. You think that's your test, and the thing is your reward. But this has not been my experience. The thing is just a plot contrivance—Hitchcock's MacGuffin, a mechanical rabbit; a diploma or heart-shaped testimonial or Triple Cross from the Legion of Courage, courtesy the Great and Powerful Oz. The test is how well you brave the journey. And the reward is your own character, which is revealed to you in beats and arcs. This is the most important thing I know to tell you: "The only reason they make it hard is to see the kind of stuff you're made of." Because as any writer will tell you, character trumps plot every time.

Nobody used this exit but us. It should have been clear. Except that near the base of the incline, the City of Austin had stretched a hose to drain the ice water from the Coke bins out onto the grassy perimeter. It caught my heel as I was coming down, so that my weight was behind me. I tried to spin around, put my hands out to break my fall, but my feet were already planted, torquing the lower half of my body. Yet even before my balance left me, my attention had already spun around back uphill, to this thing I still couldn't see, but which I was already thinking past. In my haze, I could make out a small golden idol, on an altar of polished stone, in an underground cavern in the Peruvian jungle, which I had just displaced with its exact volume in sand. Or so I thought. And now a giant boulder was barreling down on top of me.

I remembered every step in my brief, ridiculous life that had led me here. Raised in a Skinner box of movie lore and pop mythology. Tarzan and Buster Keaton and Dracula as my

3

baby-sitters. A wild, half-mad mother and a renegade, half-sane father, broken open, turned inside out in the cyclotron of the '60s, only to escape while others just like them got sucked back into the maelstrom.

"This is where Forrestal cashed in. A competitor. He was good. He was very good."

A lonesome, pining adolescence in dust-choked West Texas, reared amid a gothic power struggle that would embarrass even the scions of *Giant* or *Written on the Wind*. And then deliverance late in my teens through the aftermarket economy of those same serials and comic landscapes and 16mm dioramas into other, more opulent worlds. Life was good, finally. Maybe a little too good.

"There's nothing to fear here . . . That's what scares me."

The dolly caught me square in the small of the back. It bucked me up and threw me another seven feet, just in time for it to roll over my back and both legs, partially paralyzing me. I lay on the sidewalk and tried to roll onto my side, but I couldn't move my legs. I reached both arms back behind me and pulled my head down as far as I could into my sternum, like I'd seen a doctor do once to my mom. As I did, I could feel my vertebrae pop back into place one by one: "Pop, pop, pop, pop, pop." They sounded like rifle shots. They'd been jammed shut.

All I could think of was Tod Browning's 1932 *Freaks*. There was a character called the Human Worm, and even though he had no legs and no arms, he could fend for himself. A black man—we see him strike a match and light a cigarette with his tongue. This was going to be me. I decided then and there I was not going to burden my family or loved ones. I'd join the circus if I had to. I had worked as a falconer's assistant, and a magician's second on stage. I'd had a job helping a belly dancing troupe into and out of their costumes. (Like Woody Allen says in *What's New, Pussycat?*: It's not very much, but it's all I can afford.) I'd even been in the movies, in *The Ballad of the Sad Cafe,* from a Carson McCullers novel. I played a character called Fat Boy, with lines opposite Vanessa Redgrave, even though they accidentally cut me out of the credits. I had a SAG card and everything. There would be something for me somewhere. It just might take some legwork.

Somehow, I managed to drag myself to my car. My motor skills mobilized long enough for me to drive our second van home. That night I fell in the shower and couldn't get up again. I pulled myself into my bed, in a spare room at the back of my father's house in North Austin, where I stayed for the next six months. With no insurance to speak of, due to our gypsy existence, and without access to affordable medical care, I ventured out onto the Internet, then still in its infancy, on a Packard Bell with a 60MHz Pentium processor that I barely knew how to use, to forage for respite and cure. And before I knew it, I had spun myself into a chrysalis of fiber optics and midnight vapors, lying there dormant, reinventing myself with special powers for the better day ahead. I could hear the French-accented sibilance of Belloq, the rogue archaeologist in *Raiders of the Lost Ark,* his voice deep, mellifluous, wonderful—mocking like that of God himself:

"Dr. Jones. Again we see there is nothing you can possess which I cannot take away. And you thought I'd given up."

And so began my quest.

I am the least likely celebrity in the world. This is what I'm famous for. I dress in sandals and Hawaiian shirts—the gaudier the better. I'm roughly the size of a small European import. I have hair like an Irish setter. I look more like a cartoon than even cartoons of me do. I know this about myself. But completely by accident—and kismet, and synchronicity, and an insane amount of soul-numbing labor—I came to be at the perfect center of a universe of my own creation. One I could scarcely have imagined at any step along the way.

Every day, over a twelve-hour period, as I work on international time, I read some 1,200 e-mails, correspond with hundreds of people around the globe, chase rumors, brave innuendo, and field calls from a vast unofficial network of spies that runs the gamut of power and influence within the film industry, from the accidental to the all-encompassing. My words reach literally millions more, 365 days a year, in over a hundred countries, who tune in to find out what's the buzz. Because wherever Hollywood goes to shoot its films, I know what it's up to—my readers are everywhere, on ours and other planets, in this world and the next.

All of these people have at least one thing in common: Surreptitiously, subversively, or self-promotionally, they all wish Hollywood made better movies. And whatever its obvious faults, Hollywood itself would be hard-pressed to disagree. It just doesn't have a clue how to go about it.

Not to worry.

They have a saying among Hollywood insiders that there're two kinds of people in the creative ranks of the film industry—Geeks and Hustlers. It takes both types to make the flywheel turn. The Geeks bring an idea from inception to term. The Hustlers carry it forth out into the world. Together they're the mind/body split. Sometimes, against all odds, the Geeks rise to absolute power—Steven Spielberg or George Lucas. Sometimes the Geeks turn into Hustlers to consolidate their power—James Cameron, Michael De Luca—but inside, they're always still Geeks. Sometimes the biggest

Hustlers—Robert Evans at Paramount; Mike Medavoy at United Artists, Orion, and TriStar—seem like rogue biological agents placed here by divine providence to facilitate the spread of the Geek gospel. My feeling is, basically, the Hustlers can take care of themselves. But the Geeks are my people.

Think of a novel like *The Moviegoer* by Walker Percy. It's about a guy whose whole life is given over to movies—it opens with a Kierkegaard quote, chronicles this character's unrealized desperation as he sleepwalks through life, kind of a *Catcher in the Rye* at the protagonist's expense. A key early passage profiles his world view:

> **Other people, so I have read, treasure memorable moments in their lives: the time one climbed the Parthenon at sunrise, the summer night one met a lonely girl in Central Park and achieved with her a sweet and natural relationship, as they say in books. I too once met a girl in Central Park, but it is not much to remember. What I remember is the time John Wayne killed three men with a carbine as he was falling to the dusty street in *Stagecoach*, and the time the kitten found Orson Welles in the doorway in *The Third Man*.**

Movies in literature are often like that—the home movies that galvanize the narrator in Delmore Schwartz's "In Dreams Begin Responsibilities"; the brutal clash of images in Nathanael West's *The Day of the Locust;* the recurring poster for *The Hands of Orlac* in Malcolm Lowry's *Under the Volcano.* They're always mythical or nostalgic or enigmatic, or at the very least imbued with great portent or sadness. And who's to say they shouldn't be? The problem is that they always feel constructed as literary conceits, by someone who has no firsthand experience of what it's like to be obsessed with movies. Who doesn't live and breathe them like virtually everyone I know. *The Moviegoer* mentions maybe ten movies by name in the entire novel, not including a chance run-in with William Holden and a dog named Rosebud. And it never makes even the slightest distinction between the classics everyone knows (*It Happened One Night, All Quiet on the Western Front, Red River*) and the ones that merely seem to mirror the New Orleans setting of the novel (*Dark Waters, Panic in the Streets*).

But walk into any video store in the country and ask the guy behind the counter what he's recommending. You'll get a welter of names and italics and proper nouns, tributaries of the latest hits that lead back into the recent past through a mosquito-netting haze of thick associations and random insights, separating and recombining, forming a wild jumble of genres and competing emotions and speculative connections.

The movies are another world—a foreign place, a physical locus of sound and image whose coordinates may be shared and topography mapped through careful vigilance and an attention to the overlooked detail. And where those observations conflict or contradict one another is merely the specialized biology of that other world—like sentient insects, or silicon-based life forms, or methane-compounded atmospheres. If Tom Cruise is sometimes a testosterone flyboy and sometimes a feckless sports agent—well, he's always going to freak out and kick a wall. Jack Nicholson may be a jarhead or a juicehead or deranged or the devil, but he'll always rope us in by lifting a single eyebrow.

And Thomas Mitchell will always be Thomas Mitchell, and Warren Oates will always be Warren Oates, and Harry Dean Stanton will be Harry Dean Stanton, because they're character actors—holy men entrusted with constancy, the lifeline between films and between eras, no matter how far afield the characters they play. Just as Brando drawn through any thin braid of aspect or accent will always be Brando. That world will tolerate only what the camera allows. Sometimes it's the same as our world, and sometimes it's just the opposite. But it's always brighter, and the light is what draws us to it. Helplessly.

The best essay on film I've ever read was not by Pauline Kael, leaching all the fun out of *Citizen Kane,* for instance. It wasn't Manny Farber ranting on an adrenaline high about some dusty masterpiece; and it wasn't Andrew Sarris enumerating those objects worthy of our attention. It wasn't in *Cahiers du Cinema* or *Jump/Cut* or the *Village Voice* or fucking *Film Comment.* It was by Larry McMurtry, of all people, collected in his *Film Flam* anthology in the mid-'80s, but written on a lark for *New York* magazine sometime earlier. It's called "Movie-Tripping: My Own Private Film Festival," and it describes flying to Times Square for a weekend and watching seventeen straight movies in forty-eight hours.

The essay purports to make a distinction between "good" films (De Sica's *Umberto D,* Antonioni's *L'Avventura*) and the "bad" films he's naturally drawn to—exploitation riots like *The Velvet Vampire* and *The Night Evelyn Came Out of the Grave,* but also craftsman's jewels like *Hannie Caulder* and Sergio Leone's *Duck, You Sucker* and the next-to-last Hitchcock, *Frenzy.* It ridicules Truth in cinema in favor of the far more utilitarian Illusion. And it ends up on 42nd Street at 4 A.M. on a Sunday morning, as the author and three black teenagers marvel at the wonders implicit in a one-sheet of *Red Sun,* an "Eastern" Western much prized from my youth, with Charles Bronson as a gunfighter and Toshiro Mifune as a wayward samurai who temporarily join forces. The reason the McMurtry essay stands out in my memory is that it's some of the only film writing I've ever come across, especially of the so-called serious variety, that suggests both the wealth of the film experience as I know it, and its inevitability for people like me, who will follow it into whatever hidden fortress we have to:

> **In such theaters, anything can happen. I once saw a girl dragged out of a Doris Day movie because she was audibly in labor; and, more extraordinary, a man sitting six rows in front of me in *The Magic Voyage of Sinbad* shot himself dead during the previews while playing a friendly game of Russian roulette with his wife and a friend. His wife and the friend were not a little surprised when the gun turned out to be loaded. The panic that ensued gave one new respect for human cunning. Most parties assumed, not unnaturally, that the race war had begun, and chose to go under the seats rather than dash for the exits. The management fled, as did the friend; the wife delivered herself of a last tirade on masculine selfishness, over the corpse; and, a little later, when the panic had abated, a number of people under the seats showed their disrespect for death by getting laid. Meanwhile *The Magic***

**Voyage of Sinbad continued, as it had to, the pro-
jectionist having apparently been the first man
out.**

What's cool about that is not just the drama that effortlessly blooms all around the author; it's that he would be in
such a socially transgressive venue in the first place to see
The Magic Voyage of Sinbad. (Presumably the 1953 Russian
version, the one that Coppola rewrote the dialogue for.) It's
one thing to know everything about film because it's your
job or your field of influence. But it's something else to have
had it crawl inside you at an early age, slither deep down into
your life-support systems, and exact a more or less constant
price on your transient resources ever since.

Such people are film buffs, geeks, fanboys walking. And
what I hope to do here—now that I've finally got a moment's
reflection, and a deadline that isn't eight hours away, for
once—is chronicle the real fan's notes. I want to show how
people like me who don't connect with organized sports, institutional learning, community standards, or for the most
part even other people, find values they can live by in the accidental medium of pop culture. And how, over time, this becomes the faith that connects a loose diaspora of people like
myself, as well as the grail in whose name we conduct all of
our crusades.

I've been compared to Horatio Alger and Jefferson
Smith; to Howard Stern and fan's fan Forry Ackerman. I'm
honored. Sometimes I think of myself as maybe a kinder,
gentler Walter Winchell, an antidote to the tabloids: obses-
sive when it comes to people's professional lives, but who
could basically care less what they do on their own time. Or
maybe the opposite of Jack Valenti—the Anti-Valenti: a lob-

11

byist for the motion picture industry, only targeting the industry itself, and paid for out of my own pocket. Most of the time, I feel like the android in *The Questor Tapes* who controls the weather from his underground bunker. It's dirty, thankless work, but suppose that no one did it.

But my story is worth telling for the same reason the studios don't know what to make of me—why I'm termed a loose cannon in a closed community that doesn't trust anyone who doesn't immediately stand to gain. Because I love movies. I love Hollywood movies. I've given my whole life over to believing in them. I was bedridden, penniless, one more rip in the safety net, laid up without hope, growing fatter, drowning in my own chest. And like the twelve-year-old asthmatic Scorsese, or the wunderkind Coppola stricken with polio, I sopped up every fragment of idealized history and saturated color I could find, from the movies, and poured all of the emotion inside me back into the lifeline that movies had become for me, and into the shrine I created for them—Ain't It Cool News.

As a result, my Web site is confused, imperfect, messy, sometimes fawning, and, hopefully, indispensable—just like me. To this day, I've never spent a penny maintaining it. They told me a nice guy could never make it in the cutthroat world of media. We'll see. But I have a simple strategy that's seemed to work for me so far: Give the people what they're interested in, and they'll be back. And if they're anything like me, they'll be interested in the same things I am.

This is what makes my story inclusive: If you've ever seen the Web site, if you've followed my adventures in the papers or feel like I do about the movies I write about, then this is your story as well. Because movies should be better. And someone should be held accountable when they're not.

Movies are the last bastion of true democracy in America. People vote with their butts. (Some of us vote twice.) They're a referendum on our national identity; the incidental accretion of the zeitgeist. And they're far too important to be left in the hands of those without an emotional stake in them.

Hence, I recognize that my kooky getup and college pranks aside, this is basically my only mandate: to serve as the conscience of a system without any incentive to have one otherwise. And to state the obvious that apparently no one else is willing to say:

That the development process is debilitating and doesn't work. That event movies undermine themselves by adhering to the safety of the known variable, making them technologically groundbreaking at the same time they're emotionally pre-digested. That special effects are merely creating a new digitocracy that imprisons the slightest stirring of the human spirit. That an overattention to directors and an underattention to writers stifles creativity—and that both are merely shopworn Hollywood clichés that die hard, invented by producers and studio mavens to monopolize the profit streams. That first-week grosses measure hype, while second-week grosses measure word of mouth. That attention and popularity are not the same thing. That popularity and value are not the same thing. That a bureaucracy of institutional lies inevitably obscures even the remote possibility of objective truth. That quality is equity—in people, projects, and relationships. And that passion—the enthusiasm of directors for their vision, actors for their craft, writers for their muse, the common laborer for a job well done, and poor doomed schlubs like me for the whole damned enterprise—is as much a natural resource to be mined as weapons-grade uranium.

These days, Hollywood calls with increasing regularity to wheedle, cajole, trade gossip, and solicit my advice on projects or notes on scripts. Screenwriters adopt me to champion their work. The power elite put me on speed-dial. And basically, everyone who ever considered me a nuisance now treats me like their new best friend. Business as usual? You bet it is. Fun? You have no idea. Can I believe any of it for a second? Of course not.

I named my Web site Ain't It Cool News after John Travolta in *Broken Arrow.* Christian Slater, trapped in an open railroad car, tells bad guy Travolta he's out of his mind if he makes good on his threat to explode a stolen tactical nuclear device. "Yeah," says Travolta, his eyes glittering. "Ain't it cool?"

Broken Arrow was John Woo's first successful foray into Hollywood, proving that if you're the best in the world at what you do, then all the petulance and shallowness and psychotic ambition of the place melts away in a heartbeat, and there's a place for you at the big table. It was John Travolta's first big-money starring role after being welcomed back into the fold in *Pulp Fiction,* proving that deal memos are transient, studio favor is fickle, but movie stars are forever.

It wasn't *Citizen Kane* or *Grand Illusion* or *Los Olvidados,* something that would impress anyone else. It was just a movie I liked. The last one I'd seen before my accident, so it was on my mind. I liked the way Travolta's features lit up when he said that line, one he'd improvised, how he was suddenly animated from within by the simple self-indulgent joy of doing something he liked: playing for keeps, in a matter of life and death, and imagining how he'd look in the movie they made about it.

He's right, you know. Movies are cool.

I'm not questioning the fate of Hollywood at all. Furthest thing from it. I'm trying to offer it redemption.

Join us, comrade.

Ain't it cool?

CHAPTER ONE
The Trouble with Harry

Exactly how many movies have I seen?

I have no idea.

Paperback guides like Leonard Maltin's or Roger Ebert's list somewhere around 20,000 capsule reviews at any given time. I've seen roughly half the films on any given page. That's 10,000 titles, give or take—or a movie every day for twenty-seven years. By comparison, the *Guinness 2000: Millennium Edition* book of world records, under the heading "Fans and Followers," lists one Gwilym Hughes of Gwynedd, Wales, as Most Ardent Movie Watcher, having "seen and logged 22,990 films since he saw his first film while in the hospital in 1953." Except there are approximately 200,000 titles listed on the Internet Movie Database (www.us.imbd.com), the most comprehensive credits listings on the Internet, and much of that disparity represents genre films, in which I have a specialized interest. All I know is, for at least the past decade, I've seen on average two to four movies a day, and without really trying, I've amassed some 3,500 titles on tape, DVD, and in 16mm prints. "Enough for ten museums; the loot of the world." The final count? "No man can say."

But anyone who has electively spent upward of 50,000 hours in the dubious thrall of a sentimental education as ephemeral as this one probably has issues. Some kind of darkness visible that motivates them in ways they can't explain. Especially when there are so many other things one can choose to do with a life. The specifics never matter, except as they relate to the universal. The point is that everybody has something.

I offer this selective biography then as an X-ray of that other life—the one of Harry Jay Knowles, either pathological or blessed, lived on the fly during intermissions and before the trailers and after the crawl. My hope is that it sheds what light it can on Harry and the quixotic agenda he has before him. There is no way to tell his story without telling my own.

I was born on December 11, 1971, in Austin, Texas, a magical Brigadoon of a village at the perfect center of a vast star-shaped state, and unlike anyplace else I've ever seen. (I include the date in case you want to send me something for my birthday.) It's where the '60s really got started in these parts, back among the boho liberals of the early '50s, and where they never quite ended, through the Willie Nelson redneck renaissance of the '70s, the private manias of the long pre-*Slacker* '80s, or the fading musical and literary oasis of the '90s. It has always served as a beacon for dreamers of one stripe or another—O. Henry stopped through long enough for an unchartered prison stay for embezzlement at the turn of the last century—and that's very much the stock I come from.

I was also born at just the right time to grow up in the shadow of *Star Wars*. I was six, eight, and ten, respectively, when the first three installments came out, and they left a more or less permanent impression on my spiritual development. Even now, considering the Information Age and my humble role in it, I always return to Princess Leia's speech to the Grand Moff Tarkin while imprisoned in the bowels of the Death Star: "The more you tighten your grip, Tarkin, the more Star Systems will slip through your fingers." Information longs to be free, no less so than the rebel alliance, and I am honored to do its bidding.

My parents were nomads—itinerant vendors who rolled through the Great Southwest and across central Mexico nonstop with me in tow. At the time I was born, they were doing psychedelic light shows for touring rock bands like ZZ Top, at places like the Vulcan Gas Company and the Armadillo World Headquarters in Austin—our versions of the Avalon or the Fillmore in San Francisco. Then when disco hit and the light shows became automated, they quickly segued into comics and movie memorabilia. They were literally the first people selling movie posters in the state, and the first to organize a film festival.

Then over time, that evolved into specialized arts and crafts—jewelry, woodworking, metallurgy, macramé—anything they could sell at the various renaissance fairs or the 23rd Street Market on the Drag, which was Guadalupe Street across from the University of Texas. That's where I met most of the colorful characters who were to become my first friends—hippies and drifters and Vietnam vets who couldn't quite find their way back into society. But to a kid, they were like carnies or circus people. There were too many colors and loud explosions going off inside them for most people to handle; but for me, they were a natural extension of the cartoons I was enslaved to. I think I was four when my parents first bought me a "Question Authority" T-shirt. I was schooled young in the value of eccentricity.

We would spend up to six months of the year traveling through Mexico and Central America collecting indigenous art and native objects to resell. This was me in my Indiana Jones phase. We wouldn't have a car or a tourist pass, we'd just drive down and leave our car in El Paso and get on a bus. When we'd hit the halfway point of our money, we'd turn back. In Spanish-speaking countries, red hair is good luck, so everywhere we went people were constantly patting my head. I've been swimming with bloated alligators beneath a Yucatán waterfall, ridden on the backs of giant sea turtles, and once woke up on the floor of a grass hut with a domesticated javelina boar licking my face. We made over a dozen such trips, up until my sister, Dannie, was born.

Everything about my life from those earliest memories until the time I turned eleven was pure magic. I never really got into trouble. Mom and Dad would play good cop/bad cop with me. My mom was kind of wild—she looked just like Janis Joplin, but really pretty. (One of her college roommates was Lois Chiles, who was later the Bond girl in *Moonraker*.) When she'd get mad at me she'd say, "Jay, take him out and burn his ass," and we'd go out on the front porch, where Dad would wallop an old board with his belt while I screamed as loud as I could. Like in *Take the Money and Run,* where they whip the guy's shadow. We'd come back in and I'd be rubbing my southern side, like he'd just opened up a tallboy can of whoop-ass on me. It was our secret bond. Looking back on it,

I'm sure my mom must have known what we were up to, but she never let on.

In those days, we lived in this huge 3,000-square-foot Victorian house in Hyde Park, built in 1905, which is still my dream house. My earliest memories date from there. We lost it in the divorce—my mom sold it and bought a souped-up pickup truck, which she totaled inside of a month and a half. I plan to buy that house back someday, like Larry McMurtry— the self-appointed godfather of Texas letters—did with the big library at the center of Archer City, to house his enormous rare book collection. That's why we stay here in this cramped little shack in North Austin for now, with scripts and videotapes and movie posters all piled to the ceiling, plus ten times that amount in various storage lockers scattered around town.

That first house was haunted. We all saw things. I was there with a baby-sitter once, who was making out with his girlfriend on the couch, and a Oaxacan devil mask on the wall started talking to us. Everyone in the room saw it. Or I'd hear music playing and follow it and see this blonde lady playing my mother's organ. And I could see through her. Other people saw her four or five times in different parts of the house. It was always upstairs, where we showed films, and where all the collectibles were stored. Maybe this was some elaborately designed bit of child psychology to keep me from rummaging around and tearing up *Spider-Man* #1 or *Amazing Tales* #15. (There was also the family story that I swallowed three hits of blotter acid when I was five, which may account for both the nature of these recollections and the tortured visage you see before you.) But, I mean, I remember this stuff.

All her life, my mom had been plagued by intense nightmares. When she was three years old, she had witnessed a fire at her ranch house in North Texas that had consumed her priceless collection of several generations of antique glass and porcelain dolls. She said she could hear them crying out to her, screaming for her to come and rescue them. And of course, her family wouldn't let her do it. She was haunted by dreams of this her whole life; she used to wake up screaming in a cold sweat. They finally stopped several years after she got married, about the time I was born.

At the same time, since my parents were in the movie memorabilia trade, some of my earliest memories were spent at collectors' conventions in the company of figures who were stalwarts of the popular imagination. I met the Cisco Kid, Red Ryder, the guy who played Commander Cody in the old *Rocket Man* serial, Roddy McDowall, Spanky McFarland from *The Little Rascals*. Jack Kirby and all the comic book people. Once at a convention in Houston, Tarzan baby-sat me for three days. Literally. Johnny Weissmuller was the guest of honor at the Houston Con, and I can remember being up in his room with him and his wife and my parents. He was an alcoholic by this time, and he would tell endless stories: like how, when he would climb a tree after Maureen O'Sullivan in the movies, she wouldn't be wearing any underwear. And they'd have to shoot the scene again and again because Tarzan's mighty thunder-stick kept popping out from beneath his loincloth. Lots of stuff like that that was infinitely compelling to a kid.

This was before there were commercial videos, or even cable TV really. Especially in Austin, where the Lyndon Johnson family owned the only VHF network affiliate in town and blocked any further VHF expansion until well into the '70s. We got our first VCR in 1976. Before that, the only way you could see old movies was either to stay up all night chasing them on off-hours television, or else watch them on 16mm. So there was this whole group of maybe twenty-five friends who collected 16mm films, which were between $350 and $500 apiece. Or if you were lucky, the projectionist at some revival theater would run a print down to his buddy at the film development lab in town and strike a reduction print in 16mm, and then everybody could have a copy of *Fantasia* off the reissue.

So I was raised among this happy little band of pirates. We used to get together four times a week at somebody's house and hang up a king-size sheet and show films for ten or twelve hours at a stretch. And I was always front and center, stretched out on the floor, with my feet directly beneath the screen.

After most people had shown a print three or four times, they would sell it and buy something else. But the true collectors would hang on to their favorite prints, so some of these films I ended up seeing literally hundreds of times: *Casablanca. The Adventures of Robin Hood* and *Santa Fe Trail,* both with Errol Flynn and directed by Michael Curtiz. *Gorgo,* which was about a giant dinosaur-like creature that destroys London, very much like *Godzilla,* except made by the British instead of the Japanese. *Night of the Living Dead.* I must have seen *King Kong* over a hundred times easily by the time I was five. I was a human sponge.

This was also around the time my dad began to conduct what he called "the Experiment." He decided that the sociological premise then in vogue, which said that extended exposure to violent media can result in depraved behavior, was strictly bullshit. And moreover, he would prove it with his firstborn. So I became like a laboratory experiment for him—constantly bombarded by popular culture, and the more graphic or grotesque, the better. Looking back on it now, it was like something out of *Peeping Tom*; it's a wonder I turned out like I did. (Or maybe not.) My dad was an immense horror fan; he had me reading Forrest Ackerman's *Famous Monsters of Film-land* and *Fangoria.* We had a full-body Godzilla costume float-ing around the house from the time I was three. He even showed me *The Exorcist* at a very young age.

Everybody seemed to be in on the experiment. There was one friend of my dad's who would sit there and they would constantly drill me for ten hours while they manned a booth: What's Tom Mix's horse's name? What was Will Rogers's horse? Gene Autry's horse? Who played the Werewolf of London? Who played the Wolfman? Who was in *The Curse of the Were-wolf*? It took me forever to learn that: Henry Hull, Lon Chaney Jr., and Oliver Reed. And I don't really pride myself on that part of it—the trivia. I can't go through the whole deck of Triv-ial Pursuit movie cards like some people can—you know, like baseball statistics. But a lot of this stuff I have at my fingertips because I learned it by rote. It was like learning my multiplica-tion tables.

Everything changed when I turned eleven. The family that my mother had left behind on the dust-ridden plains of West Texas finally coerced her into coming back. And once they got their hooks into her, they never let her go again.

CHAPTER TWO

"A Boy's Best Friend Is His Mother."

Everyone has skeletons in the closet somewhere back along their family tree. All unhappy families are unhappy in their own way—that's what kept guys like Tolstoy in the sweeping historical novel business. But even so, some of my blood relatives on my mother's side still seem like the closest I've personally come to consummate evil. I mean, *Chinatown* evil. Old Man Potter in *It's a Wonderful Life* evil. Big Daddy in *Cat on a Hot Tin Roof,* or J. R. Ewing. These are people who bought up all their neighbors' land during the Depression when the banks foreclosed on them. Land barons, cattle and oil money, who take pride in their bootstrapper's ethic and saddle smarts and lack of book learning; who some devil's bargain has rendered immortal, and now they have nothing to do but count their millions and interfere in the lives of their doomed issue.

My great-grandfather Harry Halsell Portwood, born in 1903 in Decatur, Wise County, was the patriarch of this clan. He had a paralyzed right hand where somebody had stabbed it to the tabletop in a barroom fight over a whore in a Depression-era speakeasy in Mineral Wells. I'm named for the cocksucker, and I stood over him one Sunday in 1990, after he'd fallen in his kitchen and cracked open his head, and I watched him die. They had rushed him to Dallas's Parkland Hospital, the same place they took Kennedy with his brains brocaded on his waistcoat, and I caught him half in and half out of consciousness. I whispered, "Die," and he flatlined seconds later. It was like he'd been waiting for that to leave this world behind. I can't say enough against the man.

For all practical purposes, he was like my grandfather. This is the *Chinatown* part. The reason why is that his daughter— my grandmother Paula Ann Portwood—was raped at her thirteenth birthday party, and the product of that union was my mother, Helen Jane. So my mother and grandmother were virtually raised as sisters, along with my mother's aunt, Helen Lee, a rodeo trick rider.

It was my grandmother Paula Ann who was the crazy one. (Everyone in West Texas has two names; it's kind of Russian czarist. I still experience momentary tremors when sternly addressed as "Harold Jay.") In addition to alcoholism and drug addiction, she suffered from manic depression and grand mal epilepsy, and was finally institutionalized at the Wichita Falls State Mental Hospital at age fifty-two. Butch Hancock, who's a songwriter and kind of poet laureate down here, has a line about the Texas rich and their offspring in his song "Own and Own" that goes, "Now one son drives a long limousine, and another one's pumping that gasoline / One daughter don't do nothing at all 'cept talk to the walls in Wichita Falls." That was her. But she had the most amazing stories.

Like with most schizophrenics, her stories employed an almost ironclad logic, so it's impossible to tell which ones are true. She insisted Elvis Presley entertained her in his motel room after playing a dance in Seymour, Texas, in 1956, bouncing five-year-old Helen Jane on his knee till she fell asleep. Paula Ann was Elizabeth Taylor's riding double on the set of *Giant,* which filmed in nearby Marfa (that part's true), and claims she had a fling with James Dean. She played a small part as a Mexican prostitute in *The Alamo,* when they erected a three-quarter-scale replica down in Brackettville, and claims John Wayne came on to her and Laurence Harvey actually slept with her, although he could only perform after she whipped him with a riding crop.

She told long elaborate tales about how Quannah Parker's and Jesse James's gold was secretly buried on the ranch (both had been friends of Harry Portwood's father); how she and a lover robbed an Arizona Mafia poker party of $10,000 from Benny Binion, the last of the Vegas casino outlaws and owner of the Horseshoe Casino, who had them tracked to Nogales, Mexico, and her lover cut in half with a machine gun; that later Binion looked out for her and blew up an underling at his mailbox one morning who had tried to have his way with her. She accused her father of drowning one of her lovers in the Brazos River, and claimed that another died after a fight with the old man when the lugs fell off all four wheels of his pickup truck, just then loaded down with Portwood hay.

Some of these stories, like the ones about the Arizona mobster, have at least a basis in fact. Some, like how she put out Sammy Davis Jr.'s eye with a beer bottle after he insulted her at a party in Dallas's exclusive Turtle Creek, are patently

27

imaginary. Most of them, we'll never know. One story I can confirm is that after she had run off to a Fort Worth rodeo against his wishes, Harry Portwood had my grandmother's house picked up and moved into his front yard, where he could keep an eye on her.

But the story that made the strongest impression on a young boy with a lively imagination was the one she told me in confidence, years before anyone thought to call her crazy: that my mother had actually been twins, and that the evil Helen eventually killed the good Helen, dismembered her, and fed the pieces to the hogs. My grandmother swore that Helen Jane, or rather her evil twin, had tried to shoot her, had tried to beat her to death, and had tried to poison her. All were more or less true.

Actually, it's a wonder there was even time for such baroque conjecture (including the parts that were verifiable), since everyone in this family was always taking potshots at one another. Literally. In 1969, my great-grandmother Mary Helen, whom I always knew as Nan Nan, fired two shots from her pistol at a teenage niece while seated behind the wheel of her Cadillac in downtown Olney. That same year, Helen Lee tried to shoot Old Harry with a 30-30 saddle rifle in her living room, but he managed to block it with an oak coffee table, which Helen Lee later gave to my parents as a wedding present.

And one day in 1987, my mother and grandmother stood on their respective porches at the Round Timbers ranch compound, fifty yards apart from each other, and calmly emptied two .357 Magnums at each other, which my sister and I witnessed from behind a rolled-up carpet. The summer before, in front of my five-year-old sister, Dannie, a knock-down-drag-out fight between the two in Paula's living room left the old woman with three broken ribs and a bruised larynx.

The events that transpired in 1983, shortly after my eleventh birthday, which ushered my idyllic childhood to a close, were that a relative of my mother's named D. J. Brookerson, who had been like a father to her, or at least more of a father than anyone she'd ever known, killed himself on her birthday. His son (now deceased) had just called from the prostitute tank in the Dallas County jail, where they'd taken him after he was arrested for spray-painting graffiti, and they couldn't tell at first glance whether he was a man or a woman. D.J. went out and drove his diesel Mercedes straight into a parked car and snapped his neck, like Julie Harris in Robert Wise's *The Haunting,* dignity apparently having its limits.

Days later, Nan Nan (my great-grandmother) had a stroke that froze half her brain, and my grandmother suffered the first of her many nervous breakdowns, throwing this barely functioning dynasty into a tailspin. Prevailing upon a sense of familial obligation, and dangling the keys to his infernal kingdom in front of her, old Harry Portwood got my mother to come home to the family ranch in Seymour to take care of things for a while. She took Dannie with her, who was then two years old. Imagine *The Last Picture Show,* which was shot twenty miles away in Archer City. And as soon as Nan Nan came out of her coma, she said that she had seen Satan, and that Satan was laughing over my mother's soul and talking with my father about how they had stolen it away. From that point on, those folks wouldn't let up. They just basically did a Patty Hearst on her; she started drinking heavily and got hooked on prescription pills.

Dad would call and my mom would always be out in the fields doing something. He would send letters and they'd be intercepted. We'd drive up there, and she wouldn't be there. This went on for months. Finally, one day I was at school—I was in the seventh grade—and my mom showed up wearing a cowboy hat and a western shirt. She said she'd come to take me to lunch. We went to Trudy's, a breakfast diner north of campus that was always my favorite place to hang out. But then when we got outside, there were all these ranch hands, and suddenly we were on the road to the ranch. I was a Boy Scout; I'd had orientation, I had arranged hikes for my scout troop. I knew how to tell direction. When they denied where we were going, I started whaling on one of the ranch hands who was riding with us, and I broke his jaw and three of his ribs; he didn't stop yelling for the whole five and a half hours back.

This is how I found out my parents were getting a divorce. I had never seen any problems between them. They were happily married as far as I knew. Any trouble between them all happened after she went back to the ranch. I found out later that my great-grandparents threatened to withhold the millions from the Portwood family inheritance from my sister and me and to disown my mother outright unless she brought us up there to live. They hated my father, just like they hated anyone who threatened their influence, and they finally broke up this marriage like they had with all their granddaughters. It just took them fifteen years. Dad handled it the best he could. From that point on, my mother became a heavy alcoholic, and I was basically on my own.

Ranch living was an adjustment, to put it mildly. First of all, the nearest movie theater was 110 miles away, round-trip. I had visitation with my dad once every other weekend, for exactly thirty-two hours. My mother took possession of our vast collectibles store, because she argued that she would have room at the ranch to preserve them adequately. And Dad didn't fight it. But the entire collection was put in my and my sister's name.

This also meant that I had a collection of something like 175,000 comic books, 30,000 paperback books, and 5,000 videotapes at my disposal. It was a huge amount of media. And while I had never really explored this massive treasure trove before, since there was always something to do back in Austin, now I had nothing but time. It was like being in prison—you sit there and you read the entire library. To this day, I still have trouble talking to modern comics fans, because they don't know the history of it. It's the same thing with film. Because I studied all these tapes, going back to the '20s.

The other thing that was completely different about the ranch was that now I could walk into any store in town, sign my name, and get whatever I wanted. That lifestyle is very easy to get caught up in. We lived on a 76,000-acre spread, which comprised the Big House where we lived, plus seven other houses, five barns, and our own cemetery, which looked exactly like the one in *Night of the Living Dead*. There was an area in back where the fence went up and disappeared off a sandy dune that reminded me of William Cameron Menzies's *Invaders from Mars,* where people cross behind a hill and then come back completely different. We had a bomb shelter with a six-inch steel door that I turned into my secret clubhouse. My room had a full-size regulation pool table in it, and Dannie's had real arcade Donkey Kong, Pac-Man, and Ms. Pac-Man machines.

But this went hand in hand with all these twisted mind games: trying to convince me that Dad was evil, or that I should change my last name to Portwood. I kept seeing all these parallels to *Star Wars:* "Luke, I am your father. Join me." *Renounce your past and we'll buy you a car. Assume our*

31

name and we'll pay for your college. It was this constant barrage of propaganda. Except I had seen *Marathon Man, The Conversation, The Parallax View, The Manchurian Candidate*—all these paranoid thrillers where they scramble your head. I had read Philip K. Dick. So I knew to follow my convictions. In games of life, the winner is invariably the last one standing.

In the end, I picked out my great-grandfather's casket. It was lined in bright pink. Because I realized he would never be able to rest inside that pink coffin. This big rough-and-tumble cowboy, with a lump of coal for a heart and no friends to his name. My mom kept asking, "Why did you pick that color, honey?" I said, "Because it matches your Cadillac." I was at the funeral home when they were preparing the body. I kept telling the embalmer, "No, he had more red in his cheeks." By the time they were finished with him, he looked like some sort of transvestite. These people to me were the epitome of evil. They had taken a happy family and split it up over money. So let the old bastard wear his lipstick and eyeliner and rouge as he walks into hell.

Somewhere in there, Mom remarried. This guy was basically Paul Newman in *Hud* or *The Hustler*: Powder blue eyes, sly, real quick. A glass of Jack Daniel's in his hand, but never drunk. One time I saw him reach out and grab a rattlesnake before it could strike. He's the one who taught me how to play pool. It's funny, but he started taking my dad's side in a lot of the arguments, saying that he'd gotten a raw deal with Mom. But then soon enough, she divorced him too. (In fact, she was married once before my dad—to a Vietnam vet right out of college. But that was over within a month.)

Mom fell into the rut of becoming just a constant, bumbling drunk. She was usually out of it by about seven o'clock every night. I would lock her in her bedroom by wedging a chair against the door—mainly so she wouldn't hurt herself. All we needed was her tear-assing around West Texas, drunk as a lord and heavily armed. We'd hear her howling at the moon up there like a crazed banshee. It was straight out of *Jane Eyre,* with Orson Welles's first wife up in the tower. And her whole personality changed. I mean, she started talking with a heavy Texas accent: "Whut? Whut the hale you talkin' about?" She'd never talked like that before. Her walk changed, the look in her eyes was different—every single thing that told me this was my mother was no longer there to see. It's the scariest thing that ever happened to me. Because I was steeped in *Invasion of the Body Snatchers* and *Invaders from Mars*; that was always in the back of my mind.

One of the things Mom liked to do was to go stay in a hotel and get drunk while we played in the swimming pool. A real rich white trash thing to do. So one time, when I was sixteen, we were in nearby Wichita Falls, Dannie was swimming, and Mom stumbled out by the pool in her full cowgirl regalia—boots, fringe vest, everything. Drunk as hell. Drunker than all but very few people you've ever seen, who are still kind of able to walk. And she fell into the pool. Dannie was screaming, because Mom was basically a sack of bricks. I ran out and saw her, and I thought to myself, This is it. The answer to all my problems. The way out of this hellhole, and she'd done it to herself. I stood there and watched her, motionless at the bottom of the pool. She was going to drown. Then I realized, Fuck. That's my mother. I couldn't let it happen. So I dived into the pool and pulled her back to life. She wouldn't go to a hospital because she was afraid Harry Portwood would find out and there would be hell to pay. That was the closest I ever saw her come to dying. But I know there were other times.

At the same time, it's those years that taught me how to take care of myself. I virtually raised my sister. I taught her how to write, taught her about film. She still has an *E.T.* shrine in her room. I raised her to be afraid of what's in the shadows; I'd say, "I love you, darling, and I can smell your brains," which is from *Return of the Living Dead*. I'd talk to her about hydraulics and latex and molds, and how they take a cast of your face and build up a character on top of it. I got her interested in what film is. And I did what I could to deprogram her, to try to get her to understand that her father was not a bad man.

I'd never really appreciated film before; it had always just been there. Now I had time to analyze it. Contrary to what people may think, I wasn't the picked-on kid in school. I was skinny up until about the second grade, when I started to bulk up. Then I was the big kid. I was tall, stocky, and they wanted me on the football team. Also, I was never ostracized as weird just because I was a film geek, because my parents would come to school and show 16mm films, or teach leatherworking and jewelry classes, which all the kids thought was cool.

In 1977, when the first *Star Wars* was in the theaters, I was the kid who had a print of it on video. We had a 16mm theatrical trailer six months before it was released. We watched it over and over until it turned green. It never occurred to me that I was fat until the fifth grade, when a new kid at school started causing problems. That's when Dad showed me José Ferrer as Cyrano de Bergerac; when someone hurls an insult at him, he says, "Is that all? Ah, no, young sir, you're too simple. You might have said a great many things. Why waste your opportunity?" And then he names a score better himself. Or Cocteau's *La Belle et la Bête* (*Beauty and the Beast*). Or Charles Laughton in *The Hunchback of Notre Dame*. You don't have to feel bad about yourself just because you're different (boiling oil notwithstanding).

As soon as I was old enough to drive, I started coming down to Austin as much as I could, and I'd bring Dannie with me. At this time, although my mom was supposed to be overseeing all the collectibles, they were being stored in barns, and rats were pissing all over the movie posters and comic books. So every time I went home, I'd take three suitcases with me, and they'd all be loaded up with paper. I was only staying for three days. I figured all the collectibles were mine in the divorce papers anyway, and she wasn't taking care of them like she'd promised. So I felt justified. Of course, if she had ever found out I was smuggling this stuff back to Dad, she would have had him thrown in jail in a heartbeat. Out of necessity, I became real good at storytelling.

My dad looks basically like Mr. Natural from the R. Crumb comics—he's got long white hair and a droopy mustache, and usually dresses in loose-fitting clothes that suggest a robe or toga. But before he became an unreconstructed hippie, he worked on the Richard Nixon public relations staff in Texas throughout most of the late '60s. He was schooled in marketing and grassroots political organizing, ran the Young Republicans at the state level, even oversaw his share of ratfucking and dirty tricks—really mild stuff, like canceling the food at Democratic fund-raisers, or smudging the envelopes on their mass mailings so they couldn't be delivered. He was always very savvy about the workaday world—or later on, what it took to get by outside of it.

I finally left the ranch for good when I was seventeen. This was 1989. I ended up doing 110 hours at a community college in Austin, with plans to transfer over to the University of Texas for a film degree. For my dad's part, he was ecstatic that I was down there. He never thought I'd want to leave the ranch, on account of the lifestyle he imagined we led up there. He thought my sister and I had unlimited wealth and privilege, were basically the kings of all we surveyed, and couldn't fathom why we would ever want to give that up. He never saw my mom at her worst, and I never told him about it because I didn't want him to worry.

Dad was quick to involve me in the collectibles business. One of the motivating factors in his life has always been to pursue a livelihood in which the whole family could participate, because then you answer to no one but yourself. He is single-handedly the one who instilled that sense of self-sufficiency in me. And we very quickly made a very good living.

I couldn't tell my mom I just couldn't be around her anymore. Anyone who's ever been around someone who's on drugs or drinking—you still hang on because every now and then, for just a flash, they become that real person again. But it happens less and less, until finally they just disappear. So I told her I had written and optioned a vampire script. I'd tell her I couldn't come home for Thanksgiving because I had to fly up to Chicago on this movie deal. It was a project for John Candy, about an overweight vampire who wants to eat all the time. So he moves to Alaska, where it stays night for nine months out of the year. I would go into all the production details and story conferences and what the actors were really like. When nothing would happen after a while, I would say, "Oh, it's in turnaround—I don't know if it's ever going to get made. My agent has some ideas though." She was always disappointed that she wouldn't get to see me, but she was extremely proud of everything I was doing.

I was just getting ready to start college at UT when we received word that my mother had died.

We were in the middle of a show. We had had one of our worst days ever. And then that night, we get this knock at the door, and it was a cop. Being a practicing paranoid, Dad said, "You answer it."

The cop asked, "Are you Harry Knowles?"

I said, "Yes."

He said, "Well, you're supposed to call this number." I looked at it, and it was a West Texas area code. And I knew. It's the only thing it could be. We didn't have a phone at the time, because Mom would always call us up drunk and screaming. So we walked down to a payphone. Longest walk we ever took. Completely quiet. I called, and they told me Mom was dead. Dad said, "What about your sister?" He was starting to tear up, just completely devastated. I asked about Dannie, and they told me she was alright. Then I broke down.

You know, I always sort of figured it would be a drunk-driving incident. Some wreck out on the highway. But it wasn't. My mom died in a fire.

Death scenes in movies never really get it right.

In movies, death is something that happens to people you've known for less than two hours. Whereas in life, it's the enormity of something disappearing that's been there for as long as you can remember. Often, it's some polestar by which you have always navigated, and then suddenly it's gone.

My mom burned to death at my grandmother's cabin at Lake Kemp. We're not real sure if it was murder or if she set the fire herself. The alcohol in her blood level was .7—nearly comatose. She'd had this endless parade of redneck loser boyfriends and gentlemen callers. Her boyfriend at the time was named Dip. You know, the first rule is, if you meet someone named Dip, you don't talk to them. It's a simple rule.

These people are bad characters in movies. Dip was apparently some sort of cocaine cowboy drug runner. (He's dead now too.) My mom had reportedly kicked out the windshield of her car earlier that day because they'd had a fight. He was seen leaving the lake cabin about twenty-five or thirty minutes before the first smoke was spotted.

By the time the fire department got to the cabin, they couldn't do anything. The wind had whipped the fire out of control. It was so hot it blew up her car, which was parked twenty feet away. It was very weird. In my grandmother's stories, my mother's evil twin was always more beautiful than her, but she had no legs beneath the knees. And that was all they found of Mom's body—from the knees up. When I made that connection, I checked the dental records, because she was in such a financial and emotional state that you could believe she would fake her own death. If she could find this twin sister of hers, maybe that was a way out. But the dental records said it was her. She died on D. J. Brookerson's birthday, about two hundred yards from where he killed himself on hers.

Almost everybody who lived up there at the time remained permanently scarred by it. There's a real *Gone With the Wind* mentality in that part of the world about the land. Mom kept referring to that and *Giant* constantly because that was our common language. Film. She kept showing me *Giant* and *Boom Town* with Spencer Tracy and Clark Gable—all the powerful ranching or oil baron movies. And you know, I don't like *Gone With the Wind*. I don't like the racism, when Clark Gable makes fun of Butterfly McQueen outside his window, and I don't like the implied rape and smash cut to Scarlett all smiles the next morning. And I especially don't like this necrophiliac fascination with the red dirt of Tara that can make someone whore themselves out to the first available benefactor, basically compromise every other ideal they have in life, just to retain some vestige of ownership or entitlement.

"I'm going to live through this, and when it's all over, I'll never be hungry again," says Scarlett O'Hara, foreshadowing Courtney Love sixty years later. "Nor any of my folk. If I have to lie, steal, cheat, or kill, as God is my witness." I've always wondered if I dislike that film so much because I've seen this slavering devotion up close, free from the burnished hues and golden backdrops of Metro-Goldwyn-Mayer. I guess they had their fires too—Scarlett O'Hara and Vivien Leigh both.

The next day we drove up and got Dannie. We had to put up with a lot of two-facedness from people who hated my mom the entire time she lived there, but were now overcome by grief. I don't know where that kind of thinking comes from, but we saw it firsthand and it was amazing. We began excavating some of the collectibles from the barn, where the entire collection had fallen on hard times and extreme negligence. You'd dig down through two feet of dust and muck and rat excrement and you would find mint things—thousand-dollar comic books or posters. But everything above it was destroyed from being pissed and shit on by the raccoons and badgers. It was sickening.

While we were loading up some of the stuff, a guy named Markie who had been an old boyfriend of my mom's showed up. He had been out of state and didn't know anything about it—he just happened by—so he was pretty shook up. He started talking to us about this self-destructive streak that ran through her, and how hard it was even to be friends with her after they were finished. And then out of the blue, he said, "You know, it's horrible that she died the way she did—in a fire. On account of her dreams."

Dad said, "What do you mean?"

And he said, "She started having these dreams right when she moved back up here, that her dolls were burning up and they were trying to pull her back into the fire. She used to wake up every night covered in sweat—screaming."

At the time of her death, my mom's estate was in monumental disarray. She had failed to pay taxes since the divorce—almost a decade—and she was over $250,000 in debt, half of that to the IRS. She died without a will, and her inheritance from her grandfather was in probate, plus the fire destroyed most of the records that indicated exactly what she did own. There were several lawsuits pending, and she was in danger of losing the land, estimated as being worth about $4 million. This, combined with the fact that Dannie had spent maybe a hundred days with Dad in her whole life that she could actually remember, forced me to put college on hold. And before long, I began to believe that this was going to be my future—dealing with her estate.

Within a year, I had turned things around to where the estate was $40,000 in the good, and I had completely paid off my mom's debts. And all of a sudden, the rest of her family became very afraid. The Portwoods don't like it when things change, and they *really* don't like it when they're not in control of the thing that's changing. Plus I had sold off a small parcel of the land to pay off the debts, which they saw as tantamount to carpetbagging. Remember, they had this thing about the land. So just as we were preparing to inherit the estate, buy back the house in Austin, and rid ourselves of this headache once and for all, the remaining Portwoods convinced a local judge that Dad was planning on making off with my sister's inheritance and froze the entire estate in a blind trust, and had me removed as administrator. Even though I had been running a working ranch in absentia for at least a year. This suddenly left me wondering exactly what I was going to do with my life.

So against Dannie's and my professed wishes, $4 million worth of unmortgaged, income-producing land would stay in a perpetual trust until Dannie's eighteenth birthday, earning $20,000 a year in hunting leases, also escrowed, at which time they would come up with something else. Power to them. I decided pretty quickly I'd better come up with some other way of making a living.

The moral for me is that you can never go into denial. Because when you're dealing with that much money, the simplest problems suddenly seem insurmountable, and it's impossible to marshal the wherewithal to spend the money you need, or to make the sacrifices you need to make. And everyone's happy and charming and in perfect common cause with you until the last possible second, when suddenly they can't ignore the problems any longer. And then it takes ten times as much money and effort to undo all the damage that the first problem created.

Does any of this sound familiar?

CHAPTER THREE
The Abyss

And then, as it must to all men, tragedy came to Harry Jay Knowles:

I had my accident.

For reasons that I'm not entirely clear on, I sank into a real sort of screwy depression around this time. I had managed to resolve the whole ranch situation—something my mom had never been able to do—and then the folks up at the ranch basically undid everything I had accomplished. And I started to put on a monstrous amount of weight. I'd always been stocky, but this was something else entirely. Before I was done, I would weigh in at over five hundred pounds.

Now everybody who sees me for the first time, no matter what they know of me beforehand, they see a fat person. It's automatic. You know—"My God, he's huge! He's not going to live past thirty-five!" Ninety-nine percent of the time, people just can't help themselves. It's not even the things that people say; instead, it's what they don't say. It's the immediate reaction of it. You walk into a grocery store and children look at you like you're something out of a fairy tale, some creature that lives under a bridge somewhere. That's the part that's always bothered me. I hate being judged on a surface level, by how much water I can displace in a swimming pool or how many weeks I could feed the survivors of an airline crash.

At night I would have trouble breathing, and it would remind me of *The Elephant Man,* doomed to suffocation if I somehow slipped off this wall of pillows I was propped up on. I thought to myself, This is not good. I am twenty-four years old. I am not supposed to drown in my own chest. Soon they were going to have to take out a wall or something, crane-lift me out of here. I didn't want to end up as a Geraldo special.

After the accident, my dad pushed me to sue the city. I couldn't work, and the accident had happened on city property. But I didn't believe in that. I basically think everyone makes their own way in this world. What happened to me was an act of God, and God is far too busy to take a day off to have to face me in court. So this was effectively the second major chance at money in my short life that I was letting slip through my fingers, a turn of fate Dad was not shy about pointing out to me. He disagreed with my decision, if only because I had no health insurance and he wanted me to get some professional care. But ultimately, he recognized it was my decision to make.

One of the unexpected outcomes of my mom's death was that we ended up with an extra $5,000 in insurance money. This was money we hadn't planned on, and certainly not enough to make us rich, so Dad said that since I'd put so much time into rehabilitating the estate, I ought to have a major say in how we spent it. There was a new video game that had just hit—I think it was *Wing Commander III,* from Origin Systems here in Austin. It was the first of the multimedia video games that contained movie images in it, and it starred Mark Hamill—Luke Skywalker from *Star Wars*—so I was obviously all over it.

We paid about $3,000 for a Packard Bell Pentium 66 computer with a 500-meg hard drive and a scanner. I'd had a Texas Instruments computer I bought with my own money in 1982 at age eleven, but this was absolutely top-of-the-line for 1994. The one thing this family never gets tired of is its toys. Before I could even speak, the only time I ever cried or complained was when it was time to leave Toys "R" Us. But Dad was adamant that he was not going to get burned for hundreds of dollars in long-distance charges. So I was absolutely forbidden from logging on to the Internet. Then my friend Roland De-Noie convinced me that if I could get online, we could play *Doom* from home. He added me on to his account, which was $19 a month for unlimited access. That meant that now I had free Internet access.

So here I was: paralyzed from the accident, virtually bedridden, a textbook slacker in the town that coined the name, and I had no health care. Think *Time Bandits*: If somebody had a portal to access other eras, dimensions, and spheres of influence, I was ground zero on its target audience. I started spending all my time wandering around this infinite playground and prospective minefield, bumping into the oddest remnants of outlying cultures, slowly mapping it with bookmarks, and finding my way back up a trail of hyperlinks to the true believers like myself.

The first thing that took me online in a major way was to research back injuries. Christopher Reeve had just had his accident, so luckily (for me, not for him) this was much in the news. "Superman Paralyzed!" the headline writers couldn't resist trumpeting. At least I could move my arms. I began to follow links from these stories to actual chiropractors or muscle clinics. I learned that if you lie on your side, it straightens out your spine. I also learned that if nothing was broken but there was major swelling, it could be as much as six months before you regained the use of your limbs. It seemed like a matter of simple math to me: In six months, if my feet aren't working and I still can't wiggle my toes, that means my back is broken. In which case, I would have just spent the last six months in bed waiting for my spine to fuse and there's not much a doctor could have done anyway.

I started learning how to type while lying on my side. I wasn't in pain. Actually, that was the scariest part: I would take a pair of scissors and jab my foot to see if I could feel it. And I couldn't. I would massage my own legs to make sure the muscles didn't atrophy. Dad bought me a couple of canes; it was like teaching Frankenstein to walk, or Forrest Gump on the parallel bars, swaying my hips from side to side to get one foot to go in front of the other. Periodically, I could get out to work a collectibles show or see a movie, but it was still tricky.

When I first got online, it was still mostly text-based—no browsers with images. Netscape hadn't really come about yet—it was still Mosaic (the first search engine and graphics interface on the Web, just then recently developed at the University of Illinois), and I didn't know how to download images. When my friends and I would play games against one another, we would do direct computer-to-computer dialing. I could never figure out how to just type in an address and go there. So what I began doing was surfing like no one does anymore. It was all text, so the graphics sites didn't mean anything to me. I'd just go from page to page, link by link, drawing makeshift maps of my travels.

Somehow, I came into possession of one of these big generic "How to Build a Web Site" books that you find in the computer section of any bookstore. I had heard stories about guys who had broken their neck and used the nine months they were laid up to read William Gaddis's *The Recognitions* or Pynchon's *Gravity's Rainbow*. So I decided maybe this would be a good time to try and figure out this stuff. But most of it was information about design and layout. Almost none of it had anything to do with how to build a Web page. It was all about the *rules* of the Net: You can't have a document that's more than three hundred words, or people will get tired of scrolling down. This completely arbitrary protocol. It reminded me of screenwriting texts I had read: They'll spend hundreds of pages on margins and spacing and "CONTINUED" vs. no "CONTINUED," but they never discuss the differences between drafts to attract actors and drafts to secure financing, how to read and negotiate contracts—all the millions of things you need to know before wading into whatever parasite-infested swamp your work will take you. (The one exception is William Goldman's *Adventures in the Screen Trade,* which was probably published as a memoir anyway.)

In my second month of surfing, I discovered the newsgroups and IRC, or Internet Relay Chat. Newsgroups were online bulletin boards and social forums that served as virtual cauldrons of news, gossip, innuendo, and the sheerest shreds of sanctioned truth, which for the most part wound up being destroyed by spammers—mass mailings and the like. But even before that, it wasn't really news anymore, it was arguing over a fence with your busybody neighbor. If you went to alt.fan.JamesCameron, for instance, nine times out of ten they were disputing whether Harlan Ellison really invented *The Ter-minator* in his short story "Demon with the Glass Hand." That's not news. That's gossip about something that happened thirty years ago. Or worse, it was blowhards and intellectual bullies trying to prove how much smarter they were than anyone else—delusional types who imagine they're Hollywood insiders and can't wait to whip out their cybertalia to prove how long it is. It was all egotism and conjecture.

From the newsgroups, I began to develop a pretty faithful following, for a couple of reasons. First of all, in the IRCs, I would almost always post as Harry Knowles. Most people were Lord this or Sir this or Anakin that—Wallace and Gromit, that sort of stuff. Which is one of the things that's most seductive about the Internet—you can be whoever you want to be. But it also makes it very impersonal. At some point, if you plan to stand behind the information you're posting, your name has to become your bond. This was before any real personalities had emerged from cyberspace, and I think that's probably another key reason I became so popular. That's also why I put a face with my Web site when I first started it; it's like a Good Housekeeping Seal of sorts—"I am a real person (albeit an animated one). I vouch for the information to be found herein."

This was a world where most people trafficked in rumor, hyperbole, wishful thinking, where text was copied and cut and pasted until it was like one too many generations of Xerox copies—it was almost impossible to tell what had been there in the first place. I wanted to break original stories—like *Variety* or the *Hollywood Reporter*—but I really didn't have the sources. So I had to bust my ass getting industry stories and then doing a better job of researching them, picking up where they left off, or collating the various renditions. It always amazed me, reading fifteen different versions of the same

story, how much critical information could be gleaned by ex-
amining the different spins, or by connecting the dots and determining what wasn't being said.

My first exclusive was a *Star Wars: The Special Edition*
story. About two months before the accident, I had traveled
with Glen Oliver (who would later edit the Coaxial News section on the site) to Texas A&M University in College Station,
where LucasFilm was making their first presentation anywhere
outside of Skywalker Ranch. For whatever reason, there's a
surfeit of Aggies at ILM—Industrial Light+Magic, Lucas's effects company—in the technical ranks (Aggie jokes are the
Texas equivalent of Polack jokes), and they convinced Lucas to
allow the first presentation ever of footage from *Star Wars:
The Special Edition*. At this point, the *Special Edition* was still
more or less a rumor, and many people doubted its existence.
Steve Sansweet, Lucas's de facto ambassador to fans everywhere (an ex–Wall Street broker who gave it all up to write a
Star Wars making-of book and do Lucas's bidding), was the
one who made the presentation.

I suppose I should add that I thought the idea of a *Special
Edition* was stupid. The effects mistakes made in *Star Wars*
and *The Empire Strikes Back* are glorious mistakes, because
they were attempting to do something that had never been
done before. You can see maverick filmmaking physically
straining against the limits of the medium. Those mistakes are
a part of history and deserve to be preserved—proudly. Going
back and correcting them was like finding your homework
from when you were twelve and changing the answers. There
seemed something fundamentally disingenuous about it.
None of the original effects artists were even on board. But I
took copious notes and dutifully posted it on the Internet.

A couple of days later, somebody in one of the news-

49

groups where I'd posted the story—probably rec.arts.movies. starwars.misc—posted a message that said, "You asshole, that wasn't your story. That was whoever's story from Corona Coming Attractions." I went to Coming Attractions, and somebody had copied all my text and attributed it to themselves, billing it as a coup for Corona. And I got kind of pissed off about this. So I wrote Patrick Sauriol, who runs Corona, and I said, "Hey, that's my story! I fucking did that. Look at the date and time of my post versus when it was that you got your e-mail." And Patrick couldn't understand what I was upset about; *he* was upset at the idea of someone claiming information as proprietary.

For a lot of people, the whole idea of the Internet is the free flow and dissemination of information of every kind. Who the hell cares whose story it was, you know? Owning even a small part of this vast matrix of information seemed like a violation of some unwritten principle. Eventually, intellectual property rights will govern the Internet exactly like they govern traditional media now, just like they will dominate case law well into the next century. That's just not a very popular fight yet. But in my defense, I wasn't trying to profit by my story; I just wanted to build a name for myself.

The original impetus for Ain't It Cool News was very simple. I was paralyzed, laid up in bed, and I wanted someone to know who I was, in case I died. If Franklin Delano Roosevelt could be president from a wheelchair, then I ought to be able to do something. My resources were equally humble: I was capable of sitting and typing ninety words a minute for eighteen hours at a stretch. I was gifted with a free-floating obsessiveness that, if I could somehow harness it, might carry me past all the bullshit I was inevitably going to encounter. And I loved movies.

It's almost impossible to imagine now, but as recently as the mid-1990s—for me and most of the organized world—the Internet was still this uncharted ocean, the tips of vast undersea mountain ranges barely breaking its surface as isolated island atolls. For all its brave new worldliness and neuromantic glamour, no one had the slightest idea what the Internet was supposed to be used for.

Was it QVC or the Home Shopping Network, but without the chatter? Public Broadcasting, but without the pledge drives? *The Gong Show* on a global scale? Or the Minitel, the glorified directory listings/private data console floated by the French government? At that point, its only killer app was pornography, and the only reason sensible people ever went there was to see something they shouldn't, or on the off change they might get laid. (I suppose much like Hollywood itself.) The Internet was like a vast information superhighway, alright, only as if someone had erected billboards every fifteen feet of enormous vaginas. What traffic wasn't bumper-to-bumper had already pulled off on the shoulder, and was transfixed by the view.

Before long I was researching stories in earnest. If, for example, *Variety* ran a story about the new James Bond movie, saying it was actively filming in Beijing or Bangkok or something, I would go to a Web site that had a Bangkok newspaper and do a search for Bond in the Thai language. Then I would go to a newsgroup that had people from Thailand and beg for a translation of the article. They would send me one, and I would take the information from *Variety* and the information I got from the newspaper in Bangkok and mix it in with information from people on the Internet who claimed to read scripts and such, and I would fashion a report that I would post to the newsgroups. And instead of saying, "I have no life and I've just spent seven hours researching the new James Bond movie for no money," I would say, "I'm Harry Knowles and I have spies." Why? Because I wanted to be a writer, and spies sounded full of menace and intrigue. News reporting was not my primary goal. I was just learning to write in public.

Somewhere in here, I met a girl online. Her name was Rina, but I met her in a chatroom as Selena Kyle—Michelle Pfeiffer's Catwoman alias in *Batman Returns*. She monitored an Internet company in Dallas, and we used to e-mail back and forth in eight-hour marathon sessions every night. Pretty soon, we were completing each other's sentences. She said she felt trapped in her marriage, and she was pretty scarred by her experiences. I'm an incorrigible romantic—I always have been—but I found that the more time I spent trying to help her through her problems, the more I began to take an active interest in myself—what I looked like, my health, my future. Soon enough, we were exchanging photos. She was gorgeous, and she wanted to meet me. But I began to panic: No *way* would she accept someone this large.

So I went on a crash diet. I started spending eighteen hours a day typing online. Eventually, over time, this intense emotion between us mellowed into something more like a really close friendship. But because of her, I lost two hundred pounds, I mapped out the far-flung corners of the Internet, and I developed stakes in my own destiny. That's when I decided I needed my own forum. A soapbox. Something to house my diminishing girth but ever-expanding ambitions. I needed my own Web site.

Because on the Net, I wasn't a fat kid anymore; I wasn't a loser, and I wasn't a cripple—I was just Harry Knowles. It was like *Don Juan DeMarco*: Without the mask, I was Johnny

Depp as a mental patient. With the mask, I suddenly became all-powerful.

When I first put up my own Web site, I included a photo of Forry Ackerman in a Hawaiian shirt. Forrest J. Ackerman—Forry to his many minions—is the editor of *Famous Monsters of Filmland.* He is far and away my hero, and the man who pioneered fan-based movie writing for all of us. Eons before there was any forum whatsoever for the information, history, or appreciation of science fiction, horror, or fantasy in the movies, there was *Famous Monsters of Filmland.* Many of today's screenwriters, directors, effects mavens, and makeup artists—including a very young Stephen King—made their first appearance in the pages and letters column of *FMOF.* And the first e-mail I got back after the site went up, I swear to God, was from Forry. He told me that shirt had been a gift from Sarah Karloff after her father, Boris, passed away in 1968. You have no idea what kind of thrill this was at the time.

The site itself was low-tech—souped-down—the kind of thing you could put together out of an adjunct bedroom. We had one phone line—we still do. When Dad's online, I'm not. I chose orange as a primary color because—well, I am. Orange, I mean. And orange and purple seemed to capture my peculiarly visionary fashion sense. I put up little animated GIF (graphic interface format) files: eight-frame animations that were takeoffs of *Star Wars: The Special Edition* and the like. I was just learning Adobe Photoshop, so I figured if the site was a bust, I'd at least make it a job résumé.

Generally, I feel that bells and whistles are overrated. When you really get down to it, people are looking for content. That's why I have so few pictures on the site to this day. My average reader stays on the site between eighteen and twenty-two minutes. If I had thirty stills load every day, that would keep them there for maybe five minutes. Thumbnails—postage stamp–size photos—are even worse, because you lose all resolution. And the sites that excel at graphics seem to be one-way streets. They concentrate on information delivery and never on information gathering. They might as well be a broadcast medium. To me, that misses the entire point.

The least enjoyable part of this job for me has always been trying to figure out how to make any money out of it. I realize that's ass-backward as far as the Internet goes—most venture capitalists won't even look at your proposal without a prospective audience or market cap attached. But that's like pitching the movies the studios are most likely to greenlight, instead of figuring out how to pitch the movies you most want to make. This is how the system got so screwed up the last time.

Consequently, I've always been squeamish about finding the profit stream. I wasn't going to charge admission, or a subscription rate, like they do on pornography sites. I would sell advertising maybe, but I was adamant it couldn't overwhelm the site, and it couldn't influence the content. And I wasn't going to promise I could deliver some bold new demographic to potential marketers, because this site is one of the few places where you don't have to wade through a wealth of sanitized crap just to get what you came for.

I toyed with the idea, very briefly, of offering a subscription-only newsletter, completely separate from the site. This was something Matt Drudge and others do, and it would amount to patronage, or voluntary subscription. Those who wanted to could help me out, without me having to mount a weeklong fund-raising telethon. I posted a notice on the site saying we would offer a quarterly newsletter for $5 per year. The notice went up for twelve hours before the Web server asked me to take it down, since they claimed it would interfere with their efforts to sell advertising, of which they received a percentage. Rather than force the issue, I complied. (They're no longer my Web server.)

But based on that one twelve-hour notice, I received approximately 2,000 five-dollar checks over the next thirty days. Several people sent $20, two people sent $50, and one person sent $100. Of those 2,000, only one wanted their money back. The rest said keep it, it's worth it; some said, "I wish I could send more." The guy who sent $100 had a Wall Street address. I never did learn who he was. Ultimately, I decided that until we substantially expand the site, hire more employees, branch out into other areas and other media, we basically had enough money to do what we wanted. So I decided not to sweat the small stuff.

One time, about a year in, we almost lost everything because of some bad business decisions. I received word from my server at the time, Real-Times, that I was taking up as much bandwidth as DejaNews, which was their cash cow—a Web resource for searching newsgroups. They wanted me to start paying them $1,600 a month. I had never paid a penny for Internet access, plus, as I understood it, everything on the Internet was about branding, real estate, guaranteeing an audience and a demographic. This is what the online business journals were full of at the time. Charging me suitcases of cash seemed to be going against the grain.

I had met a guy at a *Star Trek* event who told me if I ever needed free access, to look him up. So I called him, and he told me he could take care of it in the blink of an eye. I didn't even need to shut down the site. Excellent. So I changed over, and since I'd been operating on less than 10 megs of space, he told me I now had room to archive. As much room as I needed. The site could become an online resource. So I began converting old word-processing files and HTML files, and for the first time, people had access to the history of the site. But the more complex I made the site, the more I began to notice that he was taking it offline at odd hours of the day. When I asked him what was going on, he told me I was overloading the server.

Then slowly, he began to reveal his master plan to me. He envisioned two areas to the site: The first would be free, but would basically be a holding area, while the second would be by credit-card access and would contain all the real dope. He envisioned scripts archived online in a top-secret area. And he thought the Talk Back section was a waste of space. Meanwhile, I could see that whatever exclusive materials I acquired came to me free of charge, and if I started asking money for them, that pipeline would dry up very quickly. Suddenly there was a crackle of free money in the air, and it invariably turns the nicest people into megalomaniacs. We went around and around on this.

Then one day, I went to the site, and there was a single message posted that read, "Harry Knowles believes that bandwidth should be free, therefore his site is no longer here." I asked him if I could at least get my files back, and he told me they had all been erased.

I was devastated. I went on the newsgroups, and I asked if someone could guarantee me free Internet access because I didn't have any money and I didn't want to charge on the site. And I got over 5,000 e-mails almost immediately—people who had 3 megs here, 2 megs there. People who offered their old computers or peripherals, or told me I could live in their home. Then David Cole contacted me from Jameson/Gold (a Web site design firm); he was a reader of the site, and they did

Disneyland.com and Sony.com, and were looking for a gateway portal site they could develop in-house (much like DEN, IFILM, and a lot of sites we've seen later). He added my domain name on their in-house employee server as a favor to me, but once they realized the amount of traffic I represented, they thought maybe I could be a gateway to their own in-house site. But my site just kept growing, until I dwarfed everything else. (Actually, what I really need is the same sort of system that was first used at the 1998 Winter Olympics in Nagano, Japan, where four or five servers were networked to operate simultaneously, because we have that many readers a day on the site.)

We worked out a compromise where I added an advertising banner at the top, but I kept a firewall between them and me. Because once content providers start talking to advertisers, all sorts of ideas start to pass for programming. So I told them I didn't want to know about it. And for the first time, I started to think of the Web site as maybe something brand-new, something that hadn't existed before, so it was impossible to predict its impact. Maybe in the evolutionary scheme of things, this was where I was meant to be. It would certainly go a long way toward explaining my ridiculous life.

Back when I happened upon it, the Internet was a byzantine place like nothing I'd ever seen. It was like the medina, the vast interconnected system of streets and warrens and cul-de-sacs in North African market districts that have been built up over 2,000 years by the necessities of commerce, and where you can find virtually anything if you know where to look for it. Once I discovered it, I was never more than a few feet away from it. And I realized that, like generations before me—through the late-night radio signal of some midwestern station, through tattered Xerox copies of out-of-print poets or long-lost manuscripts—I was not alone. There were others out there like me.

I quote Hal Holbrook in *Wall Street*:

"Bud, I like you. Just remember something. Man looks in the abyss. There's nothing staring back at him. At that moment, man finds his character. And *that* is what keeps him out of the abyss."

CHAPTER FOUR
Wild in the Streets

The word "geek" probably derives from the Low or Middle Low German word *geck,* meaning "fool." It was English slang, and later the preferred carny term for "a performer, often billed as a wild man, whose act usually consists of biting the head off a live chicken or snake." For that reason, it seems like it might have the same root as "gecko"—a small tropical lizard, and the Tarantino/George Clooney fraternal clan that wreaks havoc in the first half of *From Dusk Till Dawn*—but that word comes from the Malaysian *gekok,* and is really not our concern.

Over time, the term "geek" has come to apply rather generically to neurasthenic young white men (although not always white, and not always men) with an aptitude for or preoccupation with, first, technology, later science fiction, and now movies, comics, or any of a number of related fan-based disciplines. It has also come to be synonymous with "dweeb," "nerd," and other disparaging terms governing the strict social code of the high school caste system. I know that Quentin Tarantino and others make a formal distinction between these. But here's how I look at it: A dweeb (and by extension dork, twerp, squirrel, schlemiel, schlimazel, schmoe, and any similar epithet) describes a person who is both annoying and socially regressive. It implies no special intelligence or virtue. A nerd is similarly socially challenged, but bookish and with above-average scholastic skills. He is also reserved and generally intimidated by his circumstances.

But a geek, while also in possession of a superior intellect and often specialized affinities, is never shy or cowed by others because of it. A geek carries with him an almost hyperactive enthusiasm toward his highly proprietary subject matter, one that often comes bursting forth from him at inopportune moments, scaring the little children, and likely bonding him with others of his ilk. It's akin to "nut" or "freak" or "buff" from earlier eras—as in "hi-fi nut" or "gun freak" or "opera buff." But "geek" somehow transcends the mere preoccupation of those terms, the self-absorption of earlier times, and takes on a wholly evangelical quality, making us zealots of our own private religion. So effusive is this urge that the term "geek" transcends the category of mere noun and functions perfectly well as adjective, adverb, and ultimately action verb. My friends and I geek out when we get together, discussing the latest things that have held our attention spans hostage, and it's often disturbing or vaguely threatening to the casual observer.

Which is why it's troubling to me when I see geeks portrayed in the popular media as scared of the world, hiding out in darkened movie theaters as the nearest means of escape.

Geeks find things to celebrate in the world that most people are blind to and many actively resent. Geeks are invested in the ephemera of their environment: the trivia, the marginalia, the flotsam and jetsam, the peripheral and the parenthetical. We are the Trobriand Islanders and South Pacific cargo cults of planned obsolescence, saving our fads and castoffs, fetishizing them once they're no longer of any use to society. There's nothing to be ashamed of in being a geek. Geeks are merely our social visionaries, our psychic pioneers.

And now, the denizens of these once-isolated, overly balkanized, discrete worlds of private wonder, these fan-based pockets of enthusiasm, which have been kept subterranean and marginalized for far too long by the admen and programming czars and captains of consciousness, held apart by their lack of access and their own social failings—waiting for something like the Internet, maybe, to unleash them—seem on the verge of entering the mainstream as a newly emboldened, mutually fanatical coalition. An invisible bloc or silent army, and for once, a force to be reckoned with—geometrically expanding, and, quite possibly, entering its own golden age. A Geek Forum. Geek like me.

What makes movie geeks special is that movies are where all roads converge. Sci-fi geeks, comics geeks, technogeeks, computer geeks, kung fu and horror geeks, laserphiles and DVD junkies, videogame and Dungeons & Dragons mavens, skywalkers and trekkies and garden-variety obsessives—they all can find some sympathetic outpost in the movies.

One of the things I've always felt that was different about my Web site is the Talk Back section. Of course everybody has one now, but when I started it, it was one of the closest things you could find to pure democracy on the Internet. After every news story or review, anyone in the known universe can go on the site and post their own thoughts about it. You can scan down the list of postings by user name or subject line or time posted and get a brief history of the debate as it's raging. It's raw opinion, unmediated by me, and it excludes no one (except for a few troublemakers that Dad has had enough of).

I feel like one of the things that best prepared me for hosting the many warring factions that show up in Talk Back—and often degenerate into bloodbaths or open-air holy wars—is my history in collectibles. The collectors community is the closest thing I can think of to gathering all these different tribes under a single tent with a modicum of civility. Because what are collectors really but geeks with pocket money? What are bibliophiles but glorified book geeks? What are oenophiles but wine geeks? Or lepidopterists but net-wielding butterfly geeks? They just happen to have some expendable income to back it up.

If you walk around my house, you'll find literally thousands of images from comic books, science fiction, serials—all these competing worlds—tacked up on virtually every spare inch of wall and counter and shelf space that we have. You might find a complete set of *Star Wars* autographs. Production stills of Errol Flynn from *The Charge of the Light Brigade* or Bruce Lee from the mirror hall in *Enter the Dragon* or Charles Laughton from *Mutiny on the Bounty.* Posters or lobby cards from *The Seventh Voyage of Sinbad* or *Jason and the Argonauts.* An original *Hound of the Baskervilles* poster, which I was once offered $7,500 for. Original paintings of Robbie the Robot from *Forbidden Planet* or the 1940s *Spy Smasher.* An original bone-sculpture chair from *The Texas Chainsaw Massacre* and a Bob Burns coffin from *Poltergeist.* Tin litho *Alamo* and *Prince Valiant* Sword and Shield sets with the original Cal Foster box art. An original 1936 tube television. Animation cells of Gandalf from the Ralph Bakshi *Lord of the Rings,* the original Bart Simpson from *The Tracey Ullman Show,* Poison Ivy from the *Batman* TV show, Tinkerbell from *Peter Pan,* and Betty Boop from *Bimbo's Initiation.* A giant cube in one corner made up of 60,000 comic books. A *Last Boy Scout* poster and a Sherlock Holmes lobby card, from which I took the names Joe Hallenbeck (Bruce Willis) and Moriarty (Lionel Atwill), respectively, for my two chief spies.

In fact, most of my spies have been christened by letting my eyes glide across these surfaces. Exactly like Verbal Kint, the disguised Keyser Soze, at the end of *The Usual Suspects*—extemporaneously weaving his own safety net. Exactly like *Usual Suspects* screenwriter Christopher McQuarrie, working in the copy room of a law firm in downtown Los Angeles, staring at the bulletin board, when he came across the brand name "Quartet: Skokie, Illinois," which started him thinking. Plus a hundred times more than that which I could list, plus ten times more than that in storage. Some of this stuff has been hung up around me since literally before I was born. It's in me, and in my psychological makeup, and on my site. And it's a language I can speak with others, from having been around this stuff my whole life.

One time Bob Wayne, who is currently the head of DC Comics, was in a meeting with some Warner execs about *Batman & Robin,* and they said, "You know, we've got a problem. There's this kid on the Internet named Harry Knowles, and he's revealing all this test-screening stuff, and it's starting a real bad word of mouth." And Bob Wayne says, "Harry Knowles? In Austin, Texas? I remember that kid. He used to run around naked at conventions. Streaking conventions." My parents used to drag me along to San Diego Con or the Berkeley Underground Con and I would sleep in a dresser drawer in their motel room. I was famous for biting people on the ass. (Not a bad skill to go through life with, by the way.) I was like Calvin of *Calvin & Hobbes*.

If you go to a collectibles show today, you'll see probably 90 percent brand-new stock—action figures that people buy at Target and triple the price on as soon as they're discontinued. But you'll also find a handful of dealers who are longtimers— who have been at this gig since at least the early '70s. These are the vintage collectibles dealers. And we were at the top of that ladder. You see some really distressing things in that world: People who can't afford shoes for their kids because they have this insatiable craving for Jayne Mansfield memorabilia. Borderline stalkers who will do anything to be next to the object of their fascination. The extremes of that whole religion/addiction/fetishism side of it.

But coming of age at collectors' conventions prepared me for my singular path in a couple of important ways. First of all, if you're going to make your living in any kind of journalism, you very early have to develop a nose for news. An instinct that tells you which of your stories will pan out and which stories are too good to be true. And that's exactly the same kind of divining rod that allows you to unearth those bargains in collectibles that are going to pay the bills. My friends always referred to it as "the Force," because I have a special sense whenever there's something there. Once at the Collectors Expo in San Antonio, I had a really strong vibe that there was something in there, hiding. I let it lead me completely around the hall, into the back room, where I passed a table with a box kicked half under it. It took me forty-five minutes of rummaging, but I finally found a folded original-issue one-sheet for Howard Hawks's *The Thing*. I just opened up one corner and recognized the original ivy green color. I didn't even have to unfold it.

I asked the guy how much for the poster, and he says $8. I got that and a lobby card from *Earth vs. the Flying Saucers,* which Ray Harryhausen did the effects for, for $7 in all. I told him, "We've got a booth over there—can I bring the money back to you?" He said sure. We sold the poster almost immediately for $700, and I took his money back over to him. I would never lie to someone, tell them something wasn't valuable when I knew it was. But the guy named his own price. He never knew a thing. (Literally.) It's the same way when you're processing the gigabyte of information that comes in on e-mail on a daily basis. You have to instantly know what has a sensational value, what's going to generate controversy, and how to pick your fights, so that you invest your time in the fights you can win. Because time is always the killer.

The more you're around that world, the more you look at it with a storyteller's eye, and the more it becomes a source of material. One time at a show, a guy asked to see us out in the parking lot. He was wearing a sharkskin suit, sunglasses indoors; he had "*Miami Vice* Farm Team" stenciled on his forehead. The guy said he was a DEA agent who had raided one of Colombian drug dealer Pablo Escobar's warehouses, where they found several thousand pounds of movie paper, acquired through money laundering. The government let him take a few of these because he said he had a friend who was a collector. At least that was his story.

They were mounted on linen backs, really well preserved, and he unrolled the first one, and it was *Birth of a Nation.* This is one of those things you doubt you'll ever see in person. The exact same poster sold to Cecil B. DeMille's granddaughter at Sotheby's for $250,000, which she then donated to the

Academy of Motion Picture Arts and Sciences. He unrolled the second one, and when practically the first millimeter of it was exposed, I knew it was an original *King Kong*. The next one was for *The Hound of the Baskervilles*. *Pinocchio*. Charlie Chaplin's *The Kid*. Each one of these I had memorized from catalogues as a small child. They're like the Holy Grail of film posters.

Dad said, "Yeah, nice stuff," with this face he gets where he locks down all of his emotions, so that it looks like he's really bored, unless you happen to know him, in which case it looks like he's about to explode. The guy said, "I have to get $250 apiece out of them." This man clearly did not understand what he had in his possession. It costs $200 each just to apply the linen backing. We took everything he had except one. I think it was *Attack of the 50-Foot Woman*. We ran out of money. It came to $1,250 and he accepted $1,200. I think we sold three and settled my mom's estate-tax problem. Dad admitted later he thought we'd never be able to afford them when he told me to come outside with him. He just wanted me to see something like that once in my life. Each one was framed in snakeskin.

The other skills I appropriated from working the collectibles market are the carnival barker's ability to size up his mark, an eye for instant critical appraisal, and a storyteller's sense of what the audience requires at any given moment. You learn how to weave anecdotal history seamlessly into a sales pitch. You see somebody giving the once-over to a poster for *Mysterious Island,* you start telling them how Ray Harryhausen had his eye on the Jules Verne novel *20,000 Leagues Under the Sea* because it was in the public domain, but Walt Disney really wanted to do it, because he wanted the submarine ride for Disneyland. So in exchange for a gentlemen's agreement between them, Disney helped Harryhausen set up this other Jules Verne project at a rival studio. This is your hook. By the time you're finished, you've embellished their attraction to it with the history surrounding it, and they have to have it. This is why I started reading up on movies, learning the personalities of the different studios, tracking the various figures who kept resurfacing in all the films I liked. This has basically been my whole life, feeding on this material.

And ultimately, it's the collectors—the geeks—who will preserve this history. When an earthquake destroys that huge underground bunker the studios maintain out in the salt flats, the *Time Tunnel* complex where they store their master negatives in a perfect climate-controlled environment, it's the collectors who will reassemble the cinematic record. Why have so many great paintings survived? Because they were preserved in museums and institutional spaces? No. I think because they were in the hands of private collectors. People who loved them first, often irrationally, before time could reward them. I personally believe there's a stronger right to own collectibles than to own guns.

And you can have mine when you pry my cold clammy fingers off of them.

CHAPTER FIVE
Ace in the Hole

Not for nothing were Hollywood's earliest spectacles biblical in nature—usually something involving a pharaoh riding herd over the construction of timeless pyramids. Because this most closely approximates how Hollywood views itself: mounting great logistical efforts, breathtaking in scope, that incidentally leave behind standing monuments to those who dared envision things on such a scale—and that will invariably serve as the final resting place for such grandiose egos after they're gone. Efforts of this magnitude require pinpoint precision, unquestioning dedication and sacrifice, and absolute fealty. Everything must have its time, place, and order. The alternative is chaos.

Which is where I usually get into trouble. I show up too early in the process, hang around the margins through the long middle, and then tend to get in the way long after I've worn out my welcome. Just like everyone else in the food chain, journalists are meant to serve a function. If they point and yell too early, they dilute a film's impact. If they focus too much behind the scenes, they second-guess the product. If they hold a grudge or harbor an obsession, they divert attention from the next thing rolling down the pike. The entertainment press is entrusted with weighty concepts and heavy machinery; to behave other than as expected would be irresponsible.

But there has always been the kind of interest that I'm accused of stirring up, and that I clearly trade on. There was always a healthy market for the latest scripts, a currency exchange rate in production and casting tidbits, a handicapper's line on the weekend numbers. It has just always resided within the industry. What I help facilitate, and, more correctly, what the Internet provides for, is the expansion of that sort of ancillary interest into a universal audience. This is a good thing. That's what the studios don't get. Any interest in the offshoots and by-products, the talk soup and word salad that films marinate in and are assembled out of, just serves to bolster interest in the films themselves. This translates into "ka-ching," for those who don't traffic in the lingo.

Much is made of the publication of weekend grosses in family newspapers—as if attention to the crass commercial side of filmmaking somehow cheapens the pure film experience. Or this auteurist shorthand, which keeps everyone up on all the latest production details. But all this does is make a horse race out of it. It's an outgrowth of Oscar fever, keeping running tabs on the playing field. And it's no different—nor any less stage-managed—than insiders' scoops on the private lives of public stars in *Photoplay* magazine in the golden age of Hollywood. Or, for that matter, the latest *Vanity Fair* celebrity profile. No one claims that institutional sports is somehow compromised by people taking an active interest in the statistics. It's merely a scorecard to compare individual achievements, and to ground today's highlights in some sort of historical continuum. Presumably to encourage the level of performance.

Look at the independent film world. There is a rich, robust, insular tradition of independent and experimental cinema stretching back a century or more: Méliès, Buñuel and Dali, Maya Deren, Cassavetes, James and Sadie Benning— name your poison. But certainly one of the chief engines of the '90s explosion in independent films is as a farm team for the majors. It's the most expedient way for those born without the luxuries of access or birthright to bum rush the citadel. And part of the fun of following it is being the first on your block to recognize new talent and new voices. Entry-level films have always existed inside the industry—they've just been termed "calling-card films," and they generally weren't feature-length. But they've always made the rounds within the agencies, within the development community, among anyone who might envision a profit motive for being in this particular loop. The independent film world, for all of the other things it may be, is merely the globalization of this phenomenon. Just like it's the same showcase for writers and actors that off-Broadway theater used to be, except you don't have to take a room at the midtown Marriott or wait in line at the TKTS booth in Times Square to be a part of it.

If we extend that conceit, then for the true film fan, information streams in parallel waves, almost like light from a fading star that reaches us long after the star itself is dead. There's the hype and spin of movies as they're just about to be released, in that last pregnant moment when anything about them could still be true. Before that, there's the insiders' buzz, when things crop up in preview screenings or on the festival circuit, and where any scrap or tidbit is worth its weight in gold. Before that, there's the production buzz: What's shooting? What's the gossip from the set? How will ideas or novels or histories or mythologies or characters we're often thoroughly familiar with beforehand be translated by those entrusted with the sacred task? And before that, there's the development buzz: What are the hot scripts? Who are the up-and-coming writers? What executive at what studio with what particular set of tastes or biases will put exactly what project into play?

If you follow the *Hollywood Literary Sales Directory,* you can keep up with what spec scripts or pitches have sold quarterly. If you follow the *Variety* production charts, you know what's shooting and where. If you follow the independent film press, keep up with other film sites on the Internet, follow the festivals, you get a sense of what will be big six months, nine months, a year from now. It's like a three-ring circus—all of these are separate worlds that unfold simultaneously. It used to be that only people in the film industry knew or cared. They just tended to care a lot. But for anyone with the time or inclination, there's no difference. Knowledge is not proprietary. Knowledge is power. And power belongs to the people.

But with very few exceptions, no other journalists bother to look at it this way. One, it's a buttload more work. Two, there are official incentives from the studios for them not to get involved. And three, there is a matter of access: How do you even find a lot of this stuff, in order to have an opinion about it in the first place? It's rare among film critics to even read source novels that films are based on. Getting them to read a script, much less multiple drafts, is next to impossible.

On his Web site, Roger Ebert writes classic film reviews. He writes reviews for independent films, because he's one of the few who spends time on the festival circuit, and he writes reviews for current studio releases. What he doesn't do is cover films at the script stage that are going to come out in two years. Or five years. Or that may never come out, and why. I'm the only one I know who covers the process from the beginning to the end.

You could make the argument that it's nobody's business—or more importantly, that nobody cares. This is what you'll hear from those film industry mavens who think America is something you fly over between New York and Los Angeles, who believe the viewing public is getting dumber and dumber and who constantly pander to it, condescend to it, sink to its level. They'll tell you the Internet proves just how trivial the taste of the American public genuinely is. That's the same argument you'll get from Sammy Glick in *What Makes Sammy Run?*, which Budd Schulberg wrote sixty years ago. But in reality, just the opposite is true: We live in the Information Age. And if information is out there, someone will want to know it.

Instead, the media treats the Internet as nothing less than the Vandals on the steppes, or the Mongols at the gate. And when I say "media," I purposely use the singular, even though I know it's the plural for "medium." Because increasingly, six or seven multinational corporations—hence six or seven individuals—bring us all of our news and information, just like seven studios bring us the lion's share of our films. Often they're the very same people. And they tend to think a lot more alike than they do differently. Hence, the "media." Singular.

The journalist's profession used to be an admirable one.

How many people go out and get a story anymore—press a source or field a tip and then wander out into harm's way until something gives? The few examples of it I ever come across that fall within my purview, I always try and provide a link to. Because it's becoming a lost art. Journalism today is all sound bites, photo ops, electronic press kits, and happy news, all of it filled with late-breaking nuggets of tasty, processed pabulum that does absolutely nothing but occupy the space that all the real news stories would go in, if someone were able to tell them. Meanwhile, folks like me are treated like Jerry Lee Lewis at the dawn of rock and roll—wild animals, pounding the keyboards and howling at the moon.

I've been in arguments with print journalists on panels or online where I've been accused of not being a trained reporter, that I merely repeat everything I know, that I print lies and innuendo and rampantly run spoilers just to ruin a movie. They argue that it's unethical to recruit and encourage writers who've never worked at a newspaper or served time in the trenches, because it erodes the very foundations of journalism. They say I'm too emotional in my stories, and that it obscures my judgment—or worse yet, that I'm brazenly sentimental. That I'm some punk kid or idiot savant who turned into the 2,000-pound gorilla (literally), and now nobody can do anything about me.

Forget that *all* (and I mean *all*) traditional entertainment stories come from press releases. That pit bull publicists demand and get insane concessions for their clients—avoidance of touchy subject matter, photo approval, writer approval, question approval. Forget that a whole caste of reporters and critics spend their lives as junket whores, sopping up the free food, lavish accommodations, spoon-fed interviews, and bags full of swag—little more than glorified bribes. These aren't set visits, where you might inadvertently learn something or get a sense of the overall picture. They're not one-on-one interviews, where you have at least a sporting chance of gleaning something interesting from a star, away from their watchdogs and handlers. It's a suite in some fancy hotel, where you interview cast and crew for half an hour each at the same time as a dozen other journalists who are grateful just to be there.

Forget that the studios are extremely adept at co-opting critics by soliciting their opinions at the script or early screening stages. That studio publicists routinely call up prominent critics with a set of prefab quotes, asking, "Wouldn't you say something like this?" Or that a whole new breed of critic now exists for no other reason than to provide blurbs for the ad— people you've never heard of and will never read a review by. It's as if the Internet suddenly represents a threat to the traditional critical establishment, and somehow I make the biggest target. Yet I work a standard beat. Instead of a Rolodex, I have an e-mail in-box. I make determinations based on my instincts and my knowledge of the players. And if a story is negative, I work harder to confirm the facts, because I know what it's like to be in the media eye, and to read false stories about myself.

Once after I appeared with Ebert on his TV program, Page 6 of the *New York Post* ran a blind item saying he had called me fat, disgusting, and smelly. This was then reprinted everywhere. Ebert himself spent an entire column denying the rumor. Mind you, the *Post* isn't calling me any of those things. That would mean they'd have to take responsibility for saying it, and I could either take offense or not. They're just dispassionately reporting it. Except they *are* calling me names. That's exactly what they're doing. If they want to say I'm fat or disgusting or smelly—I mean, let's go: I'll get up on a scale.

Let's get some dogs in here, see if they can stomach me. Otherwise, it's just yellow press.

But the main difference, as I see it, between the mainstream press and myself is that we're basically interested in different things. First of all, contrary to the criticism I get, I'm not at all interested in the tabloid aspects of journalism. What people do on their own time, what lifestyle they favor off the clock, what they get caught doing or how they slip up in their personal lives, are basically of no consequence to me. Really. At a time when the bastions of the fourth estate are sliding down the raked and muddy slopes of the gutter press, I could genuinely care less. For me, it's all about the work.

To my way of thinking, all that stuff—who's gay, who's sleeping with whom, who's a cuckold or Scientologist or raging alcoholic or chronic pothead or has the tiniest of heroin problems—it's the showbiz equivalent of sports injuries: These things are worthy of our attention only to the degree that they influence the outcome of play. They're a disappointment to us when their effects become debilitating. We feel concern for those who undergo them, and wish them a happy, healthy, and wholesale recovery. But basically, it's none of our fucking business.

So Rob Lowe sleeps with a sixteen-year-old girl, because he never thought to ask for an ID? Doesn't matter. It's all about the work. Elia Kazan and naming names? It's about the work. Roman Polanski and underage sex? Robert Downey Jr. and drugs? About the work. I get notices on a more or less constant basis claiming things that I wish I hadn't heard: A very pregnant female star is seen giving a prominent director a blow job in a restaurant. Two stars, both married to other people, are caught on video in the bushes outside of Tavern on the Green in Central Park. A major actor has affairs with half the leading men in Hollywood, which his publicist just manages to keep out of the papers by the skin of her teeth. Or better yet, a journalist who covers stories exactly like these takes time off once a year to go to Thailand, where he can have sex with fourteen-year-old boys.

Did Jean Harlow shoot Paul Bern, her lover and Thalberg's theater man? Did William Randolph Hearst shoot producer Thomas Ince on his yacht, when who he meant to shoot was Charlie Chaplin for having an affair with Marion Davies? Could Kenneth Anger's private life fill at least a chapter of his own *Hollywood Babylon*? I have no idea. I cite these examples not to titillate, but because in certain circles, past or present, they're treated as common knowledge. But they're a parlor game at best, and armaments of destruction at worst. Like Coppola says in *Hearts of Darkness* about Martin Sheen's heart attack: "If Marty dies, I want to hear everything's okay until I say Marty's dead . . . What's going on is fucking gossip. And that gossip can finish me off."

So one of the principles I founded the site on, and a policy we try to uphold, is "nothing personal": If you say Bruce Willis can't act, that's fine. If you say Bruce Willis can't *fucking* act, that's fine. If you say Bruce Willis can't act, that *fascist motherfucker,* that's unacceptable. If it's a personal attack, we remove it. True, false, conjecture, lies—all the same; we remove it. The exception is when something impacts on the final product. How does Phil Hartman's death affect the final cut of *Small Soldiers*? If a famous actress has an apparent drug habit or boy problems, how did that contribute to the collapse of one of her movies, which should have been a perfect movie and wasn't? Or else when someone deserves it. If someone is letting themselves and others down—in their work—then we'll bust them on it. Then sometimes it gets kind of personal.

77

But even so, we try not to take cheap shots. And then always in context.

Because it's never fair. And when it happens to you, it sucks.

Take, for example, the strange case of Matt Drudge.

CHAPTER SIX
A Face in the Crowd

Matt Drudge was the first celebrity produced exclusively by and for the Internet. (I may have been the second.) He started out as a symbol for one thing and wound up a symbol for something entirely different. The change had as much to do with him as a person as it did with the Internet, and the forces that were brought to bear as the Internet rose in prominence. And if you follow that transition from start to finish, it's as clear a fable as we have for the morality of the media in modern times.

One day early on, while on my appointed rounds scouring the Internet, I went into a chat room where Matt Drudge was scheduled to appear. At this point, his Web site wasn't nearly so partisan as it is now, and I included myself among his regular readers. He would report on natural disasters, or various political intrigues, or the film and music industries. It was more like a newspaper format, and although you could pretty easily peg him as a moderate conservative, it didn't seem to inform so much of his content yet. Drudge was holding court in the chat room to maybe twenty people, and was at a little bit of a loss, since the barrage of questions was mildly overwhelming. The reason I never do chat rooms anymore is that if you go in as a popular Internet content provider, it's a little bit like taking your Ph.D. orals: A jury of your would-be peers sits and waits for you to drop your guard so they can show you up. Since the questions were coming fast and furious, and Drudge was struggling to keep up, and since I was a fellow information junkie—with the same CNN habit, who read the same dozen papers every morning—I jumped in to help him. And since I type really fast, I quickly came to dominate the conversation.

Pretty soon, Drudge opened up a private line with me, saying in essence, "Who the hell are you, and how do you know all this stuff?" Afterward, we went off into a private chat and talked for maybe three or four hours. He was a gift-shop clerk at the CNN Tower in Hollywood, at Sunset and Vine; I was a collectibles vendor. We were at similar places in our lives. At that point, I wasn't looking to work with Drudge; the opportunity just sort of presented itself. This was December 1995 or so.

I started off doing box-office analysis, where he would leak me the Friday numbers late Friday night or early Saturday morning once he got them from his sources, and I would project the weekend grosses, and then handicap the following weekend. Kind of like what Mr. Moviefone does now based on advance calls, or what the trades spread out over Friday, Monday, and Tuesday. And then I would suggest other stories based on things I came across—both political and film-related. I was one of the few people, I believe, to ever receive a byline on his site.

I doubt I spent more than two or three months total working for Drudge. I learned an immense amount from him: what kind of stories register with the public; how to frame a story to get people interested in both it and you. And I'll always have a special place in my heart for Matt—both for the opportunity he gave me, and on a deeper level, as someone I studied up close and had a lot in common with, and who I personally liked a great deal. But I felt like he started seeing me as his point/counterpoint—the Michael Kinsey to his Pat Buchanan, or Jane, His Ignorant Slut. The last thing I wanted to be was the liberal Matt Drudge. Even then, I could start to see his political slide. I still didn't know what I was looking for but I knew it wasn't this. So soon enough, I moved on.

Over the years, I've watched Drudge evolve from one of the sweetest, most caring guys into a prime assassin for the partisan right. Although he's rarely credited with it today, he was one of the first to implicitly understand the allure of the Internet—that people who would venture out into a new, uncharted medium like this were largely seeking community.

And Drudge was very good at shepherding people into his fold. I don't think it was calculated; I think that's just how he was. He would choose to break news inside actual newsgroups that pertained to that particular topic. If you frequented a particular newsgroup, you naturally felt an allegiance to it. Suddenly, here was someone with a minor reputation who brought something of interest to you, something newsworthy, and laid it at your feet. When he could have been trading on it almost anywhere else. And then he'd leave a link to his site behind. It was extremely validating, and it built him an incredible loyalty.

But really what attracted most people to Drudge was that his stories had such a singular perspective. They were reflective in a way that news just isn't anymore. His lead-ins always went something like: "You know, I was looking out my apartment window today, and I was thinking about the turns I've taken in my life." He made himself and his humble circumstances a character in his stories. First-person journalism doesn't always have to be gonzo—Hunter Thompson recreating himself as larger than life, blustering through his stories, pinballing off of them as they continually put themselves in his way, and as his own agenda works at crosspurposes. That only works if you're larger than life yourself. If you outweigh your material. Some of us, for lack of a better term, are smaller than life. Or at least quieter than life. That's the value of our perspective. Drudge lived in a humble apartment complex right across from the CNN Tower in Hollywood. It was the opposite of pretentious or presumptuous. It was charming.

I remember one story he did on the musical scoring session for *Waterworld*. Before going to hear the orchestra record the background music, he went out to the beach and just listened to the ocean. And then after the recording session, he went back to the beach, but this time with the music in his head. And then he went home and wrote his report. It was the most poetic thing. It had a humanism to it that is completely lacking in objective journalism. Plus it really appealed to me, because this was the way that I wrote about and experienced films: If you're going to a *Godfather* movie, you eat Italian; if you're going to see a *Living Dead* film, you eat barbecue, so you can feel flesh separating from the bone.

It just makes sense. Or at least it does to me. Whatever Drudge was covering—catastrophes, politics, film—he found a way to ground it in somebody's experiences, either his or somebody else's.

But very quickly, it became apparent to me that there is a fundamental distinction between what I do and what Drudge does, starting with why we do it. He seems very comfortable holding a partisan line. Drudge is basically like me, he's a fan—albeit of raw power. But unlike me, he has no real critical eye, which has been what has led him into league with some of the most reactionary forces in modern times. He can't see politics beyond it being a gameboard, and a zero-sum game at that. And so he can't measure his own actions as anything more or less than fealty to a higher cause— even a shamelessly misguided one.

And since this is what many people secretly suspect about me and my relationship with my industry, it's something I've thought long and carefully about: Harry's talking to Robert Rodriguez, or Dean Devlin, or Ron Howard, so obviously these people are in danger of corrupting him. That's a very real fear, and one I can completely understand. Except they haven't. They don't. Because once you sway—once you even waver—then they own you.

When I met Drudge, he told me Pat Buchanan was going to be the next president of the United States. Later on he was just as adamant that Bob Dole was going to be president, and it was impossible to explain to him why this would never be. This was back when Clinton's approval rating was something like 30 percent. I told him the Republicans were going to self-destruct, because they were arrogant and self-entitled and considered their momentary popularity a God-given right. This was why it was impossible for Dole to step aside and cede the nomination to someone who actually had a chance of winning. Because he was mean and bitter and considered himself preordained by every slight and compromise he'd ever had to put up with to get there. It had nothing to do with ideology, really. It was just the attitude these guys rode in on, and it was going to carry them out feet first. It was Nixon all over again, complete with gallows humor.

Then almost immediately, the newly empowered Republican Congress shut down the federal government, and began to dismantle the National Endowment for the Arts, and took this strident, almost schoolmarmish voice in their dealings with the American public. They became bullies, on national television no less, and the one thing Americans have zero tolerance for is bullies. Don't tread on me, motherfucker. This was something Drudge was absolutely oblivious to, while anyone who was paying attention could have seen it coming. The last time the Republicans controlled a majority in both houses of Congress, you had the House Un-American Activities Committee and charlatans like Joe McCarthy. And why not? Because to the victor go the spoils, and if your only motivation is political ambition, the only limitations you face are your own reserves of personal chutzpah—and probably free-floating hubris, somewhere out there on the horizon.

I've been in chat rooms with Drudge where Republican party leaders were stoking him and feeding him information about what was going on on the inside. And for him, it really was a Faustian deal. He saw the access sitting there, glittering, and he knew it was evil and what it would ultimately cost him, but he couldn't help himself. He lost track of what he might still call the common man. He became cynical, then dogmatic, and finally, just plain mean. He took as received orthodoxy that Clinton was an evil man, without being capable of applying the same standards to Newt Gingrich or any of these self-appointed messiahs busy clogging his side of the aisle.

I would have these insane arguments with Drudge, where he would recite this litany of charges like it had just come to him carved on tablets: Clinton deserves our wrath because he is a fornicator and a liar. Whereas I would always take the historical view: Name a standing president in this century who hasn't had a mistress in the White House. Jimmy Carter, probably. Nixon—and look what you got in exchange: an alcoholic paranoid whose madman defense may or may not have been his idea of a joke. The Brothers Kennedy took it to Roman proportions. People of privilege are seldom bound by the moral rigors of those without the same opportunities. Get used to it.

But explaining this to Drudge was like John Landis trying to explain the difference between anal intercourse and doggie style to the Motion Picture Association of America (MPAA, the guys who hand out the ratings). What parts Drudge could actually fathom, he didn't want to hear about. He finally crossed the Rubicon when I was at Sundance in 1997, on the day that Clinton announced he would balance the budget within four years—an incredible accomplishment by anyone's standards. This was the same day Drudge broke the Monica Lewinsky story.

Now, I know a few things about how to break a story; this is what Hollywood hates the most about me, is that I throw off their timing. Remember, Drudge had the story before it was in *Newsweek*. Michael Isikoff, the *Newsweek* reporter who made his reputation on it, had filed the story, but the editors had decided not to go with it until it had appeared elsewhere first.

And this was perfect for everyone. *Newsweek* needed the plausible deniability of simply following a breaking news story. The Republicans needed the story to break that day in order to bounce the budget story; a week later—in the next issue of *Newsweek,* for example—would seem too reactionary, too calculated. And the nameless patriots who had leaked the story to Isikoff in the first place needed someplace for the story to appear. Drudge was exactly what they were looking for. And it put him on the map. Of course, it was dirty politics at its worst. But it was also straight out of Frank Capra: When do they start the smear campaign against Jimmy Stewart in *Mr. Smith Goes to Washington*? The day he takes to the floor of Congress and begins his filibuster. Not only did Drudge break a nonstory, he did so at the perfect time to inflict the maximum amount of political damage.

This is the devil's bargain: Print journalism uses the Internet for its sources and to legitimize the stories it's embarrassed by. The Internet uses traditional print and broadcast journalism for publicity and credibility. Each approaches the transaction with disdain, and neither thinks it is being corrupted in the process. And both are routinely vilified by the consumer public, which understands the process instinctively. I thought there had to be a better way.

The last time I talked to Drudge was New Year's Eve several years ago, and he said, "Wow, you and I really had a year, didn't we?" And I said, "Yeah, we did." He said, "But you're taking it too easy on Hollywood." I asked him, "What do you mean? I'm the most hated man in Hollywood. Haven't you read the papers?" And he said, "Yeah, but you're letting them live in their glass houses. You need to break the glass." Like, in case of emergency, I guess.

And I said to him, "Listen, don't you want to be respected?" It literally all comes down to what you want out of life. And what you think working in this business can provide you. Do you want to become rich? Do you want to become respected? Do you want power—or friends with power, at least? Choose. In Drudge's world, Rush Limbaugh has been down that same path. And what is Rush Limbaugh? If you do a search on Amazon.com, you'll find he's a big fat idiot. He found a niche, and he can pay the rent by preaching to the converted. But he'll never, ever be respected.

Or a little closer to home, at least in the sense that he's a nominal liberal, what about Jerry Springer? I'm sure he'd like those benedictions at the end of his program to take seed in his audience. But he lowered the bar on entertainment, and now he's a standing joke—his movie tanked, every cameo he does seems tiresome and dated, and his audience has moved on to World Wrestling Federation *SmackDown*s. Where is Morton Downey Jr., these days? Well, he's dead, actually, but most of his onetime fans would be hard-pressed to tell you.

Drudge signed a half-million-dollar book advance and his book was a best-seller. He's been working really hard. But if he doesn't wake up, if he just continues with the fedora and the schtick, as the pit bull of the bulbous right, he's going to find that friends like the right wing in this country have a way of winding up safe on shore once his ship starts to list. You can already see it with the Sidney Blumenthal lawsuit (the *Time* magazine journalist turned Clinton staff member who sued Drudge for $30 million for claiming he had "a spousal abuse past"), not to mention the reception Drudge gets when he trots out the First Amendment on CNN. If they left

Joseph McCarthy and Whittaker Chambers and James J. Angleton and G. Gordon Liddy and John Mitchell and Eugene Hasenfus and William Casey and Freeway Ricky Ross and Linda Tripp dangling in the wind, they're not likely to make an exception for people like us.

I don't really talk to Drudge anymore. I've been invited on his show a number of times, but I don't want to do it. Because if I see him, I'm going to talk to him, and if I talk to him, I'll make him angry. And there's a part of me that doesn't want to wake him up, because he's forgotten a dream that we both once had, and that I'm on the verge of being able to make come true. Or else I'm still dreaming myself. Either way, I'll take my life over his any day.

To paraphrase Crispin Glover in *Back to the Future,* "Character is density." The forces that govern you, that find purchase within you, I think, are a function of moral fiber. Of how deeply or shallowly goodness runs within you. *Star Wars* teaches us that going over to the dark side is merely the inability or refusal to stay the course, to not be diverted by temporal or transient concerns—greed, power, weaknesses masquerading as strengths. Maybe the ability to focus past those things is a capacity of vision, and maybe it's a capacity of blindness. Maybe you are aided in this struggle by simplicity or naiveté or willful ignorance. I don't think it much matters. I only know the decision lies within each of us. As another '70s visionary put it in *Apocalypse Now,* another fractured masterpiece from that noble era:

"There's a conflict in every human heart between the rational and the irrational, between good and evil. The good does not always triumph. Sometimes the dark side overcomes what

Lincoln called 'the better angels of our nature.' Every man has got a breaking point. You and I have. Walter Kurtz has reached his."

We learn our lessons through films. The circumstances, the what-ifs, are always contrived. But the lessons themselves are real. And our job is to always be on our toes, because you never know where the lesson is coming from next.

CHAPTER SEVEN

The Big Carnival

Drudge is not in the minority. There isn't really any difference, other than a matter of degree, between the tabloids and the journals of record, between the *National Enquirer* and the *National Review.* Both selectively spin the facts to advance an agenda, both are heedless of where the scandal may take them, and both obviously get high off the fumes. What's the difference, ultimately, between entertainment journalism and journalism as entertainment?

But the opposite side of manufactured scandal, the other major strain in entertainment journalism today, is equally anathema to me, and may be far more insidious. It's this open-ended era of celebrity journalism we perpetually find ourselves in.

I'm not sure when it started, exactly. Maybe circa 1980, when *Rolling Stone* publisher Jann Wenner traded in rock and roll to put his newfound movie star pals on the cover. Maybe the advent of *People* magazine. More likely, as with most cases where showbiz catches up with the zeitgeist, these were more symptoms than causes. My own opinion is that celebrity journalism was an outgrowth of '70s movies. Which were themselves the place where film culture finally caught up with the cult of personality established by rock culture in the '60s. The '70s was entirely a cinema of character. Heroes, antiheroes—the morality got all kind of jumbled up. Ethics was now situational, in a way not seen since '40s noir. But unlike '40s noir, there was no longer a Production Code that spelled out in intricate detail how crime was to be punished in the final reel. Dustin Hoffman, a cheap con man and grifter, dies at the end of *Midnight Cowboy* (1969), which signaled a critical watershed of '70s-style cinema. But Jon Voight, a male prostitute, does not. So do Warren Beatty and Faye Dunaway in *Bonnie and Clyde,* and so do Dennis Hopper and presumably Peter Fonda in *Easy Rider.* But what we're left with is moral outrage at the injustice of these deaths, not the sense of fatalistic closure that comes from transgressors getting their just deserts.

And of course, character-driven cinema led to a whole new star system: all of the above, plus Robert Redford and Jane Fonda and Al Pacino and Harrison Ford and Robert De Niro and Meryl Streep and Clint Eastwood and Jack Nicholson . . . Who, with certain major exceptions, became more and more concerned with holding on to that stardom, and so with being more and more likable in their films, and so with mobilizing the publicity around them. So personal publicists and personal managers rose up to service such needs, in the absence of a studio system that took care of these things the last time there was a new generation of stars, when late-'50s/early-'60s TV actors first made the transition to film.

Entertainment journalism in the '80s also took on a certain narcissism that seems latent in the entertainments of the '70s. Maybe this was a by-product of the coming of age of auteurism: The '70s, more than previous decades in American film, was fueled by directors' personal visions and private psychologies, now projected large for all to see. And once that sort of intimacy was established between the talent and the public—a director's tortured psyche refracted through the prism of an actor's trained persona—some sort of mechanism was needed to feed and perpetuate this imagined connection. What better institution to fill that void than soft journalism? It could be financed in-house, the film production and film promotion arms being all part of the same detailed corporate strategy. And it could perfectly dovetail at the beginning of the '80s with the parallel rise of a new star system and sympathetic leading roles, the free money and class boosterism of Wall Street mania, the furious solipsism of cocaine confidence, the thousand-channel universe of the media revolution, and the emboldening of charismatic politics and the fascist right. Perfect.

So that by now, entertainment journalism serves the studios, and not the other way around. Increasingly, you see the same tepid celebrity quotes in every story, the same studio-fed Electronic Press Kit clips in every broadcast. There's no incentive to dig up and report new stories anymore; editors don't want to run them and the ad reps don't like it when they do.

Maybe it's always been like this, from the time when Louella Parsons and Hedda Hopper and Walter Winchell dominated the free flow of ideas with a flick of their poison pens. *Sweet Smell of Success:* "Light me, Sidney." "Cat's in the bag; bag's in the river." But now, as chairman emeritus John Waters says, there's a hundred times more outlets for information, and yet a hundred times less real information. Glossy magazines with four-month lead times, syndicated scoop shows, the breathless culture of E! and *ET* and *EW*—an anagram for "tweee!" by the way—all feature the same puerile stream of viscous broth that's been strained and vetted through rows and rows of sharks' teeth wielded by agents and handlers and spin engineers. Enter the Internet—and not a moment too soon.

As a matter of policy, I don't take tips from agents and I try not to deal with publicists. Why? Because my objective is to tell the truth, and publicists are basically professional liars. Or let's say paid hyperbolists. And because the agency culture is rife with disinformation, where all things are true until they can't be true any longer, and where people will lie to you just to keep in practice. There are exceptions. Terry Press from DreamWorks has always been forthright with me, and some of the independent publicists are good about not steering you wrong. And I'm sure there must be some honest agents. Somewhere. But overall, cutting them out of the loop makes for good policy.

I also don't thrive on competition. If Garth Franklin at the Dark Horizons Web site (www.darkhorizons.com) gets a detailed shot breakdown for the *Phantom Menace* trailer, I don't secretly resent it; I post a link to it and pipeline 175,000 extra readers a day to his site. I'm not possessive about the stories I break. I used to go to Patrick Sauriol's Corona site (www.corona.bc.ca/films/) and correct postings when I knew they were wrong—until he got annoyed by it. He seemed to take it personally, like I was insulting him, when I was just trying to ferret out fake sources. But whatever; I'll stop policing the universe for them if they want. At the bottom of my page I keep a standing list of links to other sites like mine that I feel do a responsible job of covering the waterfront. For me, it's all "Macy's Loves Gimbel's" (from *Miracle on 34th Street*): Promote the competition and your customers will thank you for it. It's a win-win situation.

I try to run the site on the principle "Don't hurt the little guy." Because everybody started somewhere. Just like I would never intentionally trash an independent film by a struggling filmmaker, even if it sucked. Dad and I get probably fifty unsolicited scripts or videotapes a day. We don't get around to most of them. But we do make the effort, and we do keep them on file. People think if we single them out, it could be their big break. Or maybe they just don't have anywhere else to send them. Maybe I can't greenlight someone's dream project, but the simple fact that people I admired ever took the time to offer me a moment or care about my ambitions still means a lot to me. (People like Forry Ackerman, for instance— or really, anybody I meet now that I've ever looked up to.) So we hang on to them.

I call this the Alan Ladd Jr. Principle. Alan Ladd Jr., son of the star of *Shane,* was the only guy to say yes to George Lucas for *Star Wars.* He was the head of Fox at the time, and he was their last chance. What if he'd said, "No, kid, this is stupid." Plenty of other people did. Where would the state of film be now?

There's a shot in *Finian's Rainbow,* a really execrable musical directed in 1968 by a twenty-nine-year-old Francis Coppola: Fred Astaire and all these twinkly Irish people are singing and dancing, and suddenly the camera lands on a railroad track with a locomotive racing toward it. When the train hits what would be the point of impact, the film cuts to two or three handheld undercranked POV shots that run the length of several coach cars, spliced together in quick succession, and then to a fixed shot of the train receding in the distance. The effect is as if the train has just passed through the camera. The whole thing takes maybe five seconds, and serves no discernible part of the narrative strategy. But it's breathtaking.

Or in the first part of the trilogy that makes up the *Night Gallery* pilot, directed by Steven Spielberg—before *Duel,* before *The Sugarland Express*: Joan Crawford is a blind woman and "imperious predatory dowager" who plans to buy gambler Tom Bosley's eyes so that she can see for twenty-four hours. When we first see her, she is framed from behind, sitting regally in her Fifth Avenue apartment, followed by a smash cut to an extreme close-up of her hand gripping the arm of the chair. It's the kind of thing you never, ever see on TV. And automatically, you understand everything you need to about what sort of greedy, grasping, damaged soul she really is. These movies are not very good. But those shots leap out of them—they're like holograms that suddenly unscroll in midair, with banners that read, "I am someone to watch. Ignore me at your peril."

John Sayles started with *Piranha*. James Cameron started with *Piranha II*. You never know. And if nobody ever trained a critical eye on such works, just because their origin was suspect, these people would have died in obscurity.

But probably the biggest way that I differ from most journalists is that they take an unspoken vow of objectivity. This is what's taught in the universities, and it's what prevails in the nation's dailies and broadsheets. Professionalism requires the working reporter to be dispassionate, to report all sides of the issue, to mask one's true feelings in the interest of serving the greater good.

I say bullshit.

Before the onset of the Great Depression, when Hollywood decided it needed card-carrying writers with formal literary credentials, all those writers were learning their craft elsewhere. A virtual migration of them came from the Broadway stage, spurred westward by the grim economic realities of 1929 and gushing letters from the likes of Herman Mankiewicz, an old New York literary hand who would ultimately co-script *Citizen Kane,* extolling the free money lying on the ground for the enterprising man of wit or facility. But before they discovered the bright footlights of the Broadway stage, many of those writers were newspapermen from Chicago or one of New York's dozen major dailies. It was that generation of bon vivants and raconteurs and legendary carousers who reinvigorated the movies in the Sound Era. They glorified the myth of the city newsroom and the writer's life in films like *The Front Page* and *His Girl Friday* and *Angels Over Broadway,* to name three credits for Ben Hecht, the best of his breed. At the same time, incidentally, they were depleting journalism's ranks of its finest talents in a way it would never really recover from—leaving the newspaper profession a more drab and colorless place in their absence.

I may not have been to journalism school. But I have seen *All the President's Men* and *Absence of Malice* and *His Girl Friday* and both *Front Page*s and *Citizen Kane* and Sam Fuller's *Park Row.* I've seen *Nothing Sacred* and *It Happened One Night* and *Meet John Doe; Love Is a Racket* with the great Lee Tracy, and *Woman of the Year,* the first Spencer Tracy/Katharine Hepburn, and Bogart's summation to the jury in *Deadline U.S.A.* I've seen *Superman* and *Batman, Salvador* and *Reds, The Year of Living Dangerously* and *The Killing Fields* and *Under Fire.* I've seen *Between the Lines* and *Where the Buffalo Roam* and *Perfect* and *Fear and Loathing in Las Vegas,* all with a would-be *Rolling Stone* in it. I've seen

Medium Cool, where the violence is real, and *The Man Who Shot Liberty Valance,* where the violence isn't what it seems. And I've seen *The Ghost and Mr. Chicken.*

These may just be movies, but I know what it is that journalists do. I know that when the story seems thin, you get another source; and that when the going gets weird, the weird turn pro; and that when the legend becomes fact, you print the legend; and that it would be fun to run a newspaper. In *Park Row,* set in 1900, every newspaper editor writes all his own articles, edits them, pastes them up, and prints them himself, because that was the state of the technology. That's my life story.

Here's what's really wrong with journalism today: It's bloodless. It lacks all conviction. It has become academic and soulless, and removed from the events it professes to portray. Even the average critic seems to feel it's his duty to remain distanced from something in order to judge it on a sound, level-headed basis. With all due respect—what the fuck is that about?

I believe in advocacy journalism. I am my belief system. I back up my opinions with my reputation. It doesn't mean I present biased news, or that I favor slanted sources, or that I deal in agitprop. It means that if something is right or wrong, I say so. I try to be consistent. I also try to admit when I've made a mistake. This gives my readership a standard by which to judge me. It's what creates a dialogue with the audience. This is why I answer my own phone, why I publish the address of my hotel when I'm in another city. It's ultimately why I stay in Austin. I welcome my fans. These are the people who are the most like me in the world, and whom I have the most in common with.

That's why I use the site to champion films that are in danger of never being seen. I'll often make an open plea on the site: "Somebody needs to get me a copy of this film so I can make sure it gets U.S. distribution." I'll write rave reviews, even under assumed names; I'll call up people on a film's behalf, even studio marketing departments, or address open letters to people whose opinion might benefit it. I'll make it my top story, hold it over for two days, put it in a line of sight with the latest *Star Wars* coverage. I'll do what I have to to save a film. Because anything is better than sitting there and watching it die.

Critics often take exception. They charge that I'm not a critic because I don't fit into the same literary tradition as everyone else. Maybe they're right. Maybe I'm a film booster. I certainly don't enjoy writing negative reviews as much as many of my brethren of the quill seem to. All those people—John Simon, Dwight Macdonald, Rex Reed; the Addison De-Witts of the world—who seem to take special delight in eviscerating a picture because it represents a betrayal of their youth or something. I'd rather save the orphans, those films that can't fend for themselves. I remember that *Casablanca* sat in tin cans for three months unreleased because studio bosses had no idea what they had. I remember that *Citizen Kane* was almost bought by a consortium of studio heads led by Louis B. Mayer and its negative burned, to thwart the ire of William Randolph Hearst.

This is how I distinguish myself from the fatted caftan-wearing pashas of the fourth estate who cover movie sets as if they're courtrooms. Like they really can't be bothered. Who would strip the movies of all their mystery and romance. They're as cynical and craven as Kirk Douglas exploiting the trapped miner in Billy Wilder's still-just-as-brilliant *Ace in the Hole* (re-released as *The Big Carnival* when no one went to see it the first time), while a carnival atmosphere rages outside, counting the seconds until he can put this disreputable one-horse town behind him in the rearview at 60 per. "I've met a lot of hard-boiled eggs in my time, mister," says the victim's wife, herself angling for a piece of the action, "but you're twenty minutes."

Billy Wilder, who William Holden once described as having "a mind full of razor blades." Who was a newspaper legman and three-dot journalist at twenty in his native Vienna, and then in Berlin between the wars. Who adopted wholesale that same Weimar cynicism we know from Christopher Isherwood's *Sally Bowles* and its commercial offspring, *Cabaret.* Who once showed up on Freud's doorstep to file a Sunday magazine profile, and who studied Hitler close-up enough to get out the day after the Reichstag fire in '33. Billy Wilder once said there're only two things that money is any good for: helping your friends out, and telling producers "fuck you."

I don't have fuck-you money yet, but I do have a Web site. I try to use it to help those who deserve it, and I never take work just because I need it. If this rule is good enough for Billy Wilder, it's certainly good enough for me.

And I'm ready for my close-up.

CHAPTER EIGHT
Lost Horizon

It was Quentin Tarantino who first broke me out on a national level. Quentin passed through town to show *From Dusk Till Dawn* at a benefit for the Austin Film Society, and he decided Austin might be a good place to come back and establish a private film festival (the city's third) based on the prints in his private collection. At this point, I was still largely known in town as the guy who sold movie posters to Rick Linklater. I hadn't been all that impressed with Tarantino before, just from reading his sermonizing in various interviews, but I thought his introduction for *From Dusk Till Dawn* at the Paramount Theater was amazing. At this point, I was still recovering from my back injury. I could walk for short periods with a cane. But this was my first appearance in public since being laid up for so long.

The Quentin Tarantino Film Fest was held September 1996

at the Dobie Theater, one of the great old independent theaters of Austin, down at one end of the Drag, and adjacent to the southwest corner of the UT campus. This is the theater that first showed *Slacker* through its initial four-month run, and which was situated in the actual geography of the film—across the street from where the troubadour sings about the guy who runs over his mother, and mere steps away from Quackenbush's coffee shop, where the existentialist dreamers riff on Dostoyevsky, and one of them meets the alien theorist credited as "Been on the Moon Since the '50s." The upshot was that once you walked out of the theater, you walked directly into one of the scenes from the movie. It was like a Universal Studios Tour theme ride where nothing ever happens.

It's probably no accident that I wound up in a place like Austin. Austin is popular now in the public imagination because the South by Southwest music symposium brings thousands of bands and music professionals here for one week every year, garnering it the good-time reputation of a New Orleans without the dry rot or southern decay. But there's no way to convey just what a bizarre place Austin really is, or how it acquired the values it did in this day and age. This goes back at least fifty years that I know of, and probably further. There are more bookstores, rock bands, possibly computers, and now filmmakers per capita than any other city in the country.

Austin has always been a home to regional anarchists who redlined the scale off the eccentric end: All those serial rants in *Slacker*—half of those people were local characters with their own following; the other half were ethnographic profiles of local misfits. Or our time-honored pantheon of musical geniuses: Janis Joplin, Doug Sahm, Roky Erickson, Willie Nelson, Jerry Jeff Walker, Townes Van Zandt, Gibby Haynes, Daniel Johnston, Lucinda Williams—people who, to be charitable about it, might not have been successful without a citizenry who tolerated their oddball ways, largely out of a sense of civic duty. There have always been these accidental communities: The sci-fi crowd of the early '70s—Bruce Sterling, Howard Waldrop, Steve Utley—collected by Harlan Ellison in the *Lone Star Universe* anthology, or genre guys like Joe Lansdale and Chad Oliver (Glen's father) before them. Homegrown cartoonists like Gilbert Shelton (*The Fabulous Furry Freak Brothers*) or Berke Breathed (*Bloom County*). Poster artists like Frank Kozik. Comedians like Bill Hicks. Origin Systems, which gave us the *Wing Commander* and *Ultima* series. Or before all that, state politics in the 1950s, when liberal hotheads like Willie Morris, Ronnie Dugger, Ann Richards, Bill Moyers, and Billy Lee Brammer inadvertently foisted Lyndon Johnson on an unsuspecting world.

For a city as small as this one, there has always been a tidal influx of people—first the state legislature, which washes in a new Congress every two years and a new governor every four; then the university, which siphons 50,000 students in every fall and back out every summer; now film crews who blow through at the rate of twenty a year. Or the boomtime computer industry, or itinerant rock bands, or the seaboard carpetbaggers and U-Haul gypsies who will be on their way back out again just as soon as the next bust hits. It gives this place a creative force, a perpetual invigoration to the life of the mind, and enough working writers to keep us grounded in the film business in a way we might not be otherwise. No wonder every legislative session some frustrated politico takes to calling us "the People's Republic of Austin."

But without a place like Austin, Richard Linklater couldn't have created his body of work, which from the very first flew in the face of conventional wisdom. Robert Rodriguez couldn't have created a $7,000 do-it-yourself revolution with *El Mariachi*. Mike Judge couldn't have launched MTV's poet-cretins *Beavis and Butt-head* or the gentle redneck moralism of *King of the Hill*. I suspect there would have been no *Texas Chainsaw Massacre* (whose one-minute opening narration, delivered by John Larroquette of all people, was the unsung inspiration for *The Blair Witch Project*), or the shaggy-dog comedies of Eagle Pennell, whose *The Whole Shootin' Match* was what Robert Redford was watching during the first U.S. Film Festival in Park City, Utah, when he had the epiphany to start the Sundance Festival.

Austin is where Terrence Malick hid out for twenty years, director Robert Benton was a photographer on the city daily, and screenwriters like Bud Shrake and Gary Cartwright (the Mad Dogs), Michael Ventura and Big Boy Medlin (*Austin Sun* critics), Warren Skaaren, William Wittliff, and the *Texas Monthly* Mafia (Bill Broyles and Al Reinert, Larry L. King, Lawrence Wright, and Stephen Harrigan) found a way to subsidize their craft. Jonathan Demme, David Byrne, and John Sayles all stopped through long enough to make friends and collect protégés. Joel Coen and Tsui Hark did a semester here apiece. Even Larry McMurtry lived in Austin long enough to develop a lifelong hatred of it.

And though these writers uniformly make their living elsewhere, their roots and sensibilities reside here, in a way that the people they write for could often care less about. Read Wright and Harrigan's *Moonwalkers,* about the fraternity of a dozen astronauts who have walked on the moon; or Shrake's *The Big Mamou,* a comedy about Los Alamos and the bomb, and Jonathan Demme's professed dream project; or Ventura and Medlin's *Howlin' at the Moon* (formerly *Fandango*), about the outlaw John Wesley Hardin; or Medlin's *Monroe,*

Psychic Detective, a self-explanatory comedy; or Linklater's *Rivethead,* the memoir of an assembly-line autoworker who appears in *Roger and Me;* or Rodriguez's *Madman* adaptation. None of these have been produced. Some are dead in the water. But all of them carry a little bit of the cowboy wild-dog spirit of the place that spontaneously generated them.

I put an early announcement for the Tarantino Festival on my site. There were close to thirty films, many of which I'd never seen before. But this marked the first event that I could actually cover on a daily basis. And if I hadn't seen most of these films, I was betting most other people hadn't either. I thought nobody would read it, but it was something I could provide coverage on. Then people started showing up from Chicago and New York and Oregon, and then from Germany and the Netherlands on the strength of my advance coverage. These were people who had been following the site and suddenly got excited enough to come down here. That got a lot of local attention. I would get home every night at 3 A.M. after six or seven hours of films, and then write all night until the sun came up. And then all the events began to sell out, which the people running the festival were not really expecting.

One of the reasons I've come to love and respect Quentin is that he introduced me to all this buried stuff from the '70s. The '70s were always my weakest decade, unlike just about everyone else I know. They came in between the past that I grew up studying and the present that I grew up absorbing. So the decade that every other movie enthusiast heralds as the last golden age of cinema was always the one I knew the least about. Now here was all this stuff *beneath* all that stuff; the stuff that it takes archaeology to get at. And if the last wave of auteur-obsessives came from the ranks of video clerks like Quentin and Roger Avary, comic store mavens like Kevin Smith and Scott Mosier, or film society directors like Linklater, who's to say there's not a similar movement out there even now, lurking in the sun-starved vulpine forests and subterranean chasms of the collector's world?

Over a ten-night period, we were treated to the following: Biker Night, dedicated to Adam Roarke, who had just passed away, with *The Savage Seven, Hollywood Man,* and *The Glory Stompers,* starring Dennis Hopper, and Casey Kasem as a sleazy bisexual biker. A Martin-Lewis reunion featuring *Boeing Boeing,* with Tony Curtis as Jerry Lewis and Jerry as an uncredited Buddy Love, and *All in a Night's Work,* with Dino at his most lubricated. Crime Night, featuring Robert Duvall in *The Outfit,* an uncredited sequel to *Point Blank,* from the same series of Donald Westlake novels, and *The Nickel Ride,* directed by Robert Mulligan (*To Kill a Mockingbird*) and written by Eric Roth (*Forrest Gump*), with a great '70s performance by Bo Hopkins.

There was a '70s kung fu double bill directed by Chang Cheh, kind of the John Ford of the Run Run Shaw Hong Kong studios. And Good Ol' Boy Night, with Burt Reynolds in *White Lightning,* the first appearance of *Gator*'s Gator McCluskey; *Dirty Mary Crazy Larry,* one of the best Peter Fonda roles ever (including *Ulee's Gold* and *The Limey*); and *Jackson County Jail,* which features possibly the most terrifying rape scene ever filmed, with Tommy Lee Jones trying to ignore Yvette Mimieux's screams from an adjoining cell as the local deputy brutalizes her. There was a Spaghetti Western fiesta featuring *The Hellbenders, Adios Sabata,* and, inexplicably, *The Girl from Starship Venus*; Epic Adventure Night, featuring *The Long Duel* and *March or Die,* which even *sounds* long; a six-film All-Night Horror Marathon; *The Swinging Cheerleaders,* backed with *Revenge of the Cheerleaders*; and a double bill of Jack Hill's seminal *Switchblade Sisters* and Italian horrormeister Lucio Fulci's *The Beyond*.

Quentin's rambling twenty-minute introductions gave me some real insights into this media paradox known as Quentin Tarantino. For the first time, I understood why celebrities don't want their personal lives dredged up in the pages of the tabloids. Here was someone whose work I respected greatly, whose public actions I was honestly quite often mystified by, and who I came to discover was basically just like me—a guy who lived for movies.

The thing about Quentin is that he doesn't really need to make films anymore. I sincerely hope that he does, but in a lot of ways, that's not what he's about. He's almost like a professional film geek. He knows more than virtually anyone about the kind of films he's interested in, and now he has the resources to pursue his interests. In person, I find that he oftentimes drops the pretension that comes across in the interviews. I never saw Quentin act the way I've seen him characterized in the press. Granted, he doesn't like to sign autographs, but that's because every time I've ever seen him, he's been deluged. From my side, he seems like a good guy.

On the third day of the festival, I was sitting in my second row aisle seat when an usher tapped me on the shoulder and said, "Mr. Knowles, Mr. Tarantino would like to see you." I thought, Uh-oh, now what did I do? But I clearly couldn't run, so I hobbled over to him, and he told me he had specifically discouraged the press from attending. But at the same time, he'd never had anyone cover something the way I was: I didn't focus on whether he was drinking or not; I wasn't snide or snotty about him being the wonderboy; I just reported on the films and tried to convey his enthusiasm for them. And he encouraged me to keep it up, and told me he was looking forward to the next installment. He didn't have a computer, so he asked if I could bring a printout with me every day of what I'd posted the night before. From that point on throughout the festival, whenever anybody would ask him what he was reading, Quentin would always give them the address for my Web site. So other people started reading it. And my coverage started taking on a life of its own.

Then one night, as I was coming out of the bathroom between showings, I saw this gorgeous blonde coming toward me through the lobby. Suddenly I realized it was Mira Sorvino. And she wasn't turning away, she was looking me dead in the eye. It was like in *Stardust Memories,* when Sharon Stone blows a kiss to Woody Allen from the opposite train—except Mira Sorvino was in *Mighty Aphrodite* with Woody Allen, and now here she was in the flesh. And she mouthed the words, "Hi, Harry." I was watching this all in slow motion, like a car wreck, and thinking first, Why isn't Mira Sorvino on location shooting *Mimic,* and second, how on earth does Mira Sorvino know my name? She disappeared into the theater, but at the last possible second, she turned back around and gave me this practiced killer smile—the kind that reaches all the way through you and grabs your spine from the inside. Like Bill Murray says in *Groundhog Day:* "*That* was a pretty good day."

After the screening, Mira came up to me and started talking. She had just that morning signed to do *The Replacement Killers* with Chow Yun-Fat, and I knew that she spoke Cantonese. She told me that Quentin had been faxing my daily coverage of the festival to all his friends—Samuel L. Jackson, Bruce Willis, Steven Spielberg. This was the first clue I had that I was really making any headway beyond my own borders. I was so technically naive at this point that I knew nothing about counters. I didn't realize the technology existed that would tell you exactly how many hits your site was getting. I thought what little e-mail I received was the extent of my readership. Then I learned *Premiere* had sent someone down to cover the festival based on my reports. (Actually, it was Mark Ebner, who ended up being one of my co-authors on this book.) For the first time, this whole Web site was something more than me passing time waiting to regain the use of my body, and notching marks on a prison wall. And my writing began to lose that entirely introspective tone that comes from daily journal or diary entries. Suddenly there were people listening to me speak. This more than anything took me out of myself, which is where I most wanted to be.

On the last day of the festival, Quentin had me show up early and we took pictures. And he pronounced me "the Wolf Blitzer of the Internet": the guerrilla-styled journalist (Wolf Blitzer had just made his reputation on CNN covering the Gulf War) who would report directly from the trenches, with little concern for his own personal safety. And even though I worried it was a little too self-promotional, I included his quote in my festival wrap-up. This was at the very height of Quentin's fame and glory. He had won the Academy Award two months before, he had chosen Austin as the perfect place to get out of the glare of the spotlight for a brief time; plus he had just teamed with Robert Rodriguez on a project, the indie-prod equivalent of a supergroup. No backlash had set in at this point. And Mira had just won her Oscar for *Mighty Aphrodite;* they were a golden couple, exacerbated by the fact that every geek like me the world over who had already idealized Quentin for being clearly one of them now saw him with an incredibly sexy, brilliant, Academy Award–winning actress. There were probably 20,000 Web sites at the time dedicated to him and what he was thinking. And for me at least, this became the quote heard around the world.

The Tarantino Fest became instrumental for me in another way as well. It quickly became an annual event, and when Quentin came down with the flu the next year and couldn't attend, he asked me to introduce Jack Hill. Now, Jack Hill is Quentin's guy: If there's a director from the '70s whom Quentin's world view would validate—more than Monte Hellman, who produced *Reservoir Dogs*; more than Joe Dante or Allan Arkush or Jonathan Demme, who came out of the late Corman school; more even than the Italian horror triumvirate of Lucio Fulci, Dario Argento, and Mario Bava—it's Jack Hill. Hill is the man responsible for the brilliant Eugene O'Neill–meets–*The Addams Family* horror opus *Spider Baby*; whose *Foxy Brown* was referenced in *Reservoir Dogs* and made a subtext in *Jackie Brown*; whose UCLA student film *The Host* was appropriated wholesale by Coppola madman/visionary Dennis Jakob for the last third of *Apocalypse Now.* When Miramax gave Quentin his own boutique distribution label, Rolling Thunder Films, his first re-release was Hill's *Switchblade Sisters.*

I was terrified—not just intimidated by Hill, but genuinely concerned about facing 2,500 rabid Tarantino fans who were going to start looking at me as Donner burgers if I fucked up. Plus I had to piss like a brood mare. Not the best frame of mind for a master of ceremonies. But I got up there and went into a tent revival delivery, channeling Quentin's manic energy, stepping all over myself trying to get the words out, working the crowd up into this frenetic lather, so that by the end they were all whooping and screaming. When I finally introduced him, Hill was actually embarrassed because it was so over the top.

It turns out Jeff Dowd was in the audience. Dowd was an independent producer's rep on *Blood Simple,* part of the Henry Jaglom repertory in *Someone to Love,* and, most famously, the role model for Jeff "the Dude" Lebowski in the Coen Brothers' *The Big Lebowski* (to John Goodman's John Milius—writer of *Apocalypse Now,* director of *Big Wednesday,* and legendary gun enthusiast). Dowd was so impressed by my introduction that he told his friend Roger Ebert, and that's how I was first invited to co-host *Roger Ebert at the Movies.* And what's more, the night we heard Gene Siskel had died, I was at the Tarantino Film Fest and I saw *Mighty Peking Man,* and that wound up being the film I reviewed on that first show.

But if the festival was beginning to alert me to the world peeking in, that was nothing compared to how it raised my profile out in the world at large. Little articles about Quentin and my site started cropping up in places like *Entertainment Weekly,* and the rampant attention doubled my existing audience.

And that's when "they" began watching my every move.

CHAPTER NINE

"Take Your Stinking Paws Off Me, You Damn Dirty Apes!"

McGeorge Bundy, a name forgotten to us now, once made the observation, "Vietnam was a streetcar." Bundy was an advisor to Lyndon Johnson and an advocate of our involvement in the Vietnam War. When Bob Dylan was asked what was the first thing he would do as president, he said, "Make McGeorge Bundy change his name." But then again, who's Bob Dylan?

What "McGeorge" meant was that situations like Vietnam come along at regular intervals; all you have to do is catch the right one and you're off and running. I suspect this is one of the ways history works. After the Tarantino Fest, I had 40,000 daily readers. I firmly believed that with 6 billion people on the planet, everyone has a core audience of probably 50,000, if they could just leave the right breadcrumbs out in obvious places. But real newspapers have more like a million and a half readers. To get at those kinds of numbers, I needed publicity. And to get publicity, I needed controversy. I could either go looking for it, or I could wait for it to find me. I chose to wait.

Not long afterward, in January 1997, I found a mysterious package on my front porch that contained the script and original "bug" designs for the $100 million Paul Verhoeven sci-fi epic *Starship Troopers.* These were the top-secret specs for the alien creatures, the film's most closely guarded secret— and a *major* scoop, months before anybody else had it. *Starship Troopers,* the novel by Robert Heinlein, was one of the seminal works of science fiction, with a built-in global fan base. There was no copyright information on the drawings, but they did contain the name Phil Tippett, who I knew had done stop-motion animation on *The Empire Strikes Back* and had combined stop-motion techniques with computer animation to create the dinosaurs in *Jurassic Park.* (Stop-motion animation has been around since the teens, and involves photographing static models one frame at a time to give the illusion of movement. It can be seen in such classic films as *The Lost World* or *King Kong,* and was later perfected by people like George Pal with his Puppetoons and Ray Harryhausen in *Jason and the Argonauts* and *The Seventh Voyage of Sinbad.* Computer graphics or CGI—computer-generated imagery—was developed in the late 1980s, and is done entirely with the computer. All those enormous effects movies from the '80s like *Howard the Duck* or those containing the ubiquitous "exploding fireball scene" were exclusively the product of CGI.) This was to be the first film with major CG characters, and could well be a precursor for what would appear in the next *Star Wars* trilogy. So this was the real deal.

It was clear to me from the moment I opened the envelope that this was what I had been waiting for. I needed a studio to acknowledge my existence, and this would force Sony's hand. It had to be something that people wanted to see, but also something I could champion on its own merit. And it had to be something the studio needed to protect, for the legal precedent, but which they were also secretly proud of, so they wouldn't just outright try to destroy me. I knew instinctively that this perfectly fit all the criteria. It's like when Jimmy Stewart first sees his plane in *The Spirit of St. Louis*—the look in his eyes says, "This will get me to the other side."

I spent hours scanning in the documents and optimizing their presentation. I created a whole separate sidebar to the site to house them, along with a very positive story placing them in some kind of context. I had the script, so I could tell where all these things fit in. And then I began writing my acceptance speech—the article I would post when confronted with my cease-and-desist order. I had everything all worked out.

The one flaw in my master plan turned out to be that Sony wouldn't bite. I expected to be met with pitiless retribution and an Old Testament vengeance, and instead they did nothing for four months. This was the studio that was about to be nominated for Best Picture for *Jerry Maguire*. Perhaps a little sentimentality was to be expected. I had to wait while Sony made up its mind what it wanted to do about me. And that wasn't the half of it: I kept getting furtive e-mail updates from sympathetic insiders telling me where I stood, saying things like, "I fought hard for you today." I didn't want them to fight for me. Stop with the fighting! I wanted the heat. But there was no way to convey this to friendlies behind enemy lines without blowing the whole deal.

Finally, on the very day that I went to see *The People vs. Larry Flynt,* which of course I loved, I came home to find a cease-and-desist order waiting for me from one of Sony's lawyers—along with two e-mails telling me that the order was finally on its way. And less than forty-eight hours later, after the story had hit the wire services, was when Mark Altman and Jay Babcock at *Sci-Fi Universe* asked me to be a contributing writer. *Sci-Fi Universe* was housed in an office building in Beverly Hills right across the hall from *Film Threat,* a bimonthly attack journal dedicated to making the studios sleep a little less securely at night (and where my book's other co-writer, Paul Cullum, was then an editor). Both were owned by Larry Flynt. That means that in the space of two days, I had seen a Sony film (from Mike Medavoy's Phoenix Pictures, no less) about the First Amendment, had Sony's lawyers question my own First Amendment rights, and then found my first paid writing gig because of it—ultimately hired by the subject of the original movie.

I dutifully removed the offending material from my Web site. Then I posted what I call my Uncle Remus Retraction, which was a message to my readers saying basically, Whatever you do, don't contact Sony and tell them how you feel about this. At the following address. That night, I posted the story on the various newsgroups, and sent a copy to Drudge, figuring he would probably know what to do with it. Drudge forwarded it to places like *Wired* and HotWired and MSNBC, and the next morning there were calls from all of the above and more. I did a long interview with *Wired*; for MSNBC, I went to the local affiliate and did the whole thing by satellite uplink. I posted a link from the site back to Sony and the lawyer who sent me the restraining order, and something like 100,000 people wound up writing them back.

Two weeks later, the film's producer, Jon Davison, who had also produced *RoboCop,* called and begged me to put the *Starship Troopers* material back online. This was my first real contact with a producer, if you don't count Dean Devlin from *Independence Day,* who I knew from user groups, and who I always thought of more as a writer anyway. It turns out the producers had been lobbying Sony on my behalf, which is why it took Sony so long to react.

Sony wound up calling off the dogs on their own, saying they didn't care what I did with the pictures. I had gotten a billion-dollar company to reverse a corporate decision. This was David vs. Goliath, and I had winged the big fella without even knowing it—with no money, no connections, and no legal representation. I always thought this is the thing I should have become known for, but although it spread like a prairie fire across the Internet, it was little more than a blip buried way inside most newspapers.

I knew that whatever happened next on the site, it was going to blow up big. Because I knew the media was watching me. My new Web counter could tell me how many people were visiting the site and the domain names of everyone who visited, or on whose server those people were registered. And every morning I was getting CNBC, CBS.com, lots of radio stations, all the major newspapers—not to mention Sony.com, WarnerBros.com, etc., etc. Which means that people from all those companies and media outlets were following this. At that point, I'd never paid much attention to test screenings. Reviews were starting to trickle in, but I didn't see any controversy there. I didn't realize there was an entire industry dedicated to kicking the tires on studio movies and stating where they were defective. I clearly had no idea.

There was a test screening a month and a half later for *Bat-*

man & Robin, the fourth installment of the *Batman* franchise, and, like the third, *Batman Forever,* directed by Joel Schumacher. I respect Tim Burton's *Batman,* the way the sound drops out of the trailer, as one of the great marketing breakthroughs of all time. And I know Warren Skaaren's script had more zingers per capita for Jack Nicholson than anything like it, even if the original Sam Hamm script was for me the one that got away.

But once Joel Schumacher got involved, the series became pure spectacle, with little or no concern paid to story, characters, plot—all the things that invest you in the narrative. *Batman Forever* reminded me of those films from the mid-'80s—Spielberg's *1941,* Eddie Murphy vehicles like *The Golden Child,* George Lucas's reviled *Howard the Duck*—where the actors, maybe even the entire set, were whipped up to whatever fever pitch or intensity they could muster and then turned loose on film. The result is invariably the Energizer bunny winding down. It's equally depressing and draining to have to sit through them.

When I first read the *Batman & Robin* script, there were two ways it could go: You could play it straight, and the camp value would naturally emerge. Or you could play it camp, and it would sink under its own weight. Suffice to say, Schumacher didn't opt for the first path. But the script as it was could have been great. At no point did it say anything about latex nipples, or a neon Batmobile, or guys on Rollerblades playing hockey, or Mr. Freeze as some sort of Wagnerian ice queen. The tone just completely got lost in the production design, in the costumes, in the special effects and toy tie-ins. It became a massive marketing juggernaut that the filmmakers either no longer cared about or else were powerless to stop. And no less so than the *Titanic*—the oceangoing one—once these things get some momentum up, they're a bitch to turn.

After the first *Batman & Robin* test screening, I got thirteen reviews, all saying it was abysmal. At one point, someone in the audience yelled out, "Death to Schumacher!" Columnist Liz Smith (my fellow Texan—or, as George W. Bush would have it, "Texanian") later tried to spin the story that spontaneous applause had broken out in favor of the film, but the truth was they were applauding the first catcalls, which opened the floodgates on attacking the film. It was all pretty ugly. I was still posting every important story I received in all the pertinent newsgroups, and people were getting really tired of me, because I was always pushing the Web site on people. My stories would inspire whole threads of commentary, which were the precursor of Talk Back, the interactive part of the site.

And in the course of posting this *Batman* story, I actually found the guy who had yelled out during that first screening. He had already seen all the summer movies, and this was still February or March. So I wrote him and invited him to be one of my regular contributors. He said, "Sure. I've always thought you were an asshole, but I guess you're alright." This turned out to be "Joe Hallenbeck." And he quickly began to provide the most visceral, vengeful responses on the site. People either loved him or feared him.

Of those first thirteen reviews for *Batman & Robin,* the last one I posted was Hallenbeck's, and it was virtually a call to arms. It brooked no challenge; showed no mercy; took no prisoners. In the second paragraph, our Joe called for a symbolic assassination to be carried out against Joel Schumacher. It read, in part:

> **First, let me say that Joel Schumacher should be shot and killed. I will pay a handsome bounty to the man (or woman) who delivers me the head of this Anti Christ. This man is pure evil and should be stopped at all costs! He has single-handedly destroyed what started out to be a great series of films. Someone, please . . . I beg you . . . end all of our suffering and make this man meet his maker. The same thing goes for Goldenthal's atrocious score (if you can call it that!). BRING BACK BURTON! BRING BACK ELFMAN! BRING BACK KEATON! FOR THE LOVE OF GOD, KILL SCHUMACHER!**

When I finally saw the film, I realized of course that all the reviews had been right: Joel Schumacher had taken something that was sacred to a great many people and simply eviscerated it. What could he have been thinking? I wrote a review and tried to get at the answer to that question. The press kept playing us off of each other, but we never actually spoke. Meanwhile, Warner seemed to be in major denial, with just a week to go before the premiere. When the numbers finally came in, the film fell $30 million short of its opening week box-office projections, and people were attributing this directly to me. The irony was that another Warner film I really loved, Kevin Reynolds's *187,* was slipping through the safety net because they had no idea how to sell it. So at the same time I was being accorded this newfound respect, I couldn't even save a humble little inner-city remake of *Blackboard Jungle* that starred Samuel L. Jackson in the Glenn Ford role as a concerned teacher, delivering what I thought was an Oscar-caliber performance.

So much for absolute power.

CHAPTER TEN

Sleeping with the Enemy

Newspapers started bombarding me with questions, and *Entertainment Weekly* wanted to do a story on me, Drudge, and the woman who ran the New York–based site CyberSleaze. *People* magazine promised a big feature; I must have done forty interviews in all. They all asked how I felt judging a film before it was finished. Of course, it wasn't me; I was just posting the reviews as they came in. But in the interest of drumming up controversy I said that if the studios were using these people as guinea pigs, they deserved to get bit. That's also when "Moriarty"—my other major spy, and an evil genius with henchmen in his own right—came on board. Moriarty had been posting on Corona Coming Attractions, but he recognized very early that my site had more of the sort of fighting spirit he could identify with.

The *Entertainment Weekly* story was the first to hit. I

waxed eloquent on manifest destiny and my right to do what I did. That was followed almost immediately by the *People* article, which was cut down from 1,500 to 300 words because the editors allegedly felt uneasy about posting test-screening results on a major Warner Bros. release. The same Warner Bros. whose parent company owns *People*, by the way. So I came off sounding a little bit like a kook. But they included two quotes from corporate publicists for major studios: Dennis Higgins from TriStar and Chris Pula, the head of publicity at Warner Bros. Higgins said something like, "It's scary. With the Internet, anyone can review a movie. It's like the revenge of the audience." But Pula lambasted me personally. His quote was: "They're fanatics, the nerd-geek crowd. They shouldn't be allowed to review anything other than a finished print." This was the same day they screened the final cut of *Batman & Robin,* and I had fifty-two reviews come into the site, all of them overwhelmingly negative. And since this was a finished print—like he said—I ran all fifty-two.

The next day things mushroomed. *Everyone* called. *20/20* wanted an interview. It was insane. All because of an ill-considered quote by a loose-cannon publicist in a three-hundred-word article in *People.* That quote created me. Pula didn't ask who the hell was I to have an opinion in the first place. He certainly didn't shrug me off, like you might imagine a behemoth like Time Warner would do. He treated me as an active threat. And suddenly I became one. Because that's how everybody reported it. This is when things started to get ugly.

Pula and I started being paired off in the media and on all the talking-heads news shows. They would pre-tape him and then bring me on for a live rebuttal. Pula is by all reports a nice guy, and certainly a colorful one. He was known throughout the marketing community as someone who was flamboyant, a maverick, and the opposite of a team player. He was also seen as very good at his job. I know that in between his tenures at Warner and later Disney, where he also ran up against personality clashes, he consulted on the release of *Happiness* virtually pro bono, once Universal had abandoned it. And his campaign for *The Sixth Sense*—"I see dead people," as opposed to Bruce Willis running around like in some action thriller—is as responsible as anything outside of the twist ending and word of mouth for its runaway success.

But Warner Bros. is one of the more conservative studios, and it doesn't like to be in the crosshairs of the media spotlight. And suddenly it had a holy war on its hands. *Conspiracy Theory* came out that summer, and I received a report that Richard Donner had asked point-blank why no review quotes were appearing in his ads, to which Pula allegedly replied, "Do you really think it will make any difference?" He reportedly told Kevin Reynolds he hated *187* because it made him think.

And he's famously the one who couldn't figure out how to sell *L.A. Confidential,* one of the best-reviewed films of the decade. The week before Warner Bros. fired him, he was quoted in *Entertainment Weekly* as saying, "It's really easy to piss on somebody else's campaign, but I'd like to see them market *L.A. Confidential.*" You know? Hand it over. Put Danny DeVito front and center and let him narrate the trailer, like Clint Eastwood did with *The Outlaw Josey Wales.* You already have photographs, magazines, soundtrack hits, period fashion spreads, and design details that director Curtis Hanson used as show-and-tell when he pitched the thing. Put some upbeat big-band number over the top—"In the Mood" or "Stompin' at the Savoy." And show Kim Basinger looking perfect. I mean, how hard can it be?

I ended up meeting Pula at, of all places, the *Starship*

Troopers premiere. He came up to me and gave me this long speech, something like—Harry, it's not what you do that I dislike, because on your Web site you put it in context. But when you cover a test screening, you talk about all the things that aren't finished yet. And the danger is how the real media is going to react. Because they're irresponsible. They won't report that it was a test screening, there was no score, the effects and opticals are missing, the color timing is completely off. They'll just report that the film is bad. And you have to understand that if I'm antagonistic in the press, it's because I have to be.

I told him that he ought to be criticizing the media, and he graciously invited me on any Warner junket I wanted to attend. But it was very strange meeting him. I know that almost every journalist who's ever interviewed him comes away liking him, because he's very candid and very funny. Of course, he's a publicist; that's his job. But even though I found him thoroughly charming, I sensed a definite undercurrent of hostility from him. He was clearly sizing me up, and deciding how to proceed.

The caliber of magazines, newspapers, and broadcast venues that wanted to interview me steadily continued to climb, until finally, the *New York Times* called and requested an interview. "The goddamned holy *New York Times,*" as Paddy Chayefsky called it in *Network*. They sent magazine writer Bernard Weinraub down to see me in action—to sit in this hovel I operate out of, and pore over the century's worth of movie memorabilia I have embossed on these walls. Meet the geeks—the whole nine yards.

So Bernard Weinraub came down and sat in my bedroom with me while I worked. And one of the things he asked me, which I had been asked a lot, but had never really come up with a satisfactory answer for, was how come people give me the information they do if I don't pay them. This seems to run counter to every other news-gathering operation in the world. And it occurred to me that the best way to make him understand is to tap into the same feelings that everybody shares about the movies.

So I said, "How old are you?"

He said, "I'm fifty-two."

Now, my dad was fifty-two. So I knew what it must have been like for him growing up. I said, "Do you remember in 1956, when you were thirteen or fourteen, you went to the movies maybe half a dozen times that summer? The theater was maybe six blocks from where you lived. And you saw a movie called *The Seventh Voyage of Sinbad*. You couldn't understand how they got a guy in a giant cyclops suit, and how they got his mask to blink its one eye. You had never seen a giant bird like that, but it moved and it looked real to you. You and your friends went back over and over, trying to figure this stuff out, but you never found out exactly how they did it until you were much older. Remember the next year, you went and saw something called *Blackbeard the Pirate,* and then you had a sleepover with one of your friends and stayed up all night discussing how they cut that guy's head off? And you decided it must have been some guy who was dying of cancer or had a terminal illness or something, and he wanted to be remembered or for his family to be taken care of."

And he got this really strange, faraway look in his eyes. I said, "That's the communal film memory. That's what my dad felt, because he's told me about it a thousand times. Everybody has that, because we're all brought up on the movies. The difference is that I was raised on everybody's communal memories. My whole life, I've been force-fed the cult obscurities, the collective marvels of every different age of cinema. If you're a film geek, I have your memories. Even if it's not the specific film, I know the feeling you had and the emotions it inspired in you. I know what you went through when you first found your way to where I am now. The reason I do the Web site is because I still have that enthusiasm. And the people who respond to that, respond to me. It's that simple."

I said, "The problem I have with most critics is that when they see a film now, they judge it in terms of how the public is going to respond, how much it cost to make, how it fits into its times, or the careers of the actors, director, or writer who produced it. So they're no longer susceptible to the simple joys of film; now they're simply being reactionary to it. And I think that's a real shame."

I looked at him, and he had tears in his eyes. Because suddenly he remembered what it used to be like, and what it still must be like for me.

Weinraub asked me why I hated *Batman & Robin* so much. I told him because it sucked. He told me I shouldn't hate Schumacher; he said they were friends, and that Schumacher was a prince of a guy. I said I didn't hate Joel Schumacher; that's not how it works. He said I needed to talk to him, and I said that would be great.

As it became clear that the film was going to be a bust, someone needed to emerge as a scapegoat. So then Schumacher and I started winding up on the same TV shows, doing our stock five minutes on the film. I particularly remember one interview on Australian radio, where they had me on as this kid who's taking on Warner Bros., and I just lit into the film. I tore it a new asshole, and pumped lighter fluid into its colon. And then as I was going off, I heard them introduce Schumacher, who, unbeknownst to me, had been sitting there in the studio having to listen to this tirade. And then he still had to take phone calls from viewers. I can't imagine having to go through that just to make a living.

Two weeks later, I came home to find a message from Schumacher on my answering machine. So with a certain trepidation, I called him back. I think he had read something I said about bad filmmaking being a lot like drug addiction: You have to have someone slap you out of it, or else you'll just continue down the path of bad filmmaking forever. Apparently, my metaphor struck a little close to home. He had apparently had his own experiences with drugs and their many-splendored addictions back in New York in the waning Andy Warhol disco glitter days, and he thought I was making a specific reference to him. And he wanted to tell me I was exactly right.

Of course, I had no idea what Joel Schumacher's past was, other than he was a costume designer on films like *Play It As It Lays* from the Joan Didion novel and Paul Mazursky's *Blume in Love* and Woody Allen's *Sleeper* and *Interiors*; that he wrote *D.C. Cab* and *Car Wash* and *Sparkle* and *The Wiz*, all of them black-themed projects; that he wrote and directed *St. Elmo's Fire* before he stopped writing altogether; and that he directed *The Lost Boys* and *Flatliners* and *Falling Down* and a couple of Grishams and the last two *Batman*s and a lot of stuff I'd rather not saddle him with here.

It was evident that he wasn't very happy coming off of the *Batman* experience. People were not being friendly. I can't really think of too many times in history where a director was getting death threats from his audience. But he was very honest that he had lost his way on the film. The toy manufacturers were demanding more costume changes and a new Batmobile and all kinds of gizmos they could sell; every color had to be neon and iridescent because that's what captivates

127

the preteen audience; every sound was a deafening explosion, because it had to be full sensory overload to have any effect.

Movies of this scale and magnitude, with major stars in supporting roles, automatically have go-betweens between the director and virtually everyone else. It sounds insane to the layman, perhaps, but it's much closer to building a city or waging a war. (If it's true that Hitler sent spies to the Midwest in the 1930s to study traveling circuses, to see how they could mobilize so efficiently, then something like this is clearly the logical successor to the Wehrmacht war machine.) And somewhere in there, the movie just ceased to exist.

We talked for a couple of hours. He actually shared quite a bit about himself, the things he'd been through in his life, some of it pretty heavy-duty. Of course, with show people, you're never quite sure what they're up to; the easiest way to get someone on your side is to tell them your sob stories. But he seemed very human to me, especially about the place where he was in his career. He said, "I never hated you, Harry, even when you were being brutally honest, because if I hated everyone who didn't like one of my movies, I wouldn't have any friends left." He even offered me a cameo in *8mm,* being spanked by a dominatrix, but the scheduling didn't work out. Probably just as well.

I asked him, "Why do you put up with this shit? You've made $8 million a film; you've been to the Hollywood trough enough times to have a track record—why not just stop and do something you like? You used to be an interesting writer; why don't you write something that means something to you?" I said, "Do you want to make products or do you want to make movies?"

Soon after that, he started writing again. He wrote *Flawless,* his picture with De Niro, and he's doing smaller, grittier films now—*Tigerland,* for example, about the training camp at Ft. Polk, Louisiana, for Vietnam recruits. I don't take any credit for this especially, but I do think he seems much happier. Probably after all the criticism of *Batman & Robin,* it made him take a long sober look at himself. I find it's always best to tell celebrities what you think they need to hear, rather than what they want to hear, because they get far too much of the other in the course of their day.

I still haven't really got a feel for Schumacher. He still calls me. The last time, he'd just seen the trailer for *Dogma,* and it reminded him of me for some reason. He tends to call me right before his films come out, you would think to either soften me up or feel me out on what I think about his latest work. Except we never even bring up the films. I don't know if what we have is a friendship as much as some common trauma we've both been through. I think it may be sort of a hostage/terrorist scenario—the Stockholm syndrome—where the prisoner begins to identify with his captor. I just don't know who's the hostage and who's the terrorist. I'm the one who had to sit through *Batman & Robin,* but at the same time he had to sit through its aftermath. I think we could probably go back and forth on that.

And I don't mean to pile on Warner Bros. Warner Bros. has always been my favorite studio, going back to the Warner stable of the '30s: Errol Flynn, Edward G. Robinson, Humphrey Bogart, Jimmy Cagney, Bette Davis. Not to mention *Casablanca, Yankee Doodle Dandy, The Adventures of Robin Hood, The Treasure of the Sierra Madre, The Maltese Falcon, The Big Sleep,* the cartoons, etc. They had a comeback year in '99 (*Matrix, Three Kings, Iron Giant, The Green Mile*), so that I'll end up having praised them just as they were about to publish my book. Believe me, I know how this looks.

But it makes me crazy when I see them do bush-league stuff. Like that misbegotten abortion *Quest for Camelot*. Like hanging *Iron Giant* out to dry—failing to build a specialized market through print ads, failing to capitalize on critical raves from everybody from Roger Ebert to Howard Stern, failure to push for a screenwriting nomination for Tim McCanlies. Or like sitting on the greatest treasure trove of line-drawn, comic-based superheroes in existence—all the D.C. stable, for instance: not just Batman and Superman, but Aquaman, Green Lantern, the Flash, Captain Marvel, Plastic Man, Wonder Woman, the Atom, Steel, Darkseed, Martian Manhunter . . . which everyone says is virtually frozen in the pipeline. This is free money lying around, and they can't seem to be bothered to bend down and pick it up.

I only mention this because I care.

Unless, of course, AOL Time Warner is merely buying the book to bury it, in which case you'll be reading this on my Web site instead, so never mind. I'll have some revised thoughts on the matter soon enough.

CHAPTER ELEVEN

"How Many of Those Things Are Out There?"

Newsweek once ran a photo of me in my room, carefully posed beneath a poster for John Ford's 1935 drama *The Informer.* In it, Victor McLaglen plays a hard-drinking pug in 1922 Dublin who informs on his friends in the burgeoning Irish Republican Army so he can claim a reward that will buy him passage to America, only to have to live with the consequences. The implication was that I'm the modern-day Informer, telling everything I know for my thirty pieces of silver, presumably to get where I'm going. And that someday I'll inherit my slow-building comeuppance. Except that I'm not informing on individuals for the benefit of the institutional good. If anything, I'm informing on the institutional good for the benefit of individuals. Or more aptly, for the benefit of the institutions themselves.

But maybe I should lighten up. Maybe all *Newsweek*

meant is that this is how the industry perceives me: at the perfect center of a vast network of conspirators who have infiltrated the most delicate recesses of that vast amoral abstraction known as Hollywood, and who think nothing of flinging open the doors to the inner sanctum. Perhaps they see me with a devout following of loyal readers and spies who penetrate studio security, crash private screenings, lift highly confidential photos and top-secret memos, tape ultra-secret phone conversations, and are privy to the very innermost workings of the film industry. Who stretch from the bottom to the very top of the Tinseltown pyramid—some of whose identities might be a shock to even the most disinterested of civilians.

Okay, I'm comfortable with that.

For all the damage the Internet is accused of doing today to the cause of serious journalism, one of its accidental quirks is that it now makes it possible to reclaim one of the cornerstones of an earlier era of journalism: the casual blind source. If, once upon a time, a reporter's tips came from as many shoeshine boys and cigarette girls and racetrack touts and rummies and bartenders and flatfoots and round-heeled chorines as he could cross paths with in an evening, now there is literally no limit to the number of people who can contact you by e-mail claiming they have something important to say. Unlike telephone calls, they're not traceable (except by domain name). Unlike police scanners or all-news-all-the-time cable networks, which insure up-to-the-minute currency but turn what is already a herd mentality into a series of stampedes, this latest technology expands the number of sources you can cultivate to an almost infinite degree.

Much of my daily e-mail traffic is fan mail, or updates on other business I have, or postcards from confidants and acquaintances I've developed on the job, or junk-mail spams. But a surprising number are from people who are momentarily in possession of some single, arcane piece of information that they imagine others might take an interest in, and, for whatever reason, they are motivated to share with me. These people are 100 percent the secret of my success: They literally dictate which stories I pursue, validate my editorial choices, and make their own needs heard all at once. Which is why I try to keep advertising in check, and the Talk Back section accessible and with minimal house rules, to include as many opinions as I can besides my own—if only to guarantee a cross-section of voices. Because it keeps me honest. And the minute I can sell out—that it even looks like I can sell out—is when the site no longer has any relevance.

Who are these so-called spies, then, and why would they risk their presumably much-sought-after positions for what is essentially a glorified goof, without the promise of either recognition or personal profit?

In the beginning, when I first talked about my "spies," I was usually speaking rhetorically—a little poetic license to mask the insane amount of time I spent poking around the Internet unearthing these specks and glimmers. Often, just for fun, I would do my intro to a piece, then turn myself into a spy and talk to Harry in another voice, always adding how honored I was to be a part of his crack team of international reconnaissance. It broke up the boredom a little bit, plus it was my own humble parody of these all-powerful global news organizations I was supposedly going up against. If I was reporting on some film shooting on location somewhere, I might go to one of the newsgroups for that country to see how they typed in broken English, and then adopt that as my narrative voice. It was really just to keep myself amused.

Occasionally, I still employ this tactic, if I think it will help the film. I was at Sundance a couple of years ago. (I did eighty-seven interviews in one day. Note to self: *Never* try that again.) After I'd been out to a bunch of parties one night, I got back to my hotel at 2 A.M., and there was a message from a guy named Jack Morrissey, who was Bill Condon's partner and soon-to-be co-writer. He implored me to attend a screening of *Gods and Monsters* at 7 A.M. the next morning. The film desperately needed a champion, and given the subject matter—a speculative biography of *Frankenstein* director James Whale late in life, and how an imagined gay romance echoes the story of his most famous film—he thought I might respond to it. He also knew that most critics would fail to cross the threshold imposed by the gay subject matter, while the film potentially could appeal to a much broader audience.

So I took him at his word and called him back at his hotel, which happened to be the same as mine. He answered in a groggy voice, and I said, "Hi, it's Harry. Here's the deal. I'm more than happy to come see your film, but your only screening is in another four and a half hours, and if I go to sleep, we both know I'm not going to get up again, regardless of what I promise. But I'm staying at your hotel. If you'll come over and get my key, and then see to it that I get up in time in the morning, then I'll come see your movie."

I'm sure he mentally weighed whether I was insane or not, but he came over and got my key, and then he got me to the screening on time. And I loved it! I knew everything about Whale and surrounding the original *Frankenstein,* and the film affected me very emotionally. So what could have slipped through the cracks, because Sundance buried the screening, instead ended up being the film I raved about from the entire festival. Other critics were largely prohibited from writing about it because it didn't have distribution (since most editors think their readers are only interested in the latest releases). So I made it my duty.

I filed equally glowing reviews under seventeen different names, which I think went a long way toward convincing distributors that the film appealed to a broad cross-section of people, and that it wasn't strictly a gay niche film. This in turn allowed them to mount a much broader marketing campaign. People have criticized me for this. But the object was to get the film some attention. It went on to win the Academy Award for Best Adapted Screenplay. I didn't claim to have information I didn't have, and I didn't make any claims for the film that weren't true. I just went about it creatively. In situations like that, you do what you have to.

At any rate, what I didn't count on when I first alluded to my international spy network was that people would start to believe it. Suddenly, people anywhere in the food chain could secretly control the process, if only momentarily, by the caliber of information that passed through their hands. The receptionists and personal assistants and interns and copy guys and chore whores and below-the-line crew members and executive vice presidents of whatever who actually run the place. People across the board found that this was the perfect bulletin board to post all those memos they were tempted to send out but didn't want to sign. Stripped of the burdens of caution or ambition, they could use my Web site as a place of respite, a place to atone for their sins, or just maybe the only place in their professional life where they could tell the truth without fear of reprisal.

There's a lot of working metaphors you can adopt for a place like Hollywood. One of my favorite comes from Dave Hickey, another one of those crazy Texas geniuses who have passed through this place. Hickey is currently one of the premier art critics in America, as evidenced by his book of essays *Air Guitar,* and he divides his time between Harvard and Las Vegas (by choice). But having spent time in the film trenches, he characterizes Hollywood as a "hacienda culture" that breeds contempt: The padrone looks down on his house slaves but will address no one else; the house slaves in turn look down on the field slaves; the field slaves look down on the outlying sharecroppers; and so on throughout the empire, with the distance from the source of power always determining the pecking order. Everyone is allowed to speak directly only to the person just above or just below them, and everyone puts up with this in anticipation of the day when they'll all move up a notch, so there will be one less person above that they have to suck up to, and one more person below they can terrorize mercilessly.

It seems inevitable that an inveterate system of ruthless hierarchy like this would soon drive its minions into the democratic arms of the Internet. Because in a world of arbitrary privilege such as this, information is often the only equalizer. Many of these people are in service to the industry, but pass through it invisibly. They are the cameramen, hairstylists, makeup artists, actors, agents, assistants, waiters, limo drivers, bartenders, party girls, prostitutes, professional consorts, extras, and civilians who by accident, design, or circumstance come into proximity of the facts.

Sometimes, they are the artisans, the specialized laborers out there who toil in perpetual obscurity, who never command attention but take a measure of pride in what they do: the sketch artists, production designers, art directors, model builders, animators, CGI techs, special-effects wizards, etc. And rightly so. These are the unsung authors of spectacle;

they often labor for years, craving nothing more than an audience of sympathetic observers for what they're doing. To them, it's not leaking trademarked secrets, because with genuine spectacle, nothing can undermine the finished product once it's unleashed in all its glory.

The exception are sets like Peter Jackson's *The Lord of the Rings,* where the producers or director have masterfully created a sense of camaraderie; where everyone feels like they are appreciated, that they're making the greatest film ever made, against overwhelming odds, that it's Us against Them, and that any media attention can only dilute their impact and detract from that effort. Conversely, you can't threaten genuine artists with summary execution if they talk and then expect them to remain loyal to you.

But overwhelmingly, the largest source of tips I end up using on the site are from people who are hungry for information themselves. I'm like an information exchange. People come with their bits, here and there—it might be rumor, it might be fact, it might be some grudge or agenda still grinding away, some rarefied strategy that has taken on a life of its own; often the sources themselves don't even know—and it's my job to painstakingly try and separate the gold from the lead, the metal from the dross, the wheat from the chaff.

Contrary to popular opinion, I don't just throw every juicy insinuation I get up on the site. I have a fairly involved confirmation process I use, which over time has proven remarkably effective. I archive e-mails I receive, and I've been doing so for approximately four years now. (Well, Dad does a lot of it.) I try to gauge the reliability of news tips by seeing how tips from the same source to me fared in the past. I may also try to find someone at the relevant company who has corresponded with me before and ask them what they've heard. And even though the tips I get are often incredibly specific, I have a pretty good chance of reaching someone at that particular nexus who can confirm or deny the story. Since the film industry is organized on a gigantic grid—by studio, distributor, production company, project, cast, and crew lists—I can often isolate the path by which information travels. Kind of like tracing an electrical short in a really big car.

I'm careful about accepting e-mail from Hotmail, Yahoo! or certain temporary accounts—addresses that can be set up relatively easily, without much attention paid to verification. And I check the return path at the bottom of the e-mail to try to determine its origin and legacy. I also keep an initial receptor site separate from the archive proper, where mail is subjected to virus detection software, and if any virus is detected, those addresses are red-flagged for future rejection as well. As far as I know, I've never been hit by hackers. I've been shut down, had the power turned off, and had servers break down because I was overloaded. And I've had the phone lines to my server crash and the site just fade away. But anything I can reasonably plan for, I've tried to do so.

The one story I never should have printed is the one about there being blurry footage in *Star Wars Episode I: The Phantom Menace,* which they subsequently had to correct with massive amounts of CGI. Why? Because I was wrong? No. I've never retracted that story. But ultimately, I knew right from the beginning that even though there was blurry footage, and even though the budget of the film did go from $60 to $120 million in trying to correct the problem in post-production, in the final evaluation, there would be no way I could prove the story. That ultimately, when all was said and done, LucasFilm could always say, "We just misbudgeted. We thought we could do it cheaper than we could." And they will never have to show those records to anyone, because they're a privately held company. All I had was an extremely well-placed source. The degree of loyalty at that company would make corroboration virtually impossible.

And more so than even traditional journalists, I would never betray a source. Because everyone who corresponds with me is a potential whistle-blower, if their immediate supervisor chooses to see it that way. And the last thing I need is for someone who's suddenly jobless or, God forbid, homeless to show up on my doorstep. Like Jeff Goldblum says in *Between the Lines*: "They say that rock is here to stay . . . They never say where. Certainly not at my house—I don't have the room."

For the most part, no one on the site knows who anyone else is—even when they're working in the same environment or know each other by different names. I like it better that way, and they seem to as well.

The first rule of *Fight Club* is what?

CHAPTER TWELVE
Ocean's Eleven

here are probably a dozen members now of my inner circle, whom I count on for much of my material and most of my support. Some of them are from around here and are the people I hang with. Some of them have regular jobs, some of them support themselves however they can. Some, I'm the only one who knows their real identity. Here, in no particular order, is my Last Supper Club, my *Predator* bomber crew, my A-Team, my Impossible Mission Force, my Batphone speed-dial:

Moriarty

Named for the evil genius that he is, after Sherlock Holmes's archrival. Moriarty, more than any other, is my man on the ground in L.A., although he keeps threatening to move to Austin and live at the Ain't It Cool compound. Probably the best writer I've got, his character has started to take on a life of his own—steady writing gigs for *Cinefantastique* and some German magazines, so he can vote in the Golden Globes; credentials for ShoWest as Moriarty; on-set interviews in L.A., like Brad Bird for *Iron Giant*; and now formal invitations to screenings—the first of my spies to go legit.

I finally met him in person in L.A. when he and his girl-friend picked me up at the Mondrian and took me to the Bob's Big Boy across from the *Hollywood Reporter* on Wilshire, then to Golden Apple Comics on Melrose, and then on to a whole little mini-geek tour of L.A. That was in 1998; before that, his identity was a mystery even to me. I finally got to know him when he drove some of his evil minions out here for one of the Tarantino Fests. He's also had plays produced and scripts optioned. But now he's finally able to live off his writing for the first time in his life. I'm proud of that.

Joe Hallenbeck

That's the Bruce Willis character in *The Last Boy Scout*. A lot of what we do is fun and games and carries a kind of college-prank mentality about it. That's because most of us are pretty young. But Hollywood, for all we like to idealize it, even when we're chastising it to be better, has destroyed a legion number of lives. Every missed opportunity isn't just some third-act plot trope in *It's a Wonderful Life*; it's the most productive years of people who cared enough to try and say something, who should have had the opportunity, and who were kicked in the teeth for their trouble. Hallenbeck maybe sees himself as one of those people. When he's outraged or bitter, and when he gets mean about it, he's got his reasons.

Hallenbeck's the guy most likely to take it personally when a movie fails to live up to its potential. His style is very confrontational, Us vs. Them, black and white, Good vs. Evil. I finally met him at the *Starship Troopers* premiere. He took me on the circuit of his regular haunts: his discount CD stores, his cult video stores, his used laserdisc or DVD bins, his comics stores where every counterperson knows his name (his real name). Hallenbeck has been responsible for some of the biggest coups on the Web site. And then, all of a sudden, he just disappeared. He says he found love and personal serenity. I have no reason to doubt him. But suddenly, it was like Keyser Soze in *The Usual Suspects*: "And like that—poof!—he's gone."

Hercules the Strong

Starting out, my good friend Glen Oliver used to run the Coaxial News section of the site. Coaxial was a word Glen thought up to encompass TV, cable, video, laserdisc, DVD, and everything else I can't get around to reviewing under a single heading. Of course, why he couldn't just use the word "ancillary"—a perfectly serviceable industry term—is beyond me. But there you have it. Glen was the only other one besides me who refused to adopt a secret name on the site. Eventually, Glen decided to end his "Peace Corps" years with AICN and seek greener pastures. We are still great friends, of course, but it did leave me with the need to fill the role of a Coaxial editor. El Cosmico stepped up to the plate, but his duties quickly fell into running the technical needs of the site.

Then Moriarty and I came across Hercules the Strong. Many have pondered the identity of our dear Hercules; Liz Smith sought to find him, but Hercules, like the demigod of olden times, remains unvanquished. In his palace we call

Olympus, Hercules has a bank of television screens. This is no joke. Like in the comic book panels, he has them all tuned to different channels. He has clocks with labels indicating times and locations in different areas of the world. He has a mane of hair like that of a god. He lives for television, though his real identity is actually that of a man whom all studios must bow to. He has told studio chiefs no and made them beg. However, as the saying goes: On the whole, he'd rather . . . be in television. He worships the WB girls and makes them swoon with his mack daddy stylings and lavish gifts. Hercules the Strong is a god, and no man may defy him.

RoRo

Roland I've known since I was three years old. Basically he's the hardware person on the site: He comes and sets up our new databases, and he'll network the computers when we get our fiber-optic system installed. Roland was a big fan of *The Anarchist's Cookbook* when he was a kid; he was always trying to build bombs and blow up animals—habits he thankfully left behind when he discovered movies. As kids, we were constantly getting busted in all sorts of *Little Rascals*–style shenanigans. He moved to New York with his father at the same time I left for the ranch, and his father committed suicide at about the same time my mother died. He looks like Bomber #2 in the Oklahoma City bombings—the pencil sketch of a man in sunglasses and a hat. He only lived in New York long enough to bring back the accent, which he wears now as a badge of honor. He's my Moose Malloy—the big lug looking for Velma in the Dick Powell *Murder, My Sweet*. His favorite movies are what he calls Gun-Cleaning Movies—*Lock,*

Stock and Two Smoking Barrels, Reservoir Dogs, Trainspotting—movies he can watch while cleaning his guns.

Tom Joad

Tom Joad drove down from Oklahoma for the Tarantino Fest, and then he drove down again for the South by Southwest Film Festival here in Austin just to see the movies. When I found out he was sleeping in his car in a parking garage for the length of the festival, I kind of adopted him into the group. He clerks at a video store and sharpens knives for restaurants. I dubbed him Tom Joad after Henry Fonda's character in *The Grapes of Wrath,* because he kind of looks like Henry Fonda (if Henry Fonda were ruggedly handsome and had an earring, ponytail, and Led Zeppelin tattoo), and because he left dust bowl Oklahoma in search of a better life— one where there were more movies.

He's got this John Boy demeanor, and yet he's totally in love with horror films and hardcore gore. Hence the knives, I guess. He also kind of reminds me of Bill Pullman when he turns into a zombie in the lesser Wes Craven effort *The Serpent and the Rainbow,* because he's a narcoleptic and will pitch over at the most inopportune moments. He's got this great small-town, ear-to-ear, shit-eating grin, and then suddenly—boom!—he's a ton of bricks, and you'd better get out of his way. Endless fun at parties.

Copernicus

Copernicus is a real-life astrophysicist. Or at least soon to be. I met him in Austin at the *Contact* sneak preview (where else?); he's currently finishing his doctoral thesis on the age of supernovas, as determined by gaseous emissions, and he's constantly jetting off to astronomy conventions (astrocons) all over the world. He's six foot five with platinum blond hair and extremely lanky, like Shaggy from *Scooby-Doo.* And since he's a sci-fi geek, if he detects any scientific inaccuracies at all in a film, he'll rip it to shreds. I expect big things from him in the future. I don't know what character in a movie I'd describe him as, but you know that line in *Roxanne?* Rick Rossovich says, "What am I afraid of her for? She's no rocket scientist," and Steve Martin says, "Well, actually she *is* a rocket scientist." That's Copernicus.

Robogeek

The sharp dresser of the group. Kind of our own *Where's Waldo?* He did publicity for the Paramount Theater locally—this beautiful old former opera house—so he sought me out early on in the site and offered me season passes to their vintage film series. Excellent choice! Now he's Robogeek because he's the anal retentive's anal retentive. He has the heart of a poet, yet the soul of a producer (provided, of course, that producers have souls). He is our practical savant. I think he imagines himself as William Powell from *The Thin Man.* His work has put him far behind in his drinking.

Johnny Wadd

Johnny Wadd has a taste for strange. He likes obscure things that will freak some people out—and that most people couldn't sit through. He spends his spare time in nearby San Antonio at truckers' expositions or Ham radio fests. He also plays guitar, dates strippers, and wrote as his first assignment a review of *Disco Doll,* John Holmes's first feature. Hence the name.

Quint

Quint is a high schooler whom I've taken under my wing. But one thing about him—you give him an assignment, he'll get it done. He's interviewed Elijah Wood, George Carlin, Eddie Murphy—he is tenacity multiplied. Plus he keeps me tapped in to the high school crowd. And even though he's half my age, he's an old soul. That's why I gave him the name Quint, from *Jaws.* Because half the time he's a fingernail on a blackboard. As long as he's got his quarry in sight, you can always be sure he'll catch it for five. But he'll kill it for ten.

Lobo

Lobo is my sister's name for her husband. He's a good influence on her, and a damn fine brother-in-law. But I would hope he is familiar enough with *The Godfather* to realize what fate awaits him if he ever betrays the family. My sister feels he resembles the Disney animated Tarzan, and I would absolutely agree, except add a goatee. He comes from Mexico and is a graphic designer for a sign company, and a Spanish-language video clerk by night. (It is my secret belief that Dannie fell in love with Antonio Banderas in *Desperado* and just settled on the closest thing she could find.)

John Robie

John Robie is Cary Grant in Hitchcock's *To Catch a Thief*— the Cat, a presumed cat burglar terrorizing the French Riviera.

He and a fearless Grace Kelly negotiate hairpin turns high above the Mediterranean on the same road she was to die on twenty-five years later. John Robie (ours at least) lives and works in Los Angeles. He steals his way into secret meetings and the toughest screenings. He enters mainly through skylights and ventilation shafts. Stealth and subterfuge are his only friends. For the record, I can't tell you a thing about him.

Father Geek

My illustrious father. Dad and I have an almost psychic link between us. Maybe it's just that our lives parallel each other so closely on a day-to-day basis, but when he's thinking things, I'll be thinking the same thing. We made a list of violent films one night for our Movies That Should Have Incited You to Violence but Didn't Poll. We each made separate lists in our separate rooms. His list was eighteen films long; my list was eighteen films long. And they were the same films. How do you explain that? We've been seeing mostly the same films, together, for twenty-seven years. But still.

It's weird, because when I was a kid, all of Dad's friends were my friends, and now that I'm grown, all my friends are Dad's friends. I think by his own design, he most resembles Sam Jaffe—probably as the High Lama in Capra's *Lost Horizon*. A lot of the geeks on the Web, what they're jealous of more than anything else is Dad, because—let's face it—if you plan to grow up and be a geek, you can't come up with a much better dad than mine. As I write this, he's in there right now listening to *I Spit on Your Grave* at top volume. It's all I can do to concentrate.

CHAPTER THIRTEEN
"Valhalla, Mr. Beale."

I get criticized for a lot of things. The one criticism I might possibly admit to is that I'm maybe just the tiniest bit starstruck. To have sudden access to the people who have served as your heroes for your whole life—people talk about how seductive this is, but even that doesn't begin to do it justice. A-list writers, top-flight directors, studio heads, power mavens, movie stars will drop me an e-mail or call me up in the middle of the night and want to talk about something that posted six months ago on my site. Strong drink, cash bribes, teenage hookers, plates of blow, or unlimited craft services— I think I have a pretty good handle on most of these. But when they come at you with unlimited access to the corridors of power, where you can rub shoulders with the titans that walk among us, or be seated in the great hall of Valhalla—that's pretty heady stuff.

Here's the story I tell myself to try and keep it in check:

When I was little, there were three people I wanted to be when I grew up: publisher-collector Forry Ackerman, author Ray Bradbury, and special-effects virtuoso Ray Harryhausen. A few years later, I modified that to include writer Harlan Ellison. These people were my personal deities. I grew up reading Forrest J. Ackerman and *Famous Monsters of Filmland*. I had 30,000 issues in my bedroom as a kid, because they were banned in San Antonio for being satanic, and Dad bought them up in bulk. So I've read every word he's ever written. You can look him up in the phone book to this day, on Glendale Terrace in Los Angeles. And if you call his taped information line—at (323) MOON-FAN—you'll get the date of the one Saturday morning a month when he allows the public into his house for a personal guided tour.

His house is a living museum to all the things I believe in; it's as dense-packed with information and memorabilia as my room, except his is three stories tall (not counting the secret dungeon, Grisley Land). He has everything from Lon Chaney's makeup box to smoke bombs that were thrown at the original King Kong. Now in his eighties, Forry gives a personal tour and tells anecdotes from his fifty years in this business, and there's usually a crowd of fifty or so to listen to him—visitors from all over the world, many of them the scariest-looking people you can imagine. With their children. *Entertainment Weekly* may have put me on their Hollywood power list of 101, and *Wired* in their top 25, but I'm a thousand times prouder to be there in the guestbook, on Forry's list of 35,000.

Ray Bradbury was the closest thing to a humanist out of the great postwar generation of science-fiction authors—Isaac Asimov, Robert Heinlein, Robert Silverberg, Arthur C. Clarke, Philip K. Dick, Frederick Pohl, Larry Niven (with and without

Jerry Pournelle), maybe Vonnegut or Crichton, or Frank Herbert, or Ursula K. Le Guin. "The Veldt" from *The Illustrated Man* prefigured both William Gibson and virtual reality by thirty years. *Fahrenheit 451,* filmed in English by Truffaut and recently circled again by Mel Gibson, married the dystopian novel with the First Amendment in its story of a book-burning fireman, and *The Illustrated Man,* both the collection and the movie version with Rod Steiger, are stories told by a master storyteller. His short story "Foghorn," no more than three pages, about a sea monster who is summoned from the ocean depths by a foghorn that he mistakes for a mating call, is many people my age's first introduction to pathos.

Ray Harryhausen is the modern father of stop-action animation, the special-effects genius who perfected a menagerie of wondrous beasts and creatures for the big screen—from *Mighty Joe Young* (a giant ape), to *The Beast from 20,000 Fathoms* (giant sea monsters), to Jules Verne's *Mysterious Island* (giant arachnids), to *One Million Years B.C.* and *The Valley of Gwangi* (dinosaurs), to *Jason and the Argonauts* and *The Seventh Voyage of Sinbad* (Greek and Persian epics), and finally *Clash of the Titans* (post–*Star Wars*ianesque classical spectacle). He worked in Frank Capra's film unit during World War II making propaganda films, and came home from the war with a bunch of expired Technicolor film, with which he started making little homemade stop-action animations.

And Harlan Ellison is the guy who wrote "Demon with the Glass Hand," which James Cameron sampled for *The Terminator* (and Ellison later successfully sued for, as he never tires of telling us). He wrote the best *Star Trek* episode ever, "City on the Edge of Forever"; a bunch of *Outer Limits*; some *Man from U.N.C.L.E.*s; and probably too many *Babylon 5*s. He did two books of TV criticism, *The Glass Teat* and *The Other Glass*

Teat, written as columns for the *L.A. Free Press* while he was actually working as a TV writer, and which are unparalleled. And, of course, he wrote *A Boy and His Dog.* He's also notoriously a pain in the ass to work with: He once fractured a network executive's pelvis in a story conference on *Voyage to the Bottom of the Sea,* and mailed a dead gopher to a publishing-company comptroller for inserting a cigarette ad into one of his paperbacks. Of course, anyone who claims Tom Snyder as their best friend is probably going to be complicated.

However, unlike the multitudes who grew up with the same set of private superheroes, I got to do something about it.

I moderated a panel at the Atlanta Film Festival that included Harlan Ellison, Ray Bradbury, and Ray Harryhausen. And I felt completely and utterly out of place there, because of all the reasons I've just explained, that I knew and they didn't. But the way I introduced them was like no one had ever introduced them before. I talked about when I was three, drawing an elephant on a chalkboard in College Station with Harlan Ellison during a heated round of charades, when he was trying to guess the answer "Zoot Comics." And his jaw hit the ground as the memory flooded back. I introduced Ray Harryhausen as the guy who came by my booth when I was eight at some collectors' fair and told me how *Godzilla* was a direct rip-off of his *The Beast from 20,000 Fathoms.*

I talked about one of my favorite all-time memories, when I attended my first world premiere in San Diego. My parents and I were in line for *The Golden Voyage of Sinbad*—Ray Harryhausen, in fantastic Dyno-rama. I couldn't have been more than four years old, and I had been waiting all year for this. And the theater manager wouldn't let us in because he was afraid I would disrupt the show. They were causing a big stink

about it. As luck would have it, Ray Bradbury and Forry Ackerman were right behind us in line, and they said, "Excuse me?
What's the problem here?" And the manager said, "Oh, the
kid's gonna scream in the movie. It's a scary movie." And they
looked at me and said, "This kid's seen more horror films than
you have. He's with us." And then I watched the whole movie
sitting on Ray Bradbury's lap, next to Forry Ackerman, who
was sitting with my parents because my mom was pretty and
Forry had a crush on her. And what an indelible impression
something like that makes on an already excitable four-year-
old—as I am a living testament to today.

Each of these guys just sort of looked at me quizzically, and
I said, "I was short and skinny and redheaded." And they all
went, "Oh my God!" Suddenly they all remembered me.

That's the thing about this job. You're one degree of separation from where it happens. This is an immense vantage
point. You can't really be just a fan; if anything, you need to be
a superfan, someone who knows an industrial-strength
amount about these people, to justify their attention to you.
You're a guest (although not always a popular one). You're inside the party. But you can't talk to them about what happened during your week, or your hopes and dreams, or your
innermost aspirations. At best, you can talk about *their* week
and *their* aspirations.

Consequently, I've made friends with a lot of the people I
professionally respect. Some of these are genuine, unfettered
friendships: I'm a guest in their houses and privy to their secrets and an eccentric uncle to their children. Some of them
are specialized friendships—late-night phone calls, a couple of
hours to catch up in an airport or at a film festival. Many of
them are sympathetic observers or kindred spirits I've met by
accident on sets or in my travels, who remain accessible be-

cause I amuse them or they support what I'm doing. Or else they believe in keeping their friends close but their enemies closer—Hollywood being the endlessly duplicitous, infinitely seductive place that it is. In which case, I would have no way of knowing.

My own separate peace I make with this is that if I see or am told something in confidence as a friend, which I wouldn't know about otherwise, then I respect the confidence. If I come across it independently, or if someone else unearths it as a scoop for my site, then it's fair game. A lot of times, things I've been told in confidence—off the record, if you will—appear elsewhere, and then I figure it's fair game. There's always the chance that my friends tell me stuff just so I won't find out about it on my own. But my dedication to journalism does not supersede my dedication to personal ethics.

By the same token, my loyalty is something I necessarily have to compartmentalize. Or more correctly, I can have close relationships with people who are famous, but not with their much-more-famous personas. It's my own separation of church and state, and it seems to have worked so far. My own fleeting brushes with relative fame have taught me that distinction in a clear way.

Here's generally how it happens:

The Homeboy

Sometimes you just make friends with these people. Robert Rodriguez lives in my hometown of Austin; he went to college here, he bought a farm here. At one point, he called up Mark Altman at *Sci-Fi Universe,* which was the only place I was writing at the time, and asked him what my deal was—was I a psycho or was I cool? Robert doesn't like bullshit, and he doesn't like people who pitch him things; he likes people who are like his high school friends, whom you can share your new toys with. Altman said he hadn't met me but I seemed alright. As an afterthought, he forwarded me his e-mail address.

Three months later, I got a note from the same address asking, "Do you paint models?" That was it. No name. In school, I used to think model painting was Satan's handiwork, to drive the little children insane. But I soon realized that on the collectors' circuit, you can buy some kid's handiwork for $15, all covered with globules of red for fake blood, repaint and drybrush it, and resell it for $200. So yeah, I paint models.

I wrote him back yes, plus I let slip that I knew who he was. Robert Rodriguez, famous director, possible neighbor. This really surprised him, since he puts a lot of energy into maintaining his privacy. And he hadn't given me a clue yet as to his true identity. So suddenly I was the guy who knows everything about everything—"I am the great and powerful Knowles!" Now we paint models every couple of months and I'd characterize him as a really good friend. But when *The Faculty* came out, his horror film at Dimension from a Kevin Williamson script, I gave it a qualified review: I thought it was good, but it had problems. And I was in it. (I played Mr. Knowles, the film teacher. It was a stretch.) One has got nothing to do with the other. It's all luck of the draw.

The Expatriate

Sometimes you make friends with people because what you seem to stand for is exactly what they've been seeking, even if they didn't know it. One day, I got an e-mail from Guillermo del Toro, a Mexican-born horror filmmaker who directed *Cronos,* and then *Mimic* for Miramax. It was an enthusiastic, heartfelt letter, and ended with the words, "Spread the virus. Never compromise." It turns out we're almost exactly the same person: combustible, slightly manic, too much enthusiasm for our own good. He had even written a letter to Forry Ackerman at five asking to be adopted. Soon after he wrote me that e-mail, he moved here from Mexico City, to see if this was any more of a community than where he was. And so far, it's working out: He and Rodriguez are developing a friendship, and at least he's appreciated here.

I try to share my knowledge about Hollywood politics with him, because in one sense he's just a big wide-eyed koala bear. Or a lemur, maybe. But I firmly believe he could be one of those people who define an age if he got the right break. As an April Fool's joke one year, I reported that he was preparing to remake *Curse of the Demon,* and had shot some test footage for it. Then when I met Dimension head Bob Weinstein on the set of *The Faculty*—this is shortly after I'd written an editorial involving Bob's head, his ass, and a crowbar—he confessed he swallowed the gag because people he trusted had claimed to have seen the footage. (He didn't strike me as someone who really liked practical jokes all that much.)

The Fanboy

I met Dean Devlin early on, when I was still haunting the newsgroups, because he's one of those guys. His father wrote *Thunder Island* with Jack Nicholson, and later produced *The Fortune* and *The Witches of Eastwick.* And his mother, you know, *did* Captain Kirk on the old *Star Trek* (only onscreen, as far as I know). So it's kind of his legacy. But if he wasn't writing and producing *Stargate* or *Independence Day* or *Godzilla* or *The Patriot* with Roland Emmerich, I'm pretty sure he'd be spending all day online doing what I'm doing. He's a total and unequivocal geek. My suspicion is, you can't have Captain Kirk kiss your mom and not be a geek. Just a theory.

When I started saying *Independence Day* was going to be a hit—after I'd read the script, but before I had admitted it—he started writing me from the mixing bay at four in the morning, because no one was saying this at the time. Their first test screenings had gone terribly, and at this point he didn't know. And I convinced him he had a hit. I told him it was the perfect Irwin Allen film. When it made roughly $84 million in its opening five-day tally, which is the number I had predicted, I think that went a considerable way toward convincing certain types I had my finger on some kind of pulsebeat. But I also imagine it enamored him of me quite a bit.

The Open Letter

Sometimes I observe things that I'm in a unique position to do something about. That's often when I resort to the open letter on the site. The six degrees of separation being what they are, I know the intended recipient will receive it. And I imagine it's gratifying to have someone write an open letter to you on a well-trafficked Web page—even though the same letter sent through the U.S. Mail would stand a one-in-never chance of reaching them.

When Ron Howard was planning on premiering *EdTV* at the South by Southwest festival, he was scheduled to do so at a chain theater out at Barton Creek Mall, basically a multiplex, instead of the Paramount Theater, our great grande dame theater downtown, because his techs told him it wasn't up to specification. The festival was concerned I would sour him on the whole deal if I badmouthed the other theater.

So instead, I wrote him an open letter and just talked about the Paramount—how it seats 1,500 instead of 400; how these silver-haired ladies in tuxedos take you to your seat. I cited all the people he knew who'd had stellar experiences there, including Gary Ross, who premiered *Pleasantville,* which went absolutely terribly: The film broke twice, with thirty-minute pauses each time; the sound dropped out; they had to start reels over. And by the end of it, Gary Ross was crying, because the audience was so supportive. He realized he would absolutely never have a better premiere than this. It took four and a half hours to screen a ninety-minute film, and not one person walked out. And then I said, "And this is a comedy about TV—just like yours."

Twelve hours after I posted the letter, I got a call from Ron Howard saying he was looking into it. He said, "I don't know any of the finer points of it, but your passion and love for film is so infectious, I'll take your word for it." He came with the entire cast, they had a great premiere, and he ended up donating a new projection system and sound system to the theater.

The Mogul

It's not uncommon for moguls or studio heads to want to meet me, if only to determine what all the fuss is about. Generally, when I'm going to be out in L.A., I'll put a call in to their office and they'll usually ask me to come by. Or if I'm in town and I have an hour to kill, I'll flip through the Rolodex and see who I haven't met yet. I met Jeffrey Katzenberg that way—through a DreamWorks exec who had promised me the run of the place. This was on a day's notice. He was thrilled to talk about his upcoming animation roster and the state of the art.

I constantly get notes from directors who say, "I was in a meeting with so-and-so, and we talked about you for three hours, and I got the go-ahead on my picture." It's like I'm becoming the new Masonic handshake.

The first executive who asked to meet with me, though, was Mike Medavoy. Somebody once said about Medavoy, Spielberg's first agent and the guy who greenlighted *Cuckoo's Nest,* "He's one of *them* who plays for *our* side." Until he left to form Phoenix Pictures, with offices across the street from the Sony lot, Medavoy was a senior executive at United Artists, Orion, and TriStar—one of the longest consecutive tenures of a studio head ever, and all at notoriously filmmaker-friendly studios. Even the Phoenix logo, a burning match that turns into the sun, is a direct quote from *Lawrence of Arabia,* perhaps the most famous shock cut in history. He's like the Trojan executive—somehow he got the keys to the kingdom, and he'll continue to turn out interesting movies until they take them away from him.

Medavoy told me a lot of personal things that he asked me not to divulge, so I won't. But at one point, he talked about how Spielberg was the biggest little kid he'd ever known in his life. And then he made a comment: "I don't even know what it's like to be a kid anymore." Which I thought was kind of sad. Here is a man who has had as exemplary a life as you can have in the film business. He was born in Shanghai to Russian Jews, fled the Chinese to South America as a teenager, has married more than a few breathtaking women, and ushered into existence many of the core movies that you or I were raised on. And our world would be a very different one if he had never passed through it. But this business takes it out of you. And that kid's enthusiasm was no longer there.

*   *   *

If there's a theme running through the people I talk to, that may be it. Because whether they're homeboys or expatriates or fanboys or moguls or blind copies on an open letter, they all get excited about the same thing:

They're all attracted to the same raw, unvarnished, unsophisticated, unrepentant love of the movies. It's what they all started out with—the good ones; it's what sustains them in their darkest nights; and it's what they recognize in me.

It's like a spark that never went out. That they protected all along, as something sacred inside them. And me and my kind, when we finally show up, we're like something they've been waiting for for the longest time, but were never quite sure was coming.

We're pure oxygen. And we're ready to burn.

CHAPTER FOURTEEN
Basic Instinct

Pauline Kael once said something to the effect that Steven Spielberg and George Lucas are a couple of young film-makers who, while having the best intentions in the world, have destroyed the movies forever. Except that it wasn't spectacle or extravaganza or special effects or the pure visceral thrill ride of movies like *Jaws* or *Star Wars* or *Close Encounters of the Third Kind* that wrecked the movies—or continually threatens to do so. And it wasn't the big money moving in afterward, although that was part of it. It was the crowding out of everything else. It was the hobbling of character and the streamlining of plot; it was action beats and pure sensation and perpetual climax with nothing to hang it on. So that, regardless of the changes in locale or motivation or stakes or the source of jeopardy, to a certain degree, every movie was now the same movie.

For this reason, I prefer to think of *Rocky* as the dividing point, not *Star Wars*. It won the Academy Award for Best Picture in 1976, a year before *Star Wars*. It edged out *Network*, one of the last great hyperliterate scripts. It borrowed liberally from Brando and *On the Waterfront*. And it ushered in the career of Sylvester Stallone, who seems a much better poster boy than Spielberg or Lucas for everything bad that's happened in the two decades since: the rise of the action hero, obligatory sequels, actor-auteurs. Of course, to be fair, all action heroes are throwbacks to either Tarzan or James Bond; Roman numerals in titles began with *Godfather Part II*; and a short list of actor-auteur opuses would include Charles Laughton's *The Night of the Hunter*, Richard Sarafian's *Vanishing Point*, L. Q. Jones's *A Boy and His Dog*, and Marlon Brando's *One-Eyed Jacks*, even though the latter was started by Kubrick. Not to mention everything by Welles or Cassavetes or De Sica or Robert Redford or Rob Reiner or Ron Howard or half the directors working today.

But something clearly divided the films of the '70s from the films of the '80s. It could have been the rise of film schools, and the studio development bureaucracies that sprang to life to handle the output. It could have been Creative Artists Agency and über-agent Mike Ovitz and agency packaging, or the insidious practice of studio notes that are issued by committee, or the rise of the screenwriting gurus and their focus on formulas and gimmicks, or Joe Eszterhas personally, or the emergence of high concept.

I personally choose to attribute it to the NRG.

The NRG, or National Research Group—despite a generic name that slips effortlessly beneath the film radar—is an organization that is utilized by virtually all major studios. In the course of a single day, the NRG conducts field tests of promotional materials, in the malls and elsewhere, that include trailers, TV spots, tag lines, posters, plot descriptions, print ads, entire marketing campaigns, and any other materials used in the selling of motion pictures. Toward that end, it also regularly conducts widespread tracking surveys of film awareness and preference, random phone polling on things like "must-see" factors and "recognizability" factors and "unaided awareness" (whatever that is), exit polls and movie-attendee surveys, and positioning studies on scripts, concepts, titles, and potential casting—although it is quick to claim that no projects have ever been specifically struck down as a result of the latter.

The NRG also tests the films themselves, at the behest of and paid for by the studios, with or without the consent of the directors. It routinely assigns a simple numerical value of between 1 and 100 to their probability of success in the marketplace (with 1 being the lowest and 100 being the highest), which in turn can then help determine the film's advertising budget, release pattern, and ultimately, the studio's enthusiasm toward it. It is this function, the test-screening process, that has proven the most controversial. And it is the position the NRG enjoys with all the major studios that earns it increasingly public criticism from the likes of me. In many ways, it seems a perfect microcosm of Hollywood itself: no accountability, backed by unlimited power.

The NRG enjoys an estimated annual revenue of $44 million (as last reported for fiscal year 1996, the last time I could find any public record of their earnings), has over 2,000 employees worldwide, and conducts up to twelve screenings per day. Studios will reportedly spend as much as $250,000 to test-market an individual film, with as many as ten separate recruited screenings earmarked for prestige items or those films that the studio has especially high hopes for. The NRG is currently owned by VNU, a Dutch media conglomerate and parent company of BPI Communications, publisher of such entertainment bibles as the *Hollywood Reporter, Back Stage, Billboard, Amusement Business,* and *Adweek.*

Of course, the NRG would be powerless without the full complicity of the studios. The NRG is only doing the job it is paid to do, and the studios are obviously happy with the results, or else there wouldn't be anything to complain about in the first place. And to be sure, there has always been some kind of testing process for dramatic entertainment. Broadway-bound plays routinely opened out of town—in Boston or Philadelphia or upstate New York—to determine where the weak spots were. The Marx Brothers toured their stage shows so extensively, and tried out so much material in the course of a run, that writer George S. Kaufman once famously remarked from the wings, "I thought I heard one of the original lines of the show." The most famous backstage movie of all—*All About Eve*—sets its third act in New Haven, Connecticut, where resident critic Addison DeWitt explains in voice-over: "It is here that managers have what are called out-of-town openings, which are openings for New Yorkers who want to go out of town." In fact, this is the meaning of the famous epitaph adorning W. C. Fields's tombstone—"All things considered, I'd rather be in Philadelphia"—referring to first-night preview audiences there, and their legendary toughness.

And this was no less true of the movies. Boy wonder Irving Thalberg commissioned so much footage to be reshot during his tenure as head of MGM in the '20s and early '30s that the studio eventually became known as "Retake Alley." Chaplin used to take his movies to the Alex Theater in Glendale, California, and screen them spontaneously to see how an audience responded, and both Harold Lloyd and Fatty Arbuckle routinely hung out in the back of theaters to listen for any lulls in the laughter. *Gone With the Wind* was once sneak-previewed in Fullerton, California, to a near riot, so high did the anticipation for it run. And sixty years afterward, screenwriter Billy Wilder still fondly remembers director Ernst Lubitsch collapsing in laughter after reading a preview card for *Ninotchka* that read: "So funny that I peed in my girlfriend's hand."

The difference between then and now is that most of these tests were conducted by the creative teams themselves—a director or writer standing in the back of a crowded room—or else under the auspices of a studio production chief. Either way, somebody associated with the film took responsibility. (When Harry Cohn, the first head of Columbia, announced he could tell when a picture was too long by how much he started squirming in his seat, writer Herman Mankiewicz lambasted him with, "What makes you think that your ass is wired to 140 million other American asses? Where is it written that you've got the monitor ass of the world?") George Lucas famously screens his films for his friends and peers. The Farrelly Brothers routinely take prints around to college campuses, to maximize every joke.

Yet no matter how distasteful it may have been to defer to the basic instincts of the early moguls, it still seems preferable to the present-day system—administered by some high priest of the court who can read the entrails of those who will soon enough be disemboweled by his prognostications.

The NRG is dominated by Joseph Farrell, a Brooklyn-born Irish Catholic and onetime candidate for the priesthood, who came to the task armed with a master's degree from Notre Dame, an M.F.A. from Columbia, a Harvard law degree, and a liberal pedigree accumulated as a "cultural lobbyist" for such benevolent institutions as the National Endowment for the Arts, the American Council of the Arts, and the Rockefeller Brothers Fund. Immediately before launching the NRG in 1977, he spent five years conducting political polling for Lou Harris and Associates, which administered the famed Harris Poll. Farrell is in his mid-sixties, gaunt, with the pale and circumspect demeanor of an undertaker, albeit one who has grown accustomed to the lap of luxury. He drives his choice of a Mercedes, Bentley, or Rolls-Royce. He is also a practicing sculptor and former street artist, and designs and sells upscale furniture under the name Giuseppe Farbino.

All of this will no doubt unnerve Farrell, who guards his privacy jealously. (Farrell often declines to be interviewed and in fact refused to be interviewed for this book.) Hallenbeck used to send him little personalized greetings on the preview cards at screenings he attended. I'm told Farrell *loved* that. There were times in the late '80s when he himself would recruit people for screenings out on street corners in Sherman Oaks, but those days are long gone. I've heard him described as, variously, a screamer, intoxicated with power, possessing a Napoleon complex (he's not short, but you get the idea), the Queen of Hearts from *Alice in Wonderland* ("Off with their heads!"), and Orson Welles as General Dreedle in *Catch-22* ("Take that man out and shoot him!"). He socializes with virtually all the studio heads on a regular basis, and it is to these friendships that the staying power of his professional standing can largely be attributed. This is hacienda culture at its finest.

In fact, so secure is this commitment on the part of the studios that in 1994, after an in-depth *Wall Street Journal* article reported that numerous ex-employees and others had accused the NRG of a number of improprieties, the Gallup

Organization, the research industry leader, formally took on the NRG on its own turf. Gallup expanded its tracking studies to twenty markets versus NRG's sixteen, and transferred all trailer and TV spot testing to a controlled auditorium setting, a clear improvement over NRG's handheld demo units in use in the malls (a small video player where viewers can watch film and TV ads on a tiny screen). But within a year, Gallup had thrown in the towel. More recently, a company called Market-Cast has been conducting market research and test screenings for Hollywood companies, but so far their percentage of the business is hardly threatening.

Strangely enough, fellow liberal and sometimes visionary Francis Coppola was one of Farrell's early champions, and may actually have encouraged him in the formation of his company. Of course, this last part is outright conjecture, although not mine alone. But anyone familiar with Coppola's grandiose brainstorms of the era—the manic brave new world.net techno-euphoria of his 1974 Oscar speech, his dreams of setting Goethe's *Elective Affinities* jointly in Industrial Revolution Tokyo and outer space, the booming technophilia of his Oz-styled on-set Airstream trailer command post from *One from the Heart,* his lobbying George Lucas after the success of *Star Wars* to start his own religion—can certainly see this as very much in line with his other incidental plans of world domination.

Coppola and Farrell met while working on the marketing strategy for *Apocalypse Now,* which at the time was one of the most expensive films ever produced. It was Farrell who devised the prestige ad campaign—at $9 million, the most expensive up to that point—and its striking poster with the central image of Brando, barren of any critical blurbs or awards notices. It was Coppola's contention that what the industry really needed was an independent outside agency to manage the test-screening process, then handled in-house. The thinking was that Hollywood being as insular and inbred as it is, it was next to impossible for the system to reach an impartial judgment free of the infinite tinge of connections and favoritism and mutual leverage that clings to everything out there like situational smog. And in Farrell, the Ivy League numbers wizard, arts lobbyist, liberal pedagogue, and master salesman, Coppola would naturally have seen his own Tom Hagen—Robert Duvall's character in the first two *Godfather*s: An Irish consigliere, born outside the family, and willing to carry its secrets to the grave.

But testing the way the NRG conducts it is problematic. It is subject to petty abuses and the manipulation of data, as has been alleged in the press. And it is done with a minimum of sensitivity, at best, toward the filmmakers themselves—their feelings, their needs, and their ambitions. This is why it remains so controversial within much of the creative ranks of Hollywood, or whispered about in activist cells such as ours as the new McCarthyism.

At the simplest level, the NRG can't do what it claims it can for the money. The original selling point was that by consolidating test-marketing costs into a single operation, with ensured business from all or most of the studios, the costs associated with preview screenings would be lowered for everyone. In that way, the NRG would function no differently from any other vendor—film labs, post-production facilities, etc. And initially, the studios no doubt wanted an independent arbiter they could turn to, someone who could be counted on to tell them the truth, as long as they proved to be the soul of discretion.

But a company like the NRG necessarily has budgetary

constraints. So most test screenings conducted by it are done locally, even though Los Angeles scarcely represents a cross-section of the moviegoing public. Virtually everyone in L.A. has some connection to the industry, and if you succeeded in weeding them all out, you couldn't fill the number of screenings conducted on a regular basis. The NRG now claims it can meet all sorts of demographic breakdowns intended to mirror desired audiences—half teenagers, half adults; three-quarters women; black-white mixes; gay-straight mixes; *Star Trek* vs. non–*Star Trek*—whatever. But to do this, they would have to overbook by 200–300 percent, which would deplete the pool of potential recruits for future screenings.

Audiences are routinely recruited from malls, probably the single most homogenized place in our culture. The people doing the recruiting are generally being paid minimum wage. Spies and regulars can very quickly learn the protocol and how to subvert it—whether by photocopying invitations, coming armed with different colored tickets, or persuading someone who was sympathetic to their cause to let them in. I was even recruited for a screening once—outside of Mann's Chinese Theatre on Hollywood Boulevard, for what probably would have turned out to be Kevin Costner's *The Postman*. (Luckily, I knew enough to pass.)

Filmmakers often complain that the sample size is too small (a standard three-hundred-seat audience), that no more than three screenings are held per film, that a standard set of questions are applied to every film regardless of the film's genre, tone, or intention, and that the questions are designed to root out disturbing or "unlikable" scenes, when that may be exactly the dramatic intent. And I have never heard of any attempt to follow up several days later to see if people's opinions have changed. Or at least offer that option to the filmmaker. No wonder movies these days are only made to produce a visceral response; that seems to be the only response anybody thinks to ask about.

Serious irregularities have been alleged of the NRG. And despite the company's denials and the very public hue and cry offered up by the studios, who generally claim they are shocked—shocked!—that this sort of thing has been going on right under their noses, it's not clear anything is ever done about it. A *Wall Street Journal* article of December 17, 1993, by staff reporters Richard Turner and John R. Emshwiller was headlined "Movie-Research Czar Is Said by Some to Sell Manipulated Findings." In it, the reporters interviewed some two dozen ex-employees, some of them fairly senior, who reported multiple instances of falsification or manipulation of findings. The article claims recruiters were sent into focus groups to pose as sympathetic audience members, and that "data massaging" often occurred at the behest of studio heads or as favors to filmmakers.

Farrell defended himself and the NRG in the article by saying disgruntled former employees were spreading misinformation. He also denied all charges, claiming that elaborate safeguards are in place to protect against such abuses. He pointed out there is no time to doctor screening results, since the numbers are calculated and turned over immediately, and that if such "shenanigans," as one employee termed them, were allowed, they would easily be contradicted down the line by the film's grosses. Yet in the same article, some of those interviewed claimed such safeguards weren't always implemented. And test-screening data and box-office results are often at odds with one another.

One of my major spies on the site (alright, it was Moriarty) was a theater manager in a previous life. He has personally witnessed things that would make your flesh crawl. He physically saw NRG representatives promise Barry Levinson that preview cards would not be distributed for *Jimmy Hollywood,* only to have them passed out anyway the second they could hustle him out the door. During *Scenes from a Mall,* NRG staffers didn't get a chance to distribute all of the cards, and there was a massive number of walkouts. So at least four NRG staffers went upstairs into the projection booth and filled out the cards themselves. And that's just one that I know about.

I was told that comments have been stricken from preview cards, and negative respondents have been culled from focus groups, presumably in order to appease powerful filmmakers. Perhaps some biased or lunatic or irrational remarks deserve to be thrown out. But anything more would seem to defeat the whole purpose of getting honest feedback from viewers or spotting potential problems ahead of time. (And as far as the argument of appeasing powerful filmmakers by skewing results goes, three people who review films on the site were in the actual focus group with James Cameron after the first screening of *Titanic* and indicated he welcomed their candor in saying what they really thought.)

But even if the process could be made more reliable or precise, there are still flaws that the current testing process seemingly ignores. Anyone who's ever been to a film premiere or seen films at a film festival, ahead of their hype, without the benefit of trailers or ad art, all those things that clue us in to what kind of film to expect, knows that these things often take on a life of their own. Look at the number of films that come out of Sundance or Toronto with an incredible early buzz— *Priest*; *The Spitfire Grill*; *Happy, Texas*—only to make no sense whatsoever to paying audiences later on. So much so that the Sundance Audience Award is said to have a curse on it, since it is so often a reliable indicator of poor box-office performance ahead—a fact more than one observer has attributed to the lack of oxygen at that altitude. At Sundance 1999, the year of *Blair Witch,* the Audience Award went to *Three Seasons,* a Vietnam-based trilogy directed by Tony Bui and featuring Harvey Keitel in a glorified cameo (combined total at the box office: $2,019,000).

The testing process as it's currently conducted doesn't take into consideration critical reception—film reviews, year-end critics lists, or awards and citations. It is impervious to word of mouth—how many people like the film and tell their friends. And it completely ignores the film's release pattern— what other pictures it opens up against, or how carefully a studio unveils it; whether they platform it in one or two theaters in New York or Los Angeles to generate specialized interest, start it in twenty markets nationwide and let it catch on, or saturate the marketplace and make as much money as quickly as they can. Nor does it take into consideration whatever creative promotion the marketing campaign can come up with— whether it's print ads in specialized magazines, key neighborhoods targeted for posters or events, the Internet, or whatever. All of those things help a film to find its right audience. But with standardized testing, all of this becomes moot. A film receiving an unacceptable test score is as good as dead in the water.

Historically, there have always been figures like Joe Farrell in and around the film industry. Will Hays was the postmaster general under Warren Gameliel Harding, the most corrupt presidency ever, outside of modern times. But his name will forever evoke memories of the Hays Office, enforcer of the dreaded Production Code, the in-house censorship rules enforced by the studios between 1934 and 1968 to ward off overt government or community censorship. In addition to severely limiting the incidence of sex, adultery, seduction, rape, sexual perversion, profanity, vulgarity, obscenity, and blasphemy in the movies (as the Production Code's various sections were titled), the Hays Office and its hands-on administrator, Joseph Breen, excised all words, gestures, images, and concepts it deemed unacceptable. This system was in effect for a full third of the century, until it collapsed under the cumulative weight of the '60s, and was replaced by the MPAA ratings system still in effect today. And it arguably gave rise within a generation to film noir, a chronicle of the darkest, most despicable, and most deceitful behavior in the history of motion pictures (at least in front of the camera).

Walter Winchell could make or break a career with a mere mention in his column for the Hearst newspapers or on his national Sunday night radio show—a fact he exploited liberally to settle personal grudges, and which earned him a berth in posterity as the model for Burt Lancaster's monstrous J. J. Hunsecker in *Sweet Smell of Success.* (To be fair, Winchell also shows up in *A Face in the Crowd,* Otto Preminger's *Daisy Kenyon,* and, long after his fall, *Wild in the Streets,* plus he narrated *The Untouchables* forever. And Representative John Rankin calling him "a little kike" on the floor of the House of Representatives became the creative basis for the anti-Semitism exposé *Gentleman's Agreement.*) Known variously as the Merchant of Venom, the Prince of Pep, and Little Boy Peep, Winchell enjoyed 50 million readers a day during his heyday in the '40s and '50s; by the time he finally died in 1972, his daughter was the only mourner at his funeral.

J. Parnell Thomas, the chairman of the House Un-American Activities Committee, was the man who dispatched the Hollywood Ten to their greater reward. (Of forty-one "unfriendly" or hostile film industry witnesses before the committee, eleven were singled out for questioning about their formal membership in the Communist Party; when German playwright Bertolt Brecht fled the country, the remainder— quickly christened the Hollywood Ten—were all forced to spend time in prison for contempt.) As he was still basking in his newfound public glory, a disgruntled secretary reported he was padding his payroll, and he received his own federal accommodations in a medium-security prison. (Something that bullying producers might do well to take note of.)

And Kal Rudman was a legendary figure in syndicated radio, who on the strength of his "progressive" FM/corporate rock tipsheet *Friday Morning Quarterback (FMQB)* throughout the late '70s and the '80s, became a sort of all-seeing oracle for the music industry, as if his every word was etched in stone. Allen Garfield does a wicked sendup of him in Paul Simon's film *One Trick Pony,* where his character makes such fatuous pronouncements as, "Now listen, I'm a funny kind of guy. But I will go out on a limb and I will tell you that the Stones—the Stones—are the only group that ever successfully combined music and spectacle. Maybe Springsteen."

One thing that distinguishes Farrell from this motley assortment of characters is his apparent loathing of any sort of media attention or the public spotlight. But no matter how well-meaning their intentions or just their cause, it's a bad idea to make any one human being the locus of so much power as a gatekeeper into or out of the industry—whether it's a Geoff Gilmore manning the velvet ropes at Sundance, a Harvey Weinstein doling out lottery sweepstakes prizes at Miramax, or a Steven Spielberg lining up his protégés to direct episodes of *Amazing Stories,* and someday to inherit the world.

Despite his famed reticence, I managed to talk to Joe Farrell twice. The first was the day after the first *Titanic* test screening, when I posted a handful of reports on the site from people who had been there. Farrell called me at home. He seemed like a nice enough guy, but he sounded aggravated with me for covering the test screening, and he tried to impress upon me that I was inflicting serious damage on the industry. His point was that he was only doing his job, that everyone just wanted to make the pictures better.

He reminded me of Jack Valenti, in his role as the head of the MPAA, saying that the NC-17 rating is merely a guideline and doesn't constitute censorship, when in fact it equals financial suicide by placing a film completely off-limits to most theater chains, and to all but the most maverick independent video retailers. It's why the MPAA ratings board will never expressly dictate what the offending sections of a film are, so that a filmmaker could efficiently remove them and secure the desired rating. That would constitute censorship.

What it will do instead is continue to return the film with an NC-17 rating, forcing the filmmakers to submit an endless number of cuts in hopes of securing the R rating that virtually all distributors require contractually. The MPAA does this so it can maintain the convenient fiction that it is an advisory board, selflessly guiding the filmmaker to the set of consensus community standards that he has sought all along. This is patently disingenuous. It's ludicrous on the face of it. And yet, it allows the film industry, through its unofficial spokesbody, to say one thing and do another. This is economic censorship, which completely precludes the need for political censorship: It very effectively levels a loaded gun at the offending party's head. And then charitably gives them a choice.

I listened to what Farrell had to say, and it was all pleasant enough. Then when we were finished, I dutifully copied down his number off of caller ID. Later that day, I got a call from *Variety,* asking for a quote about the screening. I told him it was strange, because Joe from the NRG had asked me to stop printing the reviews. And the reporter said, "Wait a minute— you talked to Joe Farrell? From the NRG? Joe Farrell doesn't talk to anybody. How can I confirm that you really talked to him?"

So I said, "I don't know. You want his number?" And I could hear the sound on the other end of someone ejaculating into the receiver. He couldn't believe I would just give him the private number of one of the most notoriously guarded power mavens in Hollywood. And ordinarily, he would be right. But a higher principle was at stake here. The reporter hung up and immediately called Farrell, who was now doubly pissed because he had to talk to somebody from *Variety.* And he began to speak very angrily about me. So what was going to be a five-hundred-word sidebar buried deep inside *Variety* now became front-page news, above the fold. The story began, "The paranoia in this town about Harry Knowles is so bad that studios are passing around his photo to keep him out of film previews."

Never mind that I wasn't going to the screenings. Or that I would have to commute 1,500 miles just to get to one. Forget that you don't need a Global Positioning System satellite to track my movements from space. Now I was suddenly only the second critic I'd ever heard of to be banned specifically from test screenings. (The first, Jeffrey Wells, currently a columnist for Reel.com online, was banished by the Guber-Peters regime at Sony after he reported test-screening findings on *The Last Action Hero,* at which Sony first learned they had an albatross for their big summer release.) And directly as a result of Farrell's challenge, two things immediately happened: (1) I became a symbol for the people crashing the screenings who had serious reservations about the testing process. They began to photocopy caricatures of me off the site with the URL address and put them up in the bathrooms at screenings, or on people's windshields. And (2) Now people who attended screenings who had never heard of me, and chances are never would have, suddenly had someplace to register their opinions, and a community they automatically qualified to be a part of.

At one point, an anonymous woman who claimed to be an NRG staffer contacted me and said the company had hired a private investigator to try and find some dirt on me. I took the "high road." I posted a notice on the site that set out in detail all the women I'd ever slept with, any outstanding debts I knew of, basically anything I could think of that a private investigator might turn up. I titled it "This Is My Life, Mr. Farrell." And within six or seven hours of the posting, someone identifying himself as Farrell called again. This time he sounded *really* angry.

He said, "I have *not* put a P.I. on you!"

I said, "Well, that's not what the P.I. said." Of course, this was all a bluff, but the best defense is to make them think you have a smoking gun (one way or another). I asked him, "Don't you think it's kind of rude to engage in this sort of thing?" And there was just silence. Finally he hung up. And I noticed from caller ID that the phone number was different. So I dutifully copied it down again, for any reporters who might want it later.

Now every person attending a screening has to sign a piece of paper containing what some folks have referred to as "the Harry Knowles Clause," which states that you agree not to discuss the picture screened with anyone in the entertainment industry or in the media, or share your opinion on an Internet Web site. But since so many people don't even use their real names—when attending the screenings, and especially when writing about them afterward—this is pretty much a hollow threat.

The NRG claims that filmmakers are largely grateful for the set of fresh eyes that its screening process provides them. But filmmakers as diverse as Woody Allen, Oliver Stone, Ed Pressman, Brian De Palma, Sydney Pollack, Ron Shelton, Barry Levinson, and Steven Seagal have all been vocal critics of the NRG. Robert Altman was reportedly so incensed when the NRG recruited a test audience against his wishes that he allowed the audience to stay but made the NRG representatives leave. As the head of 20th Century-Fox, Barry Diller was reportedly so enraged over the NRG's failure to predict the success of the dark comedy *The War of the Roses* that he moved to sever all ties with the company—an action that was effectively tabled by deft back-channel diplomacy. A similar action two years later was stymied when Diller's tenure at the studio came to an abrupt end.

And director Sydney Lumet, whose four-decade career began in the golden age of television drama in the late '50s, and who is responsible for many of the finest films of the '70s—*Serpico, Dog Day Afternoon, Network, Equus,* virtually all of which couldn't have been made in any other decade—saw the NRG's rise to power as so historically damaging that he spent the entire last chapter of his memoir, *Making Movies,* demonstrating in detail how the process works. In it, he manages to indict the concept far more eloquently than I can:

"I have no idea what the correlation is between the 'numbers' and the eventual financial success of any movie. I once asked Joe Farrell, whose organization, the National Research Group, conducts most of these tests, if he didn't have a breakdown of this vital piece of information. Almost all the major studios use him, so by now there must be hundreds of movies on file. But no. He said he has no such breakdown." Lumet goes on to print verbatim the disclaimer at the top of every NRG audience report, which says that data derived from audience reaction surveys cannot successfully predict box-office success, nor can it gauge the size of any potential audience. "So what the hell use is it?" Lumet asks.

The number of films where the NRG's predictions were dead wrong are infamous. *Hearts and Souls* with Robert Downey Jr., Howard Stern's *Private Parts, Billy Bathgate, Mrs. Winterbourne*—or more recently, *Opportunity Knocks, October Sky,* and *Simon Birch*—all tested well and then severely underperformed at the box office. Test-screening respondents significantly bid up the prospects of *Tribute,* where Jack Lemmon is dying of cancer, and then stayed away in droves.

Meanwhile, test audiences couldn't predict the dark appeal of spousal revenge in *War of the Roses,* the crossover potential of *Boyz N the Hood,* the success of sports comedies like *White Men Can't Jump* or *Bull Durham,* left-field surprises like *Pulp Fiction, 12 Monkeys,* or *Goodfellas,* or the alternative audience for *Seven,* which received some of the lowest numbers ever recorded in a test screening and yet grossed over $100 million. It's the same reason why "It tested through the roof!" has become a punch line on television sitcoms. Because it's the next best thing to say when you can't realistically claim, "People seem to like it."

In fact, the whole notion of "sleepers" and "bombs"—films that do much better or much worse than expected at the box office—couldn't even exist if research firms could guarantee their methodology. It's like the weather: If they could really predict it, there would never be any surprises. Like Robert Ryan says in *The Wild Bunch:* "What I like and what I need are two different things."

Brian Helgeland's *Payback,* Lee Tamahori's *Mulholland Falls,* and David Nutter's *Disturbing Behavior,* from a Scott Rosenberg script, were all changed extensively as a result of the screening process. All started from strong to excellent scripts, and all suffered mightily in their final release versions. Perhaps all were ruined in the execution, or somehow slipped through the cracks, and the NRG valiantly did what it could to restore a modicum of their potential glory. But it doesn't seem very likely.

Even *Fatal Attraction,* which is universally cited as a shining moment for the NRG in maximizing audience response, is a specious example. In the original, Glenn Close's character commits suicide when faced with the prospect of losing Michael Douglas. And test audiences found that ending disturbing. Then the ending was changed, so that after several false endings, she gets blown away by Anne Archer, Michael Douglas's wife. And the film made $200 million for Paramount. So in that respect, the NRG did its job. Except that now it's a damaged film. And what was a rather elegant retelling of *Madame Butterfly* and doomed passion now becomes an advertisement for adultery. If you cheat on your wife, don't worry about the repercussions, because your wife can always blow the bitch away.

All *Fatal Attraction* did was standardize the trapdoor ending. What I have come to think of as the Joe Eszterhas ending. Meaning that, regardless of what has come before it, regardless of what kind of characters you are portraying, any character can now justify any sort of behavior, as long as it sets up what you're supposed to think of as the ending, but what really just drops through to another ending, which may or may not be the real one. And so on. *Jagged Edge, Betrayed, Music Box, Basic Instinct, Sliver, Jade*—they all work exactly the same way. These are no longer whodunits; now they're did-he-or-didn't-he's. They're a shell game, or three-card monte. No matter which card you pick, you're always going to lose. How many times in a row do you think an audience will fall for that?

Weigh that $200 million that Paramount basically made off a gimmick against all the people who stopped seeing movies altogether, because now they know how the trick is done. Or better yet, weigh the approximately $30 million total that Eszterhas reportedly received for the spec scripts *Gangland, Land of the Free, Reliable Sources, Foreplay, Evil Empire, Original Sin, Trapped, Sacred Cows,* or *Male Pattern Baldness* against the chances of most of them ever getting made.

How many studio executives did George Lucas go to before he got a green light for *Star Wars*? The answer is all of them. And what sort of advice did he get along the way? "Lose the robots; no one wants to see a cute robot." "It's too far out." "It's too retro." "Never mix genres." "You've basically got nothing more than a comic book." William Goldman coined the phrase "Nobody knows anything," to explain the folly of just this sort of grandstanding. But what that maxim means to me is that no one will ever get it down to a science, no matter how big their annual bonus or how current their decor, because if they do, there's too much incentive for someone else to come along and reinvent the wheel.

In James L. Brooks's would-be musical *I'll Do Anything* (it started out with original songs by Prince, back when he was first Prince, only to have them unceremoniously removed after its own test screenings were a disaster), there is actually a Joe Farrell character in the person of Harry Shearer. Albert Brooks plays a Joel Silver–like action producer who makes the following proclamation:

> **"I believe in screen tests. I believe in cutting people out if the dailies are bad. I believe in replacing people if the previews aren't there. Because I don't make movies for theaters that sell cappuccino in the lobby. I make popcorn movies. You want to know what I like, come to my house, look at my lamps. That's what I like. But you won't see it in my movies. In my movies, you'll see what I know. And what I know is detail, and what I don't know, I discover."**

This is how movies stopped having a point of view. Because in the service of this greater market-driven meta-aesthetic, which everyone seems to believe in but nobody knows where it comes from, somewhere along the way personal taste became a personal luxury. Later on in the same film, Nick Nolte as a disgruntled actor dresses down a smug creative exec, barely out of adolescence, by saying, "It's not your fault, this stupidity of yours. You're just a scared little shit that gets to say he's making movies. And the only thing they ever taught you is that what you really like doesn't matter." Tastes, values, touchstones—all become points of weakness, Achilles' heels, and so things that must be defended. And so all of them are jettisoned, just like any other sentimentality in time of war.

But in the case of Farrell, the virtual architect of this world view, we know what he likes. His personal preferences. Or at least, we know those hallmarks by which he wishes to be judged. How? Because they're on public display, for any and all to see. Where? A one-sheet "Official Biography," submitted in his own handwriting, and dated April 1986, is on file at the Academy of Motion Picture Arts and Sciences Library in Beverly Hills, the one on La Cienega just south of the Larry Flynt Tower, with the belltower from *Vertigo* built into its facade. The form provides education, employment history, and spaces for names of spouse and children, which, like other questions about his personal life, he left blank. (Farrell is remarried, with three grown sons from a first marriage.) But under "Film Credits," he prints the following list, verbatim:

FILM CREDITS: Marketing consultant/research analyst on the majority of the movies distributed by the majors in the late '70s and '80s, including the *Rocky* series, *Bond* movies, *BH Cop*, *Terms of Endearment*, *War Games*, *Jagged Edge*, *Indiana Jones and the Temple of Doom*, *Four Seasons*, *An Officer and a Gentleman*, *Down and Out in Beverly Hills*, *Deer Hunter*, *Top Gun*, *Ruthless People*, *Greystoke*, *Garp*, etc.

Study that list. Not a bad body of work, to be sure. There are many fine films on that list—many of which have come up so far in our discussions, or will surface in the chapters ahead: *Rocky* and its many sequels. The James Bond series. *Jagged Edge*, with a script by Joe Eszterhas. The *Indiana Jones* series, although he manages to pick the worst of the three. *Greystoke*, a cerebral Tarzan film originally conceived by Robert Towne, although he lost control of it long before it reached the screen. Note the chummy, almost affectionate references to *Beverly Hills Cop* and *The World According to Garp.* But then ask yourself—where are the classics? Where are the films on that list that you would be proud to have promoted, or that you can imagine taking credit for? *Rocky* (but without the sequels)? *The Deer Hunter? Terms of Endearment?* Possibly. By comparison, look at the credits someone like Mike Medavoy cites in his bio: *Annie Hall, The Sting, One Flew Over the Cuckoo's Nest, Coming Home, Apocalypse Now, Raging Bull, Amadeus, Dances With Wolves, RoboCop, Bull Durham, The Silence of the Lambs, Philadelphia, Sleepless in Seattle, The People vs. Larry Flynt,* and *Apt Pupil,* just to name an identical fifteen at random.

But perhaps that's not fair. The time periods don't overlap exactly. To ask the question another way: In the period between 1978, when we know Farrell worked on the marketing campaign for *Apocalypse Now,* and April 1986, when this biography was filed, where are the films of quality? Those films that might charitably be remembered for something more than the money they made their makers?

Where are *Alien* or *Aliens* or *Blade Runner* or *The Terminator* or *Mad Max* or Cronenberg's *The Fly* or *Repo Man* or *Blue Velvet?* Where are *Atlantic City, Being There, The Big Chill, Blood Simple, Breaking Away, Coal Miner's Daughter, The Executioner's Song, The Killing Fields,* or *Local Hero?* Or *Mask; Once Upon a Time in America; Ordinary People; Paris, Texas; The Shining; Stand by Me; Thief; Under the Volcano;* or *Witness?* Or simple comedies like *Airplane!, Back to the Future, The Blues Brothers, Tootsie, The Life of Brian, Real Life, Lost in America, Fast Times at Ridgemont High, Diner,* or *This Is Spinal Tap?* Where are Oliver Stone's *Salvador* or *Platoon,* Scorsese's *Raging Bull* or *The King of Comedy,* any Woody Allen between *Manhattan* and *Hannah and Her Sis-*

ters, or *Raiders of the Lost Ark,* or *E.T.,* for chrissakes? Or *Apoc-alypse Now,* for that matter? Or a single one of the *Star Wars* trilogy?

Perhaps these weren't among the films Farrell worked on. But then, he claims to work on "the majority of the movies distributed by the majors . . ." I thought that was the whole point. Perhaps he did work on many of these films, but just chose not to list them among his credits, or didn't recognize them as classics at the time. That makes the point all the better. Or perhaps in those days, many of these filmmakers still possessed such cachet that they were able to forgo the testing process altogether, preventing him from sharing in their success. That makes my point best of all.

But even this may be too abstract. Because we know empirically exactly what kind of films Farrell would like to see made if he had the chance. In 1987, halfway into his two-decade tenure atop the NRG, Farrell executive-produced his own film, meaning he helped secure the financing for *Mannequin,* starring then Brat Packer Andrew McCarthy as a lovelorn window dresser and Kim Cattrall as a department store mannequin inhabited by the disembodied spirit of Egyptian royalty.

A poor man's *Splash* or *Date with an Angel,* or *Teen Wolf* if you reverse the genders, *Mannequin* features sub-TV production values, on a par with straight-to-video fare, suggesting that most of the $8 million production costs were spent on trendy cast and other "elements." The tone is all over the place: McCarthy plays it for dramatic depth, second lead James Spader is pure farce, and Cattrall remains strangely insular, locked in a wide-eyed, breathy Marilyn Monroe delivery. Also bought and paid for were musical tracks by Belinda Carlisle and Starship and animated titles by Sally Cruikshank (just off *The Twilight Zone*).

And the film is knee-deep in scatological jokes and offensive material: "hemorrhoids," "camel dung," "fart blossoms," characters being bludgeoned in the testicles or shoved face-first into a mannequin's butt-crack. There is rampant racism and sexism (Persian studs, jive-talking black janitors, "flamboyant" designers). And at the end, apropos of nothing, a janitor finds an unconscious woman literally in the trash, and a Prince Charming moment suddenly becomes a simulated rape, played for laughs. Perhaps even more disagreeable is the ex-girlfriend who out of sheer boredom agrees to have sex with someone she clearly finds despicable.

What might be called homophobia in any other context is here almost a weird unarticulated subtext: McCarthy's character, constantly mistaken as homosexual, is named Jonathan "Switcher," there are numerous jokes about "getting wood" and sex with mannequins, a rent-a-cop constantly minces and lisps while making fun of the "marys," and Meschach Taylor, as a flamboyantly gay black man, holds police at bay with a large firehose while screaming, "This is what being a man is all about—oh yeah, honey!" or, in case the point is lost on us, "Mine's bigger than yours is!" Creepier even still is the fetishistic devotion, bordering on necrophilia, that McCarthy pays to the lifeless mannequin, which he never lets leave his sight.

It would not be an overstatement to say that everything wrong with movies in general breathtakingly converges in this one film.

But this was more than just youthful folly; Farrell's second-in-command at the NRG, Catherine Paura, also served as associate producer, and virtually everything about the film, from cast to subject matter to intended audience, seems thoroughly researched and market-tested beforehand. And with a $7.9 million negative cost (the total production cost) and $41 million in domestic rentals, the film brought in more than a five-fold return on its initial investment—a feat that Farrell remains extremely proud of to this day.

In a 1992 *Los Angeles Times* interview, Farrell took the opportunity to brag about his one foray into filmmaking: "Most people think my financial success came out of this company. That's not true. When Lou Harris's company was sold to Gannett, I had some participation. Then little *Mannequin* came along and popped for a lot of it. Still, I don't aspire to do another movie. This way I can have a perfect track record."

That's what he thinks.

How can someone refer to a work of this appallingly substandard caliber as constituting a perfect track record, regardless of how much money it "popped for"? But don't take my word for it. Really. Forget that Leonard Maltin—one of the most generous of reviewers—gave it his lowest BOMB rating, adding, "Attempt to re-create the feeling of old screwball comedies is absolute rock-bottom fare. Dispiriting to anyone who remembers what movie comedy ought to be." Forget that Roger Ebert reviewed it as "dead," and Paul Attanasio, the screenwriter of *Donnie Brasco* and *Quiz Show,* then reviewing for the *Washington Post,* called it "a movie of nearly thrilling obviousness." Rent it for yourself. Go ahead. I presume Farrell still has "participation"—a percentage of the profits. Make Joe Farrell a wealthy man all over again.

"It was light, frivolous entertainment for seven-year-old girls," Farrell went on to say in his defense, as quoted in the same *Los Angeles Times* article, "a variation on the *Pygmalion* story, which has been done in various forms since the beginning of time. It works for a certain type of person—young, optimistic about life, which is a big part of the population, since aspirations know no social bounds. Every actor in the movie had been successful in a youth movie before. Kids like familiarity. They like what they like."

Yet unlike the Pygmalion myth as found in Ovid, or the George Bernard Shaw play based on it, or *My Fair Lady,* or *Pretty Woman,* or *She's All That,* here the heroine is at one point rescued from a grinding machine, at another is seen having sex in a pup tent, sex in a hammock, sex on a bed of furs, and in an unguarded moment claims to her mentor/creator, "You've got good hands—I like the way they felt when you were putting me together." Promoting this to an audience of seven-year-old girls would seem to border on the criminal.

But just for fun, let's run the numbers. Farrell's mysterious database is allegedly cross-referenced by actor, director, box office, genre, studio, and who knows what else—the ultimate "Six Degrees of Kevin Bacon" cheat sheet. Let's use "little *Mannequin*" as a test case. McCarthy made his name in *St. Elmo's Fire* in 1985 and John Hughes's *Pretty in Pink* a year later, as did Spader. Cattrall, already in her thirties at this point, and despite some nine made-for-TV movies, had been in *Porky's* in 1981 and *Police Academy* in 1984, although she admirably opted out of the sequels for both. And no doubt, much or all of that $41 million gross was brought in on the good faith that this film would be on a par with those previous credits—clearly some kind of marketing coup.

However, let's look at it another way. What became of these actors' careers, in the years and projects that immediately followed? McCarthy tried to segue into serious drama with *Less Than Zero, Kansas,* and *Fresh Horses,* a direction in which his fans clearly did not follow him, and was reduced to doing *Weekend at Bernie's* by decade's end, which, along with its sequel in 1993, appears to have supported him throughout much of the '90s. Spader continued his signature yuppie-scum roles in *Less Than Zero, Baby Boom, Wall Street,* and to lesser effect in *Jack's Back,* before reinventing himself in 1990 with *sex, lies and videotape.* Cattrall starred in a series of increasingly less memorable melodramas—*Palais Royale, Midnight Crossing, Masquerade,* even the big-budget bomb *The Bonfire of the Vanities*—before eventually finding her way back into long-form television.

It's possible to read too much into these things—stooping to the same sort of bad science and inexactitude of which the NRG has been accused. And I certainly don't mean to embarrass or belittle the actors; actors have to work, and it's only at the very top of their profession that they can uniformly steer their own destiny. McCarthy was good in *Mulholland Falls,* or at least would have been if the test screenings hadn't significantly truncated his part, and he had possibly a career best in 1999 with *I'm Losing You,* which you might have seen if the test scores had been good enough for a major distributor to promote it. Spader works well and often, and Cattrall later vindicated herself on TV in the *Wild Palms* miniseries and currently on HBO's *Sex and the City.* But one possible interpretation of these various paths is that the laws of physics are not a joke, that every action has an opposite and equal reaction, and that fans of these actors, once burned to the tune of $41 million, were twice shy. And that a certain type of person—young and optimistic about life—will get the picture if you disappoint them enough, and if you cheat them out of that optimism. You can't prove it, of course. That's the beauty of it. It's just a theory.

The thing that seems to crystallize much of the resentment against testing though, and to point up the difference in world view between it and Hollywood's creative elements, is the numbers. And rightly so. It's this thoroughly arrogant insistence that research companies like the NRG can take something as mercurial and ephemeral and ineffable as art and graph it on a curve. Yet it is exactly that promise that makes the testing process so appealing to the studios. The numbers are primarily what the studios consider when allocating marketing budgets, which in turn makes those films with the lowest test scores the most poorly attended—a self-fulfilling prophecy. And not just self-fulfilling, but the sort of prophecy they can point to as proof that the system really works. By accepting the NRG's numbers then, what the studios are effectively doing is giving it huge influence over their marketing budgets. And reducing their in-house marketing divisions to glorified copywriters.

Why they would ever agree to something so patently ridiculous at face value is because executives at the top of the studio hierarchy, with too few exceptions, don't understand the history of movies, much less what makes a single movie work. What they do understand is numbers. Numbers are their friends. They are empirical, quantifiable things, grounded in nature, that invariably provide certainty. Most executives can't watch a film and tell you if it's any good, even though that's something you or I or everyone we know can do. So to the modern studio executive, Louis Mayer's gut or Harry Cohn's ass are colorful eccentricities, and vaguely suggestive of bad management principles. They can't be verified on a spreadsheet.

But numbers imply exactitude. They promise scientific rigor. And above all, they give the illusion of something tangible, concrete, validating. So that when some Harvard M.B.A. with a mid-six-figure salary pulls out their linear programming charts and statistical decision theories and minimax solutions and computes the price-cost probabilities of their transactions and investments, and the whole thing comes up terribly, tragically wrong—and it will—they can always point to the numbers and say, "It should have worked. Look at these numbers. We don't know what went wrong." They take it on faith. And without the benefit even of knowing the relationship between faith and common sense.

What the NRG is most like to these people, then, is Star Wars—not the movie, but the Strategic Defense Initiative implemented during the Reagan era that quickly inherited its name. It was conceived out of an almost cosmic hubris; it was begrudgingly accepted out of fear and desperation; and it will last only as long as the latest emperor still believes in it. But man, wouldn't it be cool if it really worked?

Math and English, as they were applied to opposing lifestyles back in my high school, exist in separate hemispheres—of the brain, and probably of reality. On the subatomic or galactic levels, there's still no portal where one converts into the other. And regardless of how they spin it, the NRG still takes raw data and interprets it. They claim to rely on their comprehensive database, which has been painstakingly assembled over the past twenty years and gives them an analytical advantage over their competition, but they won't tell you what's in it. The alchemy of it occurs at the exact point that Farrell takes this data and converts it back into his report to the studio. He looks at the numbers and makes his recommendations, not on the basis of what the numbers mean—after all, they're merely numbers—but rather on the basis of his interpretation of the numbers, given his experience of doing this, his mysterious database, or whatever other magical implements he has brought with him on his journey. It's creative speculation. And this makes it Joe Farrell's art form. It is his means of personal expression. As such, he opens himself up to the same criticisms—and the same unsentimental dismissal—with which he summarily greets the artistic vision of virtually everyone else.

Fine. I challenge. The emperor has no clothes. His arguments are specious. Maybe what he was pushing was a good idea at the time, a decent alternative to the way the studios used to be—like every other innovation that ultimately slips into torpor and corpulence after twenty years, and then is incapable of letting go. But its time—his time—is drawing nigh.

Some NRG supporters call what it does no different than the Nielsens, which assess television viewership. Except the Nielsens are used to extrapolate ratings, which are the television equivalent of box-office grosses. They predict the past, not the future. Farrell has called his focus groups a "town meeting of sorts," a chance for filmmakers to interact with their natural constituency. Except they're more like a town meeting in someone else's town, one with an understandable hostility toward outsiders.

Mathematics, like the law, is not an absolute; it can be twisted into whatever pretzel logic its manipulators are capable of pulling off. If studio executives are so all-fired sophisticated in their appreciation of numbers, then how is it they can hold youth in such high esteem, even to the extent of turning the true talents of the industry out to pasture once they hit their forties or fifties, and still put such consummate faith in Farrell, who is sixty-five years old—the mandatory retirement age in most industries?

I suppose, to be objective about it, there is a chance I'm lying to you. Or that I believe sources that aren't to be trusted. Maybe I've got it all wrong; maybe it's me who's been duped, and I'm the one doing the bidding of the dark side. Okay, I'll go that far. Then that should be easily enough remedied.

Have the NRG release their data.

Not their proprietary database and whatever secrets it holds, and not the tortuous record of midwifing any given film into existence. I mean their success rates. There are a hundred Web sites out there now handicapping the weekend grosses; Mr. Moviefone even does it based on the number of calls they get for showtimes. As stated in the *Wall Street Journal* article, Farrell claims to be some kind of wizard—that he comes within 10 percent of predicting a film's final gross 80 percent of the time. The NRG is defended as a risk-management tool, to better calculate the house odds. Okay. Have them tell their predictions on every film, and let us judge the ratio of success. Let's see where they were right and where they were wrong, and the margins for each. Stop hiding behind arcane distinctions like "playability" vs. "marketability," when marketing is basically the only thing Hollywood can still do right, this process notwithstanding. A casino may not open up their books if you ask them, but I guarantee you they can show you the house advantage down to the tenth decimal place.

Or if you want to see if testing works or not, test-screen old movies. Ones that everyone can agree are classics. Get a number on *The Wizard of Oz* or *Citizen Kane* or *Gone With the Wind* or *Casablanca*. They should automatically have near-perfect scores, right? Or *Yojimbo,* or *Persona,* or *The Rules of the Game.* Let's have those numbers so we know what we're dealing with here. Even if it's just to determine what people like and don't like about successful films from other eras. What would actual scientists do if they were trying to prove this technology? Establish a control group. Determine some standard that they could judge their effectiveness against. Choose any film, outside of those that have already been tested, meaning any film before 1978. What I predict this would show is that even the proven winners of the past, whether judged by critical consensus, popularity, or cold hard profits, wouldn't even test well enough today to justify a studio's attention.

What this says is that history is of no use to us, and that it teaches us nothing. But I know that Mr. Coppola doesn't feel this way, because he quotes Eisenstein's *The Battleship Potemkin* in *The Godfather* and Herzog's *Aguirre, the Wrath of God* in *Apocalypse Now*. In fact, go visit his estate in the Napa Valley, and the first thing you see is the PBX patrol boat *Erebus* from *Apocalypse Now*—named for one of the guardians of the gates of hell in Greek myth—suspended in a tree, just like the boat in *Aguirre* and the helicopter in *Apocalypse*. And I can't believe he would be willingly complicit in having launched a process that will make all of history no longer relevant.

Better yet, if you really want to determine what people want to see, then pass out the cards before the screening. I'm serious. Spending $80 million to make a film and then finding out what people don't like about it is massively ineffectual. Ask them what they want to see before you make the movie. Distribute blank cards and tell them we've got $80 million to spend. I promise you you'll get some variation on the answer "I want to see Madonna get fucked in the ass." This has no real bearing on anything, other than that when there are no consequences, most people will stoop to their basest instincts every time. People want to see whatever they haven't seen before, the raunchier the better. If you purposely won't show them something, that's what they'll most want to see. It's like Pottersville in *It's a Wonderful Life,* once Jimmy Stewart is no longer around to influence the town of Bedford Falls. It doesn't mean people want a steady diet of sleaze, or even that they'll feel especially healthy about it afterward. If anything, it just means they're sick of being imprisoned in such a narrow bandwidth in their entertainments, and given the opportunity would blow the whole thing wide open. But it's the answer you'll most likely get.

But even this doesn't quite get to the crux of it. The real reason the studios shell out seemingly infinite amounts of money on test marketing is because it gives them a pretext to say and do whatever they want. It lets them have the final word with a filmmaker, without having to bear the brunt of the filmmaker's animosity the next time out. And it gives them a sound business reason to meddle. Because that's what people in charge do. They control. Freedom of the press means the freedom to own one. And as the price of speech rises exponentially, so does the argument for owning it.

As the NRG conducts it, the testing process is just an elaborate justification for high concept. It allows the studios to manufacture pure drivel to market to cretins, in the mistaken belief that cretins are more easily controlled as consumers. Except that real people aren't cretins. They just have better things to do than have to come up with their own entertainment: They have children to raise and livings to make and lives to live. They're more than willing to pay for their diversions. But once the diversions no longer divert, people can't be blamed for going somewhere else.

So it turns out that Joe Farrell and the NRG aren't really the problem at all. They're just the messenger. The real problem—big surprise here—is the studios. And maybe not even the studios. Just the multinational, meta-commerce, vertically integrated corporate entities that have hoovered up the film business like so much freebase, and now have to justify such ill-considered travel and entertainment expenditures to skeptical shareholders, to whom they are infinitely suspect. Those same craven, deracinated interests who flaunt their latest event films like diamond pinkie rings; who abdicate all responsibility to the fan base and the common good alike; and who have presided over a disintegration of the American moviegoing audience to roughly half of what it was—in raw numbers—more than fifty years ago.

In September 2000, when Senator Joseph Lieberman and others were intent on punishing the film industry for marketing R-rated product to minors, a confidential memo from the NRG to Columbia/TriStar on marketing the self-reflexive slasher film *I Still Know What You Did Last Summer* was leaked to the *New York Times*. It stated, in part: "Although the original movie was R-rated and the sequel will also be R-rated, there is evidence to indicate that attendance in the original movie dipped down to the age of 10. Therefore, it seems to make sense to interview 10- to 11-year-olds." And for once, Farrell and his company were right. Not for marketing horror swill to preteens—that part is reprehensible. But rather, given the interests he serves and the mandate he was given, that makes perfect sense. The only thing stopping him would be conscience.

I think that's why the NRG reacts so vehemently toward us. Because they know their reasons why critics shouldn't review an unfinished film—no titles or end credits, temp music tracks, scenes missing, incomplete optical or special effects—are the same reasons a test audience shouldn't decide its fate. We, the fans, are the thin blue line that separates the public from anarchy. We are the *Consumer Reports* of road-tested movies. We are the checks and balances for saturation book-ing. And we challenge the hype. Because hype is the safety net.

Even if the movie is irredeemably bad, a certain return is guaranteed on their investment on opening weekend, on the sheer strength of pure hype. That is, unless someone spills the beans. But if a studio is entitled to income from people who unwittingly go to see a bad film, that isn't revenue. It's taxation. And taxation without representation was settled a long time ago.

The most cogent definition of hype I've ever heard is again from Butch Hancock, the poet laureate songwriter we've got down here. Butch is a practicing architect, and back in a more reactionary time this is how he described the difference between what you could hear on the radio and the music he chooses to make—and by extension, between hype and those things of lasting value:

> **I see it as the difference between compression and tension. Compressive structure has strength, but it will buckle under too much pressure. But tension can hold just an incredible strength. Hype is all compression; that's why so much of the stuff on the radio falls apart. But if there's some sort of mandate for it, it can support any kind of weight that follows.**

I can't say it any better than that.

And this is the reason why people like me have such a Texas-size beef with Joe Farrell and the NRG:

Because it totally discounts the fans. The geeks. The people who care about this stuff in their sleep, and every hour of their waking day. The studios want it both ways. If the film tests well, they want you to tell your friends, get on the Internet, alert the user groups. They just don't want you doing so if the screening didn't go the way they planned. But you can't have one without the other. And by relying so heavily on young males between fifteen and thirty-five with too much time on their hands, especially those chosen at random, who are hanging around in malls in the first place—this in turn skews the numbers toward that bias, which creates films being made almost exclusively for that demographic, which in turn attracts only that demographic to the movies. And everyone else finds something else to do with the time they used to spend going to the movies. Like go on the Internet, for instance. And chat with millions of others who feel the same way they do. And figure out how to get even.

Test marketing has been a staple of the packaged goods and service industries for over half a century. Ever since Edward Bernays, the father of modern public relations, used to sit around the dinner table and pick the brain of his father-in-law, Sigmund Freud. But traditional businesses will usually try and change their marketing to reflect the product, and not the other way around. And they certainly would never fill their advertising with specious claims, flood the marketplace with inferior product, and try to keep the shelf life short enough that hopefully no one will notice. Such a strategy would be professional suicide.

I get all sorts of grudges and agendas attributed to me in judging a film. But it doesn't work like that. I always start out wanting a film to be good. Always. And the Internet, at least at the hot points of fan-based sites, is like sampling without error. It's exactly the people the studios want to reach, who are more than willing to receive. It's the perfect economic model.

Of course, without the NRG, maybe Ain't It Cool News wouldn't have any reason to exist—we are locked into a cycle of co-dependency and can't survive without each other.

I can't speak for the other guy. But I'll take my chances.

CHAPTER FIFTEEN
A Night to Remember

Then there was *Titanic*.

The thing about *Titanic* was, given its crushing $200 million price tag, and since it had been pushed back so many times, people were ready to see it as damaged goods. There were all sorts of wild rumors: that Mexico's lax safety laws had resulted in multiple stunt deaths on the set; that a vengeful caterer had doused the crew with homemade psychedelics; that James Cameron was rearranging the deck chairs on the *Titanic*—literally: demanding authentic brand-name china or carpets from the original manifest, or last-minute computer work to add period hairstyles or clouds of frosted breath.

What no one knew at the time was that Digital Domain, the effects house that Cameron had founded, was busy completing effects for Luc Besson's *The Fifth Element,* to honor a promise from one filmmaker to another, and that secretly

Cameron had preferred a Christmas release all along. But because the summer had been such a bust, there was already blood in the water. Everyone with a vested interest in film was circling this would-be bloated cadaver, ready to sink their teeth into the carcass, and anxious to be the first to call it the new *Waterworld*.

The problem with that was threefold:

(1) James Cameron, if nothing else, understands an audience. *Aliens* trumped a classic, which only a handful of sequels have done in modern times. This is the man, after all, who scripted the *Rambo* phenomenon. He may make a film like *True Lies* that's sexually creepy and politically reprehensible (lovers in the clinch frame a tactical nuclear explosion, and no one even bothers to look). *The Abyss* may underperform in the marketplace, although he'll be critically vindicated once twenty minutes is restored on laserdisc. But he will not misjudge his audience.

(2) Leo Mania was all set to bust out. Virtually every review of *What's Eating Gilbert Grape?* had compared DiCaprio to James Dean. He was already in the Japanese fan mags and tabloids on the strength of *Romeo & Juliet*—presumably because of those Asian eyes.

(Moriarty had a story about the *Phantom Menace* premiere at the Mann's Chinese on Hollywood Boulevard in Los Angeles. Reportedly, George Lucas slipped into the private balcony for the first showing at midnight on Wednesday with Fox domestic chairman Tom Sherak and Leonardo DiCaprio, who was currently being wooed for the role of Anakin Skywalker in the second and third installments. Before the feature, a trailer for *The Beach* played, which opened with a close-up of DiCaprio's face. And people booed. Why? Because in their minds, DiCaprio represented *Titanic,* and *Titanic* was the enemy if *The Phantom Menace* was to become the highest-grossing film of all time. Of course, to be fair, they had no way of knowing that DiCaprio was in attendance. But these finer points were lost on the VIPs, and DiCaprio reportedly left not only the theater but the entire country to put the memory behind him.)

(3) And I had read the script. Cameron was traditionally an executor of what's on the written page. I knew you couldn't count this one down and out. Which suited me just fine. I was sick of triaging movies and dismissing the ones that weren't going to make it. Nobody was more ready than me for the *Gone With the Wind* of our time. So, of all people, I suddenly became the voice of reason, demanding that judgment be withheld until we had proof that the patient was terminal. "If Marty dies, I want to hear everything's okay until I say Marty's dead."

In November 1997, I went to the *Alien Resurrection* premiere in L.A. And I absolutely detested the film. Leaving the screening, I was terrified they were going to stop me and ask my opinion. Because I don't want to dis somebody at their own premiere. This is your one night where people have to be nice to you; I think it's a union thing. Plus I didn't want to be rude, being a guest and all.

So I was looking down at my shoes, trying to get out of there, when I felt a tap on my shoulder. It was Fox's then head of production, Bill Mechanic, who has been a very vocal critic of the Web site and of me; he tells a number of anecdotes in public that involve me threatening him or baiting him in some way that are kind of patently absurd. Mainly because I don't threaten people; I rarely even lose my temper without considering the consequences first. But he asked me point-blank, "What did you think?"

And I was at a loss. I finally just said, "How could you make a bad *Alien* movie? How was this possible? It was horrible."

He said, "Yeah, yeah."

I said, "I hope *Titanic* isn't going to be the same story."

And he said, "Oh, no, *Titanic* is the real deal."

So, of course, my first instinct was to believe this was doomed as well.

The first test screening of *Titanic* was to take place in September. Before that, the word on the film was that it was over four hours long, that it was a film no one was interested in seeing, and that everyone—alive or dead—already knew the ending. They called it Cameron's Folly; it was Clive Cussler's *Raise the Titanic!* all over again. Movies on water are cursed; the *Titanic* itself was cursed. How could film versions of it fare any better?

Then one day, according to popular legend, I got a call from an anonymous woman who said, "If you want to find the *Titanic,* you need to search the Twin Cities." Someone who had seen *All the President's Men* one too many times, I might add. She probably meant Minneapolis–St. Paul. But I couldn't send someone there, and I couldn't call my local Minneapolis affiliate and ask them to send out a SWAT team. And I was getting conflicting information from my moles at Digital Domain and NRG.

So I did the next best thing. I posted a message on the site that read, "Attention Minneapolis–St. Paul residents: Contact me immediately! Important life-saving spy mission to occur in your city!"

I got 150 e-mails back saying, "Okay, I'm getting off work. What do I have to do?"

I began to coordinate the reconnaissance efforts. Between calling every theater in the Twin Cities area and monitoring local radio stations, we determined there were two test screenings being held the same day: One was for a Martin Lawrence comedy called *Nothing to Lose* and one was for *Great Expectations.* Both titles were ripe with irony. But *Nothing to Lose* was a Disney film, and opened the next weekend. *Great Expectations,* however, didn't open until the following February. And it was from Fox.

Just to be sure, I divided my spies between the two screenings. I knew when each one started, and that *Titanic* was a four-hour movie. At first I was giddy that I'd actually pulled it off. And then as the hours wore on, I started to develop a sinking feeling (not unlike the *Titanic* itself). What if it was an unmitigated disaster?

Then the first response came in. All it said was, "Utterly, unbelievably fantastic. I'll write you later." That was it. That may have been the worst part, knowing that it was great, but not being able to hear anything else about it. Eventually, thirty-five people wrote back saying they had gotten into the first screening. All thirty-five loved it; the only criticism was that the modern-day section at the beginning and end might have been a little too long.

So I posted the results. But not just that. I started saying *Titanic* was going to be the highest-grossing movie of all time. What I was spouting was absolute heresy; it was at odds with every other critic in the world, but I secretly knew I was right. The feeling was indescribable. Media calls started flooding in. This was right when the *New York Times Magazine* piece on me was about to come out, and so once the *Wall Street Journal* learned that, they decided to scoop the Sunday profile with a Friday article of their own. That was when it all supernovaed.

After those two pieces ran, my regular circulation jumped

to 100,000. Before the frenzy over *Titanic* was done, I'd be up to half a million daily readers. (Although hot stories will create momentary surges in circulation, that usually falls off in a couple of days. In the days leading up to *The Phantom Menace,* we would sometimes register 4 or 5 million hits. More recently, when we broke the *X-Men* costume photos, we got 20 million hits in one day, which crashed not only our server, but all the sites linking to ours as well. So, once again, we moved to a bigger server. But generally, we have about 15 million page views a month, representing approximately two million unique viewers.)

I had reports from Digital Domain that they were posting the reviews on bulletin boards in-house. Employees were ecstatic; there was a newfound camaraderie in the hallways, since the buzz had been so bad that the company was losing business. No one thought they could deliver their effects on time.

Now suddenly, the media was crediting me with *Titanic*'s success, just like they had blamed me for *Batman & Robin*'s failure. They couldn't seem to fathom that, in the first place, I didn't write the reviews, I just collected them and put them up on the Web site; and that second, *I don't make the movies!* The movies are either bad or they're good; there's not too much that's subjective in the process. People are either going to know going into the first weekend, or they're going to know going into the second weekend. But they're going to know.

Titanic topped all existing box-office records. It tied *Ben-Hur* for most Oscars ever. And for better or worse, I earned my own weird species of celebrity in the process. Here I could care less about actors' or directors' or producers' personal lives, since learning about them so often upset the fragile alchemy onscreen, and suddenly I found myself in the middle of a media feeding frenzy. People wanted to know everything about *me*—a fat cartoony guy with a bright red beard—when I was completely the product of my interests. I was also one more story good to go before journalists ever lifted pen to paper or mic to mouth. Word got around that Harry was good copy, that I knew how to lay up a pull quote or deliver a sound bite, and that you could sell a two-page story on me if you'd just call me up and chat for half an hour.

And suddenly, I was the story, not the storyteller. I found myself inside this fantastic, deafening, blinding bell chamber of flashbulbs and spotlights and hyperattention and rarefied, razor-thin atmosphere that all celebrities must consider second nature. No wonder these people are so messed up. I was like Tom Hanks at the end of *Splash,* plunging into the East River, suddenly in some soundless, beautiful underwater kingdom; or Tom Hanks in *Apollo 13,* shot into space, where the old rules of gravity no longer apply; or Tom Hanks at the end of *Saving Private Ryan,* shell-shocked, ears ringing, cut off from his senses, oblivious to the danger all around him. And people like Tom Hanks do this every day.

I also learned what the media is looking for. A couple of all-purpose rules for the next time you inadvertently attract world attention and need to plead your case in the international press:

They used to say the reason there's so much violence in film is because eighteen-year-old actors think it's cool to play with guns, so if you want to get one interested in your script, give them a gun to play with. Same thing with the global media. You want to get on these people's wavelength? Learn to speak their lingo.

For instance, always speak in metaphor. And somehow

plug the metaphor back in to what you're doing. Now, suddenly, you're a trope—a literary embellishment—and such are the tools of the working journalist. If you're doing a rock-and-roll site, paint yourself as a pinball wizard, sitting at home in front of your console, blind and deaf and dumb to all but the impulses and intuitions you take from the open wire. If you're fighting the system in some way, draw a parallel to a Frank Capra character. If you're excavating the latest gleaming factoids from a desert of archaeology, see yourself as Indiana Jones digging up the Well of Souls, searching for the Lost Ark of the Covenant. Or a three-quarter-ton dolly happens to be barreling down on top of you? Make it the giant boulder from *Raiders of the Lost Ark*. This isn't rocket science. It's free association, and anyone can do it with a little practice. But it looks great when all of a sudden you do it in an interview.

Always refer back to something you've said in a previous interview. This validates the efforts of earlier reporters, lets them know you have an appreciation of their work, and tends to make them keep up with you. Recognize the value of the political maxim "Free money screams," since publicity that comes without having to go look for it is better than any publicity money can buy. And if you should ever find yourself on some industry power list published in an entertainment magazine, take amusement from the fact that there is probably a difference of at least two decimal points in mean income between you and anyone else on the list.

Did I ever meet James Cameron? No. But at the first test screening in Los Angeles, out in Yorba Linda in Orange County, a week or two after the Minneapolis screening, the great Joe Hallenbeck walked up to him—caught up with him outside the theater.

Hallenbeck said, "Excuse me, Mr. Cameron, I just want to

say it's an honor to meet you. I'm a big fan. I just came out of *Titanic,* and I have to say this: Congratulations—you just won yourself your first Oscar."

Cameron started laughing. He said, "There's no way in hell the Academy will go for this movie. It's too popcorn."

And Hallenbeck told him, "You mark my words. This movie is going to walk away with several Academy Awards, and when it does, I get to say I told you so."

Cameron said, "Okay, fine," and that was it.

Confidential to James Cameron: Consider yourself told.

CHAPTER SIXTEEN

"To George Bailey, the Richest Man in Town. Hee-Haw!"

The easiest job in the world is armchair general. Anyone can make fatuous pronouncements after the fact or second-guess the opposition from the ridge above the plain of battle. "The men died wonderfully," says George Macready in Stanley Kubrick's *Paths of Glory.* "I'm not saying we wouldn't get our hair mussed," concurs George C. Scott in *Dr. Strangelove,* echoing the identical sentiment as a vaudeville gag. But until you've been down there in the trenches, tasted the blood and smoke and sting of battle, yada yada yada.

Alright.

I've been taking a lot of hits of late in the would-be populist press and from my enemies, real and imagined, for all sorts of speculative lapses on my part. Some of them, I've tried to address in this book. Some of them, they hardly seem worth the bother. A lot of them, frankly, seem like sour grapes.

Or maybe just inevitable: You can't have the rise without the fall. The heat without the chill. "The only reason they make it hard is to see the kind of stuff you're made of." I still believe that. All of 200 pages later.

But for the benefit of my critics—the faceless studio hierarchies and strident archnemeses I have tweaked and vexed over time, the pretenders and usurpers, the apostates who have parted ways with the faith—I offer up the following stories for your reading pleasure. Sample them in broad spirit.

I get a lot of freebies through the site—swag, I call it. I've had computer problems and people have sent me hardware or memory; I get free videotapes, CDs, DVDs, scripts, laserdiscs—either from companies, the filmmakers themselves, or from zealous fans. I got lots of baked cookies and desserts, after I started posting recipes on the site. Not to mention the plaintive, pitiful begging for presents on my birthday. I'm not Louella Parsons, taking the limo around to the studios, demanding Christmas presents (and then when they're stolen, doing it all over again). If I was strategic about it, I could double or triple the amount of swag I pocketed, but then that would defeat the whole purpose. Obviously, I'm not in it for the money—or the swag.

And as if that were ever really in doubt: I was once offered a substantial sum of money to favorably review a script on the site. When I told Roger Ebert this, when it came up in conversation, he was astounded. Someone who had written a comedy script knew I had a copy of it already, and also knew that a certain studio boss he hoped would give it the green light followed the site religiously and respected my opinion. He offered me $20,000 cash, no questions asked, if I would post a positive review. Furthermore, I had already passed the thing along to Quint, because I don't read comedy well, and he was on record as having liked it. So I could have, entirely in good conscience, posted an honest review, had no moral qualms about it afterward, and pocketed a quick $20K in the bargain.

Except that like all crimes, the first one's easy; it's the last one that's hard, because it's impossible to stop until it's too late. And all it takes is one person who can prove I've taken a bribe, traded a favor, scratched a back, or greased a skid, and my opinion is never again worth a Liberty dime. Twenty grand isn't enough; $2 million isn't enough, because if my word is for sale, then that puts me in the same line of work as every other assembly-line chemist out there who processes raw information into corporate hype. These include some of the largest mergers and zaibatsus and megalopolies on the planet, whose resources are infinite. There is no way I can compete with that. My only protection is that I offer something different.

I went to London on a press junket to visit *The Mummy* set. I decided I'd like to see London, and I wanted to see what a big fancy studio junket was really like—where the studio flies you out first-class, puts you up in an $800-a-night hotel, walks you onto the set, takes care of your every need. There are film writers for whom this is a way of life, and I wanted to experience it firsthand. It was common knowledge what hotel I was staying at, because I always post it on my Web site, in case any fans want to track me down or come by. So one night at about two in the morning, I got a call from the front desk. It was a girl who called herself Chastity, who it turns out was sixteen, and who wanted to come up and see me.

I said, "It's two o'clock in the morning—don't you think someone is liable to get the wrong idea?"

She said, "There is no wrong idea. I'm a working girl."

I said, "Like a prostitute? I didn't order a prostitute."

213

And she said, "Oh, no, sir, that's all been taken care of. I'm a gift from an admirer. Let me come up and I'll show you."

Apparently prostitutes are not only legal in the United Kingdom, but they can ply their wondrous trade at the age of sixteen. I told her, "You know, it's not that I'm not honored, but I'm going to have to pass. I don't know you or who sent you. I'm sorry I brought you all the way down here." She said no problem; if you change your mind, call this number. Then the next day, I told someone who lives there what had happened. And they said, "For God's sake, man, that's how they do it! The tabloids send these young prostitutes around, and then they sell their story for publication. Including a blow-by-blow of the sex. You would have been the laughingstock of Fleet Street."

I'm not saying I won't do something stupid someday and wish I could take it back. Or haven't already, for that matter. But I am saying it would take something like a protracted lawsuit at this point to bring the Web site down. Some studio that dangles the bait of a story that's too good to be true, waiting to pounce on me as soon as I commit it to cyberprint. Some individual or entity who tries to prove I acted with willful or malicious intent, to knowingly commit slander or fraud. I mean, if they can almost take down the president, they can probably figure out how to get to me. But I try to be very, very careful, in my conduct and my ambitions, to avoid just that kind of standoff.

So for anyone tempted to send private detectives around to dig up the local dirt: The thing about me is—once you get past the waist size and the long hair, the house full of sacred junk, and the raised by feral hippies stuff—I'm an Eagle Scout. I'm trustworthy, loyal, helpful, friendly, courteous, kind, obedient, cheerful, thrifty, brave, clean, and reverent. Or at least I try to be.

I got dinged for my flip-flop on *Godzilla,* and probably rightly so. But not for the reasons people think. As chance would have it, mainly through my acquaintanceship with writer-producer Dean Devlin, Glen Oliver and I were invited to the *Godzilla* premiere at New York's Madison Square Garden, which is summarily destroyed at the end of the movie. Five weeks earlier, I had run five extremely negative reviews from the first test screening. But Glen had been in touch with Devlin's people, and so even after the reviews had run, Devlin put us on a plane and brought us up for the event. Which I thought was a sign of character on his part. This was my first trip to New York, by the way—staying on the fifty-second floor of some fabulous hotel in midtown, two blocks over from David Letterman's theater. I had to watch for falling apes every time I went outside.

And the premiere itself was like nothing I'd ever seen before. It was insane. They had 18–20,000 fans crammed into Madison Square Garden, with an immense screen and high-tech sound system worthy of a rock concert. In fact, that's what it was most like: people tossing beach balls, throwing Frisbees, smoking dope, chanting. We were down front, right at the back of the celebrity rows, but next to all these kids attending through some special urban outreach program. And every time a beach ball would bounce over into their section, they would deflate it and put it under their jacket to take home with them. Every time Godzilla appeared onscreen, these kids would stand up on their chairs and do the Arsenio Hall whoop. It was one of the greatest film experiences I've ever had. I don't even know how much of the film I really saw.

But just to feel 20,000 fans screaming in unison at a movie—it was incredible.

Then as soon as they showed Madison Square Garden on-screen, the place went nuts. Just total deafening screams; I was having a Leni Riefenstahl moment. And then at the party afterward—I met Muhammad Ali. I met Chow Yun-Fat. I met Jackie Chan. I mean, do they make cooler people than this? These are the virtual gods of coolness for over three-quarters of the planet. The next day we flew home, and I filed my first review on the cab ride back to La Guardia. I still stand by it. It just didn't have very much to do with the movie.

The first thing I did when we got home was tell Dad, "You've got to see *Godzilla*—it's amazing!" So we went, right then; there was a show starting in thirty-five minutes. And I was shocked. Not at how bad it was, although it was, but at the difference in my perception of it, then and now. Suddenly, there were all these glaring problems: Godzilla runs away from the military, when no self-respecting Godzilla had ever done that. The acting was the stiffest I'd ever seen in a big-budget extravaganza. The effects looked good, and Godzilla himself looked great. But the movie was flat.

I walked out feeling terrible; I realized what I'd done. So I rushed home and immediately began writing a second review. I shredded the film, took it to task for all the inconsistencies and insensitivity to the source material, and posted it. Then I thought to check the Talk Back section. And I saw that people who had seen the film on the strength of my first review were starting to write in now, and they were leveling charges of sell-out against me. I had my first insurrection on my hands. And it was going to get worse, because I had just flip-flopped. I had changed my mind in a very public way, and it looked like I'd done so trying to lead my troops from the rear.

But actually, this makes my point. Because that's one of my big things—taking into account the screening experience when you're reviewing the film. Every review I've ever posted has probably at least paid lip service to the circumstances in which I saw the film: going there, who you're with, what it reminds you of, how it reconnects you with the continuum of your life. I just think that's endlessly relevant. And conversely, I think one of the reasons so many bad films come out of Hollywood, or at least why they make it past their fail-safes, is because everybody out there sees films in private screening rooms—with plush seats and optimal sound systems and one of twenty brands of sparkling water at their disposal if they just buzz for it. You can watch the worst film ever made, but if you do it at Robert Evans's house, with Warren Beatty on your left, Jack Nicholson on your right, and the ghost of the first two *Godfather*s clinging to the upholstery, I guarantee you you're going to remember it. And now, even though I kind of backed into it, I had become an example of this same principle.

Critics change their minds. It happens. Not Pauline Kael maybe, because she claimed to never see films twice. But Ebert's done it three or four times. Joe Morgenstern at *Newsweek* did it for *Bonnie and Clyde* at a crucial juncture in the life of that film, as reported in *Easy Riders, Raging Bulls.* I tend to do it with John Carpenter films: *They Live* with Rowdy Roddy Piper was a movie about a guy who didn't want to put on a pair of sunglasses. Then the second time, it was a social parody that claimed that yuppies were really aliens. Which actually explains a lot. And then there are films like *Speed,* which are a fantastic ride the first time through, but once you know where all the bumps and pylons are, it's like standing in line for Space Mountain a second time.

Glen still argues with me about this. He says, "Man, you

fucking loved that film when you came out of it." I tell him, "The second time, I saw a different movie." We're both right.

And then there was the Academy Awards brouhaha. The whole thing was explained in detail on the site at the time, but basically, I got a tip that someone had gotten hold of the 2000 Academy Award nominations the day before they were to be announced, from an Academy computer set to download the info onto their official Web site. I was duly skeptical, although I did confirm that all the names and films listed were both eligible and likely. Then I asked a tech person I trusted whether it seemed as though the initial message had actually originated from the Academy server. They assured me it did. I had a handful of hours before the nominations were going to be announced. I had to make a choice. The correct choice was, "It seems thin; get another source." This is not the choice I opted for. I posted the names, they turned out to have come from the home computer of an ABC.com freelancer-underling who had compiled an early list of potential winners. The guy who got them for me was just a kid who thought he had something and overstated its importance, and I wound up wearing a three-egg omelet for a facial moisturizer.

This was the same year that the Oscar ballots went missing, the awards themselves were stolen, and nine months later the network news divisions faced a similar decision on deadline when they called the presidential election both ways on the basis of Florida. Not to try and downplay my responsibility. I obviously regret the entire incident, and basically deserved all the criticism I got. I had to apologize to the Academy of Motion Picture Arts and Sciences; to Roger Ebert, who thought I had hacked into the Academy's mainframe; to my faithful readers, who counted on the site; and to my dad, who suddenly looked like he had sired an imbecile. "God, son, it must have been the milkman after all, 'cause you ain't no part of me," says Kennedy clan–style patriarch John Huston to Jeff Bridges in *Winter Kills*.

Maybe there's something to this redheaded stepchild business after all.

CHAPTER SEVENTEEN
Skin Game

But that's not to say there aren't things I'm not embarrassed about. Situations where I knew better, where I was raised to be smarter, and where through hubris or wishful thinking or sheer boneheaded guilelessness, I belly-flopped smack into the deep end. Maybe this stuff can happen to anybody whose attentions are diffused elsewhere; or more likely, maybe anybody else would have better sense than to trundle it up as an anecdote about themselves. But apparently not me. As a cautionary tale, then, I respectfully submit the following:

It all started in December 1997. I got a call one night from some guy—we'll call him "Ray." (That's not his real name.) He said he had adapted Tolkien's *The Hobbit* into a screenplay. He knew the rights were held by producer Saul Zaentz, the San Francisco music manager turned highbrow film producer who had just done *The English Patient,* as well as *One Flew Over the Cuckoo's Nest, Amadeus,* and Ralph Bakshi's 1978 animated *The Lord of the Rings.* All he wanted to know was how to get in touch with Zaentz. So I looked it up in the *Hollywood Creative Directory* and read him the number. I told him his chances were a million to one, especially since the Peter Jackson *Lord of the Rings* trilogy was being set up at Miramax, but, you know, go forth, advance the cinema. He thanked me and that was it.

About a month and a half later, I got another call from this guy, and he was positively effusive. He said, "Mr. Knowles, I can't thank you enough. I had to deal with a million secretaries and creative execs and development execs and whatever, but I did it—I'm in business with Saul Zaentz! You changed my life! You have to let me buy you dinner."

Now, this was intriguing. I can't say it was very likely, but this guy was over the moon. So I met him at a local restaurant. All I knew at that point was he was in his twenties and he drove a nice car. And he spun this wild tale.

Initially, the Zaentz people hadn't wanted anything to do with him, but he said he convinced them that he held none of the underlying rights, so he wasn't a threat to them. He got them to send the script out for independent coverage, and it came back glowing. It slowly made its way up the ladder, until Zaentz himself read and liked it, and since it dovetailed with the Peter Jackson/Miramax deal (this was before New Line came on board, after Miramax had put it in turnaround), all the Tolkien novels suddenly had cachet.

Zaentz didn't want to proceed without the approval of the Tolkien estate, so on his own initiative, Ray had flown to France to present his case to Christopher Tolkien, the principal heir. And Tolkien had gotten spontaneously caught up in his enthusiasm as well. Ray could describe Zaentz's offices and he knew everybody's name; he could describe the Tolkien estate in France. Everything I asked him, he could answer, and all of it jibed with what I knew or could confirm. He promised to keep me informed, and we parted company. He picked up the check.

At that point, there were all sorts of wild speculations in the press and on the Internet about Peter Jackson's *The Lord of the Rings*—casting, script revisions, etc.—and I was beginning to get a lot of back-channel feedback from Jackson himself. I e-mailed Peter and said, "Heads up, somebody else may have a *Hobbit* project," and he said, "Yeah, I've heard the same rumors." Then I ran into Ray at breakfast—Robogeek was with me—and Ray claimed that, since the Miramax deal wasn't set yet (they still didn't know if it would be one film or three), and since any other Tolkien deal would jeopardize that one, Zaentz wanted to get things going off the Hollywood radar. Zaentz wanted Ray to start developing this as an independent project, scramble a crack team of local Austin talent that nobody had ever heard of, and to informally start preproduction. Zaentz would still be godfathering the project, but he wouldn't announce his involvement until the other deal was on firmer footing.

Ray wanted me to partner with him on the project. We could split everything fifty-fifty, and he would even let me take the reins, since I knew more about this stuff than he did. We could involve any of my friends, or whatever talent I knew of locally, and he would defer to my judgment. Robogeek was incredulous. I told Ray I'd need to see a script first.

Frankly, I thought things were getting a little ahead of themselves. On the one hand, it seemed highly improbable that anyone, much less a seasoned producer, would turn over a project as prestigious as this to a neophyte, regardless of his reasoning. On the other hand, as Ray had pointed out, Zaentz completely controlled the rights; if Christopher Tolkien was on board, what harm was there? Plus *The English Patient* had just swept the Oscars; of all the old-guard producers likely to buy into the new evangelism of independent film, Zaentz had perhaps the best incentive. And if there was even a remote chance of getting *The Hobbit* made, and I was close enough to see that it didn't get fucked up—well, this was advocacy journalism with some teeth in it.

I thought about calling up Saul Zaentz and seeing if he had any plans to make *The Hobbit.* But then I got to thinking. I had been privy to far too many confidential phone calls just like this one to imagine that I could keep it under wraps. First of all, Zaentz was supposed to already know all about me; if I called and asked for confirmation, that said that I implicitly didn't trust the person who had brought me to the table. That's a bad way to start out doing business. And second, if someone were to overhear my phone call, or intercept any record of it or fax relating to it, then I ran the risk of having that information all over Hollywood inside of half an hour. Not only could this jeopardize the project itself, but this was at a point when I was posting open letters to Miramax on the site trying to get *The Lord of the Rings* made. How was this going to look?

Ray called me back to say he had just gotten some seed money from Zaentz to set up a production company. They finessed the rights issue by Zaentz's taking out an option on one of his other scripts, a science-fiction spec, so that no one would get suspicious. And Ray wanted to split this money with me, because he felt duty-bound. He wanted to set up a bank account in both of our names, so that we both could access the funds. Soon he started coming over every day to talk about the project, and to work out the details. Where were we going to set up offices? How do we go about preproduction? What artists do we need to contact? Who could we get to handle the advance publicity and initial marketing?

Since he was over at my house every day, naturally he met all my friends, and proceeded to tell them about everything as well, so that before long, Roland was our accountant, Robogeek was the project coordinator, and Glen was enlisted to bring in a marketing guy he knew who had logged some time with LucasFilm on *The Phantom Menace*. Startup mania was just beginning to grip the Internet, and all of these rock-solid foundations of a dozen interrelated industries that had ruled entertainment for over a century were suddenly revealed to be standing on shaky ground. Ray was thrilled, and took a copy of all our suggestions back to Zaentz.

Once a month, he would fly back to San Francisco for three days or so. I had been treating the whole thing casually so far; it wasn't costing me any money, it wasn't trading on my name, and I figured if it happens, it happens. But I began to realize that my friends were starting to take this all really seriously. This made me nervous, and the more nervous I got, the more suspicious I was about the project. I had yet to see a script, see any real money, see any sort of independent confirmation from outside sources.

I tried to articulate some of my concerns to Ray. He responded by ratcheting up our timetable: Let's go out and meet Zaentz; when I couldn't go because of other business with the site, he offered to take Robogeek. But one thing or another always seemed to come up. At this point, we had the movie hammered out—we could see it taking shape in our mind's eye. We knew how to make it work, who to hire, who to talk to.

One night, while Ray was on the phone from Zaentz's, I heard a computer sign online, and I thought it was his linkup at home, because I recognized the local provider tones. At that exact moment, Roland beeped through on call waiting. I told him, "I can't explain now, but call Ray at home and tell me if he's there." Roland didn't understand why—Ray was in California—but he did it, and then when I was back on with Ray, I heard a second call beep in. Ray said, "Who would be calling an old man's house at this hour?" When he came back on, he said it was one of Zaentz's granddaughters and he had to go. When he called me back the next day, Robogeek happened to beep through, and I had him do the same thing. The same thing happened.

To make a long story short, I had a weird feeling about it. So I bailed out. I advised my friends to do the same. And since they were excited about being involved now, they acted like I had just peed on the Baby Jesus. Plus there's the simple protocol of movies and TV: Who stands to gain? What was the motive? Does it outweigh the cost? Ray had spent a fair amount of money over the course of our brief time together—several hundred dollars alone on film festival passes for my friends. If he was trying to con us, wouldn't *we* be giving *him* money?

The next morning, Ray showed up at my house with a script and a contract. The contract looked legitimate, but then I was a layman, so how would I know? Then I looked at the script. It was good, but it was taken almost entirely from the book. It was the right length and the right format, but there was almost nothing original about it. Then again, if someone weren't as familiar with the book as I was, maybe they wouldn't know that. And maybe that would explain why

Christopher Tolkien responded so well to it, because it was such a faithful adaptation of his father's work.

I told Ray I didn't want to be involved in the project anymore. His feelings were clearly hurt, but he hoped we could still be friends. When he heard that my computer was broken, he offered to buy me another one out of their development fund. Since this was his first offer of actual money, and I suppose to humor him, I told him sure, that would be fine. He showed up instead with a compatible hard drive, which seemed to work great.

Later that night, I was sitting in my room staring at my computer screen. I tried to pinpoint exactly what the root of my concern was: Here a dream project literally falls into my lap, and all I can do is try to pick at the corners to see if it unravels. Was this a fear of success? A fear of failure? Was I projecting my own inadequacies onto the sort of opportunity that comes along certainly no more than once or twice in a lifetime? What exactly was my problem? As I was contemplating the nature of my existence, I started to poke around on the computer. And I started to see evidence that the hard drive had been reformatted. Suddenly, it occurred to me that this wasn't a new hard drive at all—it was an old hard drive with all the memory erased. I called Roland, my in-house tech adviser, and he said that even if the memory had been erased, there would still be a complete record of it somewhere, and he could probably find it.

Roland determined that this was the hard drive that Ray's Netscape had been on, and he hadn't bothered to empty his trash before he deleted all his files. That means that suddenly we had access to his e-mail records for the three months before he contacted me. And this stuff was unbelievable. For instance, he had contacted me under various different names during that period. These blind sources would always have tips on Peter Jackson or *The Lord of the Rings*. It was never information that I could independently verify. Sometimes, the kind of rumors I get are so exclusive that you couldn't possibly get a second confirmation on it. Usually, these things go into the crackpot file, but once in a while, they turn out to be true, and I kick myself for not having gone with them. But then months later, every time Ray let drop some pearl he had gleaned from the Zaentz camp, it was something that I had already been told by a covert source. Ingenious, no?

And before that, he had been hanging out for *years* in newsgroups on all these subjects. He wasn't posting in the newsgroups themselves, but rather silently monitoring them for things he could use, and then establishing back-channel e-mail communications with people in the various groups, vacuuming up the crumbs, and leveraging them against one another with each person separately.

For instance: He had been logging on to the *Buffy, the Vampire Slayer* groups, getting tidbits from stunt coordinators or guys on the set. He had these people convinced he'd been having an affair with Charisma Carpenter, who played Cordelia Chase. Apparently, he could identify a tattoo in some personal place that was rumored but had never been confirmed. And he could describe it in detail. He had all these intimate facts that he had allegedly gotten directly from her, during pillow talk supposedly, that fans would swoon over. And they would give up whatever they knew, whatever pearls they'd been hoarding, just to hold up their side of the conversation. He had this entire cosmology, these spinning plates of separate universes, which he could perpetuate with the tiniest dregs of gossip, and which he would then use as hard currency. (I guess to be fair, someone else could have logged on to Ray's computer and sent these messages. But I don't buy that.) There were also rumors about movies that were never made, which I recognized from international newspaper items or online chats. When we checked the dates, we discovered that every time Ray had allegedly been in San Francisco dealing with Saul Zaentz, he had actually been here. I guess he thought if he could just keep it going, somehow it would come true.

And suddenly, I realized what this reminded me of: my grandmother, all over again. Effortless, soaring stories that had to be true, because no one could make all this stuff up, where if you accept the premise, then you have to accept the conclusion. It's what Mr. Orange is drilled on in *Reservoir Dogs*: "Now, the things you got to remember are the details. It's the details that sell your story."

No one ever really talks about Internet scams. Stories about a new Superman movie ran in Australian newspapers, but my sources at Warner Bros. had never heard of the guy. It turned out to be someone who had whipped up these rumors in the hopes that someone would read his script. A similar situation arose with a script called *Indiana Jones and the Sons of Darkness,* which appeared online and was allegedly written by Jeffrey Boam, a co-writer of *Indiana Jones and the Last Crusade.* It was later attributed to an unproduced screenwriter.

I've left out a lot of identifying details about Ray—some of them confidential things he told me, and some of them things I dug up after the fact. Ray isn't the important part of the story. He's entitled to his dignity the same as anybody else. But with people like Ray, if you think about it, it's not that far from what filmmakers do in general, on a constant basis. They convince investors to give them money, people to do them favors, studios to offer them patronage or protection, audiences to extend them the benefit of the doubt. It's how they survive. And any independent producer or director worth their salt will tell you that when you're ready to be taken seriously, you forge ahead regardless of whether the money's in place or not. The world has a way of catching up.

The kicker, as they like to say in the pitch meetings, came four months later. I got an e-mail from Peter Jackson, whom I was corresponding with fairly regularly. It said, "Hey, no time to talk, but there's this guy down here in New Zealand who keeps saying he's an associate of yours and that now he works for New Line. He's going around trying to buy a bunch of stuff on New Line credit. He's driving a new BMW. He says his name is 'Ray.' Do you know anything about this guy?"

So I told him everything I knew. New Zealand, like Hollywood, is a really small place, and very quickly, Jackson saw to it that everybody knew about this guy and could see him coming a mile away. So whenever he got back to his hotel room, he would get an anonymous phone call that said, "We know all about you. The police are on their way. You're going to wind up in the kooky ward forever." Finally, Ray left the country, and I was told he can never apply for readmittance without winding up on some red-flag list. So now he's effectively banned from an entire country. The last I heard, he was a used-car salesman somewhere.

As for me, I filed a story for Planet Hollywood Online about all these crazy rumors that were spontaneously combusting on the Internet about *The Lord of the Rings*: That a reunited Pink Floyd was doing the soundtrack. That Enya was writing some music. That Rowan Atkinson would play Bilbo Baggins. I never said how, exactly, but I was in a unique position to shoot these down with reasonable authority.

I've never gone public with this story before. I'm sure some of my friends would rather I wouldn't do so now. Mainly because it makes us look like idiots. The whole thing played out in probably three months, tops. But this was the inspiration for archiving and cross-referencing my e-mail as I do, so that I can see exactly who has told me what. It takes an immense amount of time just to log it in. But the alternative is still too creepy to consider.

I tell this story because I believe in full disclosure, and because I don't want to see it someday in a six-hundred-word sidebar or cut and pasted on the Internet. Because I want to make the point that if you don't check your sources, or you're gullible even when it seems too good to be true, you basically deserve what happens to you—a fact I learn over and over again. And because I want to clarify the difference between dreams and lies.

Lies hurt people. But when you let go of your dream, you die.

That's from *Flashdance*, with a script by Joe Eszterhas. It doesn't make it any less true.

CHAPTER EIGHTEEN

Born Yesterday
(or the Geek Manifesto)

America is really the property of the world, and not only of
the Americans, who, among other things, have the habit of
diluting the wine of their mythical ideas with the water of
the American Way of Life. America was something dreamed
by philosophers, vagabonds and the wretched of the earth
before it was discovered by Spanish ships and populated by
colonies from all the world. The Americans have only rented
it temporarily. If they don't behave well, if the mythical level
is lowered, if their movies don't work anymore and history
takes on an ordinary day-to-day quality, then we can always
evict them. Or discover another America. The contract can always be withheld.

—Sergio Leone
American Film,
June 1984

I t's possible, I suppose, in plowing through these
dystopian screeds, to come to believe that the end is upon us.
That the movies as we know and love them are done for. In
the first place, there's nothing wrong with the film business
that a good-size earthquake couldn't fix. But secondly, as it is
with so many things, the problem *is* the solution.

Because I firmly believe that the industry's saving grace
will always be what has driven it from the very beginning—the
sword it has continually beaten into ploughshares, and the li-
ability it repeatedly distills into an asset: greed. Greed is what

keeps Hollywood honest. Greed works. Greed transcends race and class and values and ethics and pride and morals and humanity. Just as you can't fault nature for natural selection or survival of the fittest, you can't fault the film industry for pursuing the almighty dollar into whatever God-abandoned recesses it leads them and slitting its sexy little throat. Or for rooting around on all fours snout first until they unearth it from the sacred muck.

Because there isn't anything too wild, too radical, too critical or prescient or outrageous or controversial that Hollywood won't assimilate, as long as it thinks it might somehow lead to buried treasure. It will adopt world views to which it is diametrically opposed, like it did in the '70s. It will promote the most vilifying, excoriating, self-immolating piece of agit-prop that argues against its very existence—*Sweet Smell of Success* or *Network* or *The Player*—and gladly take the money. It will freeze out black, Latino, Asian, gay, women directors without a moment's hesitation, in self-defense even, until the unlikely day when Spike Lee or Robert Rodriguez or John Woo or Don Roos or Kathryn Bigelow inadvertently makes someone some money, in which case the floodgates will clang open. It will ransack its own masterpieces, release criminally truncated versions of *Touch of Evil* or *Blade Runner,* and then canonize its own complicity with celebrated restorations of both—with equal abandon, and without a second thought.

Someone like Sherwood Schwartz can produce a sitcom in 1969 as banal and vacuous as *The Brady Bunch,* which is breathtakingly oblivious to the world and times around it. He can revive it in 1977 as *The Brady Bunch Hour,* a mawkish spinoff in loose-knit variety format, which trades on curdled nostalgia and the freak show of seeing child actors who largely didn't survive the transition to working adults. And then he can revive it as a film parody franchise in 1995—*The Brady Bunch Movie, A Very Brady Sequel,* ad infinitum—which ridicules not only the series itself, but the very impulse behind having floated such a ludicrous premise in the first place. And why? Because the money all spends exactly the same. Because there was life still in the property; because the franchise had legs. The goal is to get the money. Assigning any other values to people in this position is merely anthropomorphism.

And that even includes making movies smart again, if that's what it takes. If dumbing down and high concept have run aground, if even textbook liberals now are bemoaning the pervasive raunch and sleaze, then go the other way. TV did it; there's still no program on the air as consistently intelligent or consistently popular as *The Simpsons.* The Emmys routinely reward the smartest, best shows out there—*The West Wing* and *The Sopranos, Seinfeld* and *ER* before it, *The Larry Sanders Show* before that. If television, everyone's favorite vast wasteland, can become a meritocracy again, there's no reason film can't follow suit.

And if smart audiences can't find the smart movies that are out there, then it's only because they have been systematically alienated from movies over a hard-fought twenty years. Films didn't get stupid all on their own; they were beaten and blood-ied into submission in the mistaken belief that it would gen-erate greater profits. And what the studios don't seem to understand is that just because their numbers are up (no pun intended), just because they are making more money each year than the year before, and more money now than ever be-fore in the history of the motion picture industry, *it still doesn't mean they're doing anything right.*

Look. What's the yardstick? *Titanic,* okay? Everybody still talks about that as if it was this grand success. But forgetting for a moment even that *Titanic* carried a $200 million price tag; it only reached 75–80 million viewers—and that's not even counting the fourteen-year-old girls who saw it five times in the throes of Leo Mania. Because $600 million divided by $7.50 is 80 million. That's still shy of the 100 million people who saw *Star Wars* when it first came out. That means there are still 190 million people in this country alone who didn't see *Titanic*. By comparison, *Gone With the Wind*, which *Titanic* is often credited with being the modern equivalent of, reached approximately 75 percent of all Americans in its day.

This means that there is a huge, enormous, untapped potential audience out there, if somebody would just start making the movies they want to see. And conversely, that making every single movie for an audience of adolescent males, just because they happen to be the single largest category you can subdivide out, even though all categories are ultimately arbitrary, is a victory for the marketing analysts, but not necessarily for the accountants. And this comes from someone who couldn't be more at ground zero on the demographic they're targeting. Plus, I'm just asking, but how can adolescent males be the salvation of the film industry, to the exclusion of every other filmgoing group, when it was adolescent girls who turned out in droves for *Titanic*? Or how can production slates be aimed exclusively at young males, on the strength of repeat business (teenage zealots who will see a film anywhere from two to ten times), while marketing strategies and screen allotment (how many screens; how long to book them) are geared to the big bang—making as big a splash as possible on your opening weekend, creating a "film event" where people don't want to miss out on the Monday morning water-cooler discussions about it, and then getting out of the theaters as soon as possible? I mean, do teenage males even have any concept of what a water cooler is, much less why you would discuss things around it?

The only thing the studios can be accused of then is short-sightedness. So it's just a matter of showing them they're really missing out on profits—all the people who have become disenfranchised over this long era of favoritism toward some imagined golden consumer niche. And that once these people are welcomed back into the fold, the profits will cascade and supernova.

One common criticism often made on the studios' behalf is that there's too much attention being paid to the film industry, that with the amount of money at stake, the studios are no longer free to experiment. When box-office receipts are published in family newspapers, and the studio chain of command occupies the sort of attention that it does, then people with the power to greenlight rightly feel as if a world full of armchair CEOs and Monday morning mavens are staring over their shoulder. The other shoe dropping on that argument is that if people like me would just take a powder, maybe relax, then the film business could get on about the business of film. But people like me make it easier, not harder.

The problem, small or large, in a nutshell or on the macro level, is fear. Fear is the reactor core of the Hollywood dynamo, the unacknowledged fuel that drives everything. (Like Pauline Kael says: "The movie industry is always frightened, and is always proudest of films that celebrate courage.") Fear divests people of their opinions, causes studios to throw themselves at people or projects lest someone else does first, stymies creative thought or impulse once those people or projects are in place, and ghettoizes simple stories told well at the very bottom of the price structure by taking a value-added approach to elements of any kind (human, machine, other)—as if bigger stars or bolder effects are going to buy them any kind of a guarantee. It ultimately makes studios throw money at the spinning turbines of a moving film, for no other reason than the desperate hope that some simple naked likability will adhere to the sides as it steamrolls by—much like those "sticky bombs" they use at the end of *Saving Private Ryan* to separate tank treads. And with pretty much the same results.

It's this culture of resolute dread, this unhealthy preoccupation with big money, getting and keeping a good job, and second- and third-guessing every decision, no matter how minuscule, out of fear of jeopardizing the job or the money, or out of sheer anxiety over the amount of money being spent, that is reflected in the kinds of films being made. It's not just a storm, it's *The Perfect Storm*; it can't just be a wave, it has to be the biggest wave ever. Everything about movies these days is hyperbolic, hence cartoonish—everything is the biggest, boldest, baddest, brightest, strongest, smartest, prettiest. Every sound is immaculate and amped. Every surface is polished and positively gleaming. Every actor is gorgeous; every extra is perfect; every motivation is imperative and action compulsory. It's centrifugal force; everything is being pulled to its most extreme point on the orbit, in every possible direction, because of the intensity demanded of it. Because no other dramatic solution can possibly justify all of this preternatural attention. And this intensity—or better, this desperation—stretches to the planning and making of films as well.

But sunlight is the best disinfectant. And as long as all creative decisions receive a full airing, meaning if all you have to do is go to some Web site to get the latest updates on script drafts, pitches, casting, early cuts, release schedules, marketing strategies—not to mention raw opinions every step of the way, from right-thinking people—the studios ought to find this incredibly liberating. Now no longer can an executive be bamboozled by whoever stands to gain, or bullied by someone with a private agenda, or leveraged by peer pressure, or swayed by consensus at the weekend read (where everyone discusses the scripts they read over the weekend), or swept away by high hopes or nightmare scenarios. And no longer do studio executives need to dread their own instincts and how they measure up. Now they can see what others believe, and why.

And not just others who are talking in pretexts, or floating ulterior motives, or weaseling and worming and wiggling their way inside. No—true believers! People whose allegiance is to the material first. My Web site allows executives to finally behave in the manner they'd like to behave, to heed the better angels of their nature, if they just didn't have a million other things to worry about first.

There also seems to be a sense among studio heads that allowing filmmakers their freedom is somehow a weakness, that artists are basically children who have to be constantly disciplined and reprimanded, or else things will descend into chaos. People like Mike Medavoy, when he was at TriStar, or John Calley, now at Sony, are sometimes characterized as out of touch, starstruck, unable or unwilling to exercise the strict discipline that ensures both a tight financial ship and a predictable flow of product. But look at someone like Mike De Luca at New Line or now DreamWorks. In his heyday, De Luca was clearly a golden boy; he could do no wrong—he proved that empirically. He lived by his instincts, he was not anyone whom you would attribute weakness to (or at least not and live to tell about it), and his track record was impeccable—for the eight years of his New Line stewardship, at least as good as anybody's in the business. But above and beyond that, De Luca seems to have figured out that if you can't have some fun with a position like his once in a while, then what's the point of all the aggravation?

And so within parameters of budget and subject matter, he gave self-proclaimed artists their way. Sometimes, as with loose cannons like Tony Kaye and *American History X,* he got bit in the ass. Sometimes, as with brash lightning rods like Paul Thomas Anderson and *Boogie Nights* or *Magnolia,* he wound up with lightning in a bottle, and the endlessly entertaining spectacle of watching a true original growing up in public. But anyplace else, authentic voices like Tony Kaye or P.T.A. would be starved into submission—would have waited around literally for years until they got their mind right, boss, like in *Cool Hand Luke,* or until their spirit was broken. For better or worse, these folks got to cut to the head of the line. That wasn't a sign of weakness on New Line's part. That's all testicle.

It used to be that studios produced certain films—John Ford's *The Grapes of Wrath,* let's say—as prestige pictures, designed to collect Academy Awards and reap audience goodwill rather than simply make their money back. The modern equivalent is the Woody Allen film—made for a fixed budget, on a yearly cycle, and starring the finest actors of the day, who revel in the privilege. Forget that so many of his efforts these days seem thin and uninspired. Quentin Crisp once called Woody Allen a chain filmmaker, which is to say that he lights each new project from the smoldering butt-end of the last. But Woody Allen keeps up the pace he does first of all because he can, and second because he serves a function that no one else does.

It's the deal that most filmmakers—the ones who aren't in

it to get rich, at least—would prefer, and it was a by-product of the golden era at Orion, "the way it used to be," as Jonathan Demme said in his Oscar speech for *The Silence of the Lambs.* That was the period beginning in 1978 when Arthur Krim, Eric Pleskow, and Mike Medavoy left United Artists to form a company where filmmakers could make the films they wanted to, once everyone agreed on a script, free from constant studio meddling. The reason it worked then, and the reason it would work again, is that those films were all made for a price everyone could agree on.

The problem isn't that movies cost too much to make. Or even that actors are paid too much, or executives, or directors, or that writers are paid too little (although they are). It's that no one seems to be able to match a project with its appropriate budget. *Titanic* cost $200 million because that's what it took to produce the visceral reaction that would make it required viewing. *Waterworld* cost $176 million, conservatively, under the mistaken impression that its star would overcome whatever production difficulties arose, through the sheer strength of his will and charisma. This didn't prove to be quite as safe a bet. But the problem with *Waterworld* may have been that it didn't cost enough—especially since a big chunk of that was for the underwater hydraulics of a sea monster that is only glimpsed in the finished film for possibly one second. And it may have been that particular effect—regardless of how much money it cost—that would have made *Waterworld* indispensable viewing. Meanwhile, small character-driven dramas featuring prominent actors in roles they clearly want to play, and distributed by boutique arms of the major studios, basically ask all the participants to work for free. This is how we've come to have two separate film industries—so-called studio and so-called independent. And even though the independent world of the '90s has largely been successfully assimilated into the existing studio system, there still aren't mid-size pictures for specialized audiences. Or there haven't been until very recently.

The prevailing wisdom, at least since the nadir of the '80s, when the studios were making a dozen films apiece per year, all of them prospective blockbusters, is that above a certain budget, all films cost the same in P&A costs—prints and advertising—so why not try for the home run every time out? Percentagewise, eleven out of twelve films may not find purchase in the general audience, but it gives you a one-in-twelve chance at the gold—much better odds than one in forty or fifty. The flaw in that reasoning is that very soon now, all films won't have the same P&A costs.

The whole reason for the Internet, at least from the point of view of the commercial titans dumping billions of dollars into it, is that instead of shotgun marketing, where you fire at as broad a target as you can and hope you hit as many consumers as possible, now there is the capacity for rifle-shot marketing, even laser pinpoint marketing. Once the infrastructure is in place, advertisers will be able to target you individually; they can divide their demographics into an infinite number of marketing slots, based on what they know about you from your purchase history. Some of this may be clandestine or transgressive or border on invasion-of-privacy issues. But an unanticipated reward may be that someday soon, people will automatically find their way to those products that interest them, and vice versa. It could be the advent of friction-free commerce. The only thing bad about advertising, outside of questions of style or taste, is that it's dishonest; it tries to sell you things you don't want or need. If suddenly you wanted or needed those things, then the advertiser is no longer trying to twist your arm. Now he's performing a public service.

And since the film business is basically a new product launch every time out, it means theoretically that each new film could now reach exactly the audience that is most likely to respond to it. Big-ticket items such as television ad campaigns would become superfluous. Literally any film could now be made, just by assessing its potential audience and adjusting the budget accordingly.

Soon a natural median will form. Films made for below the median amount will herald authorial voice, carte blanche, idiosyncrasy, and means of expression as paramount virtues, to be encouraged by the studio. Films made for amounts above the median will require a common-denominator audience; they will appeal to the things the audience has in common instead of the audience in all its diversity. Instead of the artist's voice and freedom of expression, these films will rely on genre conventions and formulaic rigor. They will try for popular consensus rather than willful idiosyncrasy. They will be objective rather than subjective, in order to attract the numbers that their size will make necessary.

And rather than divide these two worlds permanently, the median will encourage a cross-pollination between the camps. A free-form experimentalism from below will slowly begin to trickle its way up. A muscular discipline to order and clarity from above will slowly trickle its way down. Filmmakers like John Sayles and Jonathan Demme who have spent their entire careers passing freely between these two worlds may become the paradigm for the emerging artist. Those who can demonstrate the greatest flexibility in circumnavigating these worlds will become greatest in demand. Audiences will gravitate to either or both, according to their needs. Actors, directors, writers, and artisans may dip freely into either world, as their financial and emotional needs require, approximating the division that stage and screen once did for a previous generation of entertainers.

Each season will offer new success stories of journeymen suddenly liberated by their newfound artistic freedom—Mike Figgis brainstorming *Timecode,* for example—as well as mavericks equally liberated by structure and conformity—Orson Welles and his pulp masterpiece *Touch of Evil,* or Steven Soderbergh's genre breakthroughs in *Out of Sight* and *Erin Brockovich.* Market forces will set the median, and it may fluctuate from one season to the next, depending on the prevailing mood of the public. As the public craves more formulaic entertainment, or an art that takes more chances, the bar for event films or the untraditional will rise or fall accordingly. And since the same people will administer the budgets and reap the profits in both worlds, any competition between them now becomes superfluous.

The other thing this will require is some system in place like Soundscan for CD sales to monitor gross ticket sales, to ensure accuracy. As it stands, almost one-fifth of all ticket sales are the result of independent, nonchain, mom-and-pop theaters, and their profits are reported every weekend and week by phone solicitation, virtually on the honor system (that is, somebody from ACNielsen or EDI, for instance, calls them up and asks them what the week's grosses were, without any sort of control mechanism in place to monitor this independently). This means that as much as one-fifth of all ticket sales we take on faith. Once this is no longer left to chance, like it suddenly was when Soundscan started electronically monitoring record-store sales—the technological innovation that overnight created Garth Brooks and Kurt Cobain in the public consciousness, when it became apparent that niche country or grunge audiences were the ones buying all the records, once you subtracted all those Michael Jackson units being returned—then it will be crystal clear who's seeing what.

My suspicion is that if such a world were to freely evolve into being, it would come as a welcome relief to the business side of the industry. Because people in the business of marketing rarely care about content. We care about content. You and me; the end users. Marketing people believe that content-driven businesses are unstable: The Japanese learned it the hard way; Wall Street learned it the hard way; dotcom zillionaires learned it the hard way. That's the way it's always been. It's the single main reason why the world-class bandits and snake oil salesmen and carnival barkers and medicine-show drummers and arms dealers and loan sharks and drug kingpins and gang impresarios and pornographers and confidence artists who flourish in the fecund muck of the killing floor of Hollywood will always have their day. Because content is beside the point. Content is for suckers. Or zealots. All that the people in charge really want—the Global Content Conspiracy, if you prefer—is your money. They want it bad enough that they'll even produce quality entertainment, if that's what it's going to take.

But however we decide to carve up the future, the old way doesn't work anymore. In fact, it more than just doesn't work: The old way of counting on blockbusters to see you through the lean times is not just foolhardy; it's dangerous. Between superstar salaries and the costs assigned to digital effects, computer animation, and the like, the bar on event movies has finally been raised to a point that's prohibitive. (Digital technology, shooting against blue and green screens, the creation of as many as several thousand shots in post-production, was universally adopted by the studios two decades ago because it was going to revolutionize the cost of making movies. And yet the cost of making movies has more than doubled. *Heaven's Gate* cost $44 million in 1979 and brought down United Artists. Today, $44 million wouldn't even get you two top stars and a name director.)

Studios have now taken to co-financing their biggest films, putting domestic and foreign in the same pot, and splitting the profits evenly, rather than taking their chances solo on making a killing. Because the failure of even one $200 million juggernaut could bankrupt a studio. It's like arms buildup: Whatever the original arguments for deterrence, the caliber of destruction now available makes any use of our nuclear arsenal obsolete. We've finally reached the house limit. The game is too rich for even the boldest gambler's blood. I suspect that given the choice, Fox wouldn't even roll the dice on *Titanic* again. (Although Fox and Paramount split the bills on the *Titanic* financing, with Paramount taking North American rights and Fox foreign, Paramount's investment was capped at $65 million plus P&A (prints and advertising). When the working budget began to stretch toward the $200 million mark, Paramount refused to cover the cost overruns, making for some tense weeks among Fox upper management. *Titanic* eventually grossed $600 million domestically and $1.234 billion overseas.)

So rather than simply getting bigger, films must find a way to grow in some other direction: deeper, broader, wider, brighter, denser. They have to expand on different planes than the ones they're used to. One thing that could help allay anxiety and settle the stakes down for everyone is to routinely build most above-the-line salary structures into the back end. That is, for stars, directors, writers, and producers (the creative elements on the film, as opposed to the hired artisans and other budget considerations that make up below-the-line) to make their profit participation contingent on a film's performance. Big or small. Rather than pay Jim Carrey $20 million up front, pay him the equivalent of $20 million-plus to come out of the film's profits. Same with the actors in *Blair Witch*: You're going to starve these people in the woods for two weeks, make sure they see some money once everybody comes in from the cold.

Two problems there: All the big guys—Stallone, Schwarzenegger, Travolta, Carrey, Cruise, Ford, Hanks, Willis—won't go for it. (So the argument goes.) Except for Stallone with *Cop Land*. Or Carrey with *Man on the Moon*. Or Cruise with *Magnolia* and *Eyes Wide Shut*. Or Hanks with *That Thing You Do* or his HBO series (*From the Earth to the Moon, Band of Brothers*) or Travolta with *Battlefield Earth*, or Willis, who sacrifices his quote probably as often as he gets it. So then, stars are willing to compromise, but only when it suits their needs. Simply make this the norm. The incentive is that in the event of runaway success, above-the-line elements will now be equal participants, sharing in profits accordingly. And as for those stars who won't play along? Get new stars. I'm serious. Whoever wishes to see themselves priced out of the film business, my advice is to enjoy your free time immensely. Take long walks; meet the neighbors. Check out that whole new Internet deal the kids are raving about. But stand out of the way.

The second problem is with the infamous studio accounting, which has made net points virtually worthless to the neophytes who fall for them. It would take a braver man than me to attempt to break down studio financing, but suffice to say that gross points—percentage of all monies taken in on a film—are good, while net points—percentage of a film's profits—are not so good. This is because so much of a studio's cost of doing business—distribution, advertising, studio overhead—is charged back against the cost of a film that many films never show a profit. This led Eddie Murphy while under oath to coin the term "monkey points" for net points. Studio accounting is a privileged science, inscrutable to the layman, and the studios like it that way. But take a day's drive up through Malibu or Benedict Canyon to see if anybody is making any money off this stuff.

There are ways to burrow through the thicket. Jack Nicholson forwent his upfront salary on the original *Batman* and reportedly pocketed $50 million. Both the Writers and Directors Guilds currently offer seminars to instruct their members where net-profit loopholes are generally buried. That part just seems a matter of education. Or else develop a formula that's part net, part first-dollar gross; or part up-front and part back-end. By paying people out of their profits (and really paying them, rather than cheating them later on), the studios would simultaneously decrease their exposure and limit the incentive for actors to make terrible movies.

Many people might claim that the kinds of films that have come to dominate over the past twenty years—special-effects films, those monuments to the second law of thermodynamics, all mass and momentum—can be attributed exclusively to the cult of marketing. They seem to picture cabals of numbers theorists and brooding drinkers of other people's blood, huddled over cauldrons, gleaning form and meaning from arcane shifting patterns and ominous mists. And who's to say these people are wrong? Their solution is generally of the *Taxi Driver*/Old Testament variety: "Someday a rain will come and flush it all down the fucking sewer." Or barring that, they suggest erecting some kind of firewall between the marketing and

creative sides, much like there has always been between pub-
lishing and editorial in print journalism. (At least before that
went bad as well, at the very same time as movies did, and for
all the same reasons—too many layers of human cannon fod-
der standing between the fusillade and the point of impact.)

The problem, as these people might describe it, is that the
marketing and creative sides really do opposite things. If you
go into a creative meeting, you're dead in the water as soon as
they say, "We've seen that before." But in marketing confabs,
it's exactly the opposite; they want you to provide shorthand
to tell them what it's already like: "It's *The Graduate* in high
school"; "It's like *Mrs. Doubtfire* meets *The Man Who Would
Be King*." And if it's too original, the easiest thing in the world
for them to say is, "We really love it . . . but we don't know
how to sell it," on your way out the door. Creative execs want
to believe they're approving something that's never been seen
before, at least in the specific, even if it has to adhere to three-
act structure, character arcs, action beats, and all the other de-
vices designed to make it feel familiar. But the marketing
hierarchy wants that familiarity branded on the outside, so
they can sell it as a proven commodity. Those are two different things, and they work at loggerheads.

However, I am not one of those people. I don't think a
firewall solves the problem. I think the marketing arms of too
many studios have calcified, ossified, grown moribund and se-
date, like an alcoholic cat. I think they're just now getting the
whole indie revolution, ten years too late. I think most movie
trailers say either too much or too little: They either give away
the entire plot and all the money shots in sixty seconds, or
else they try to convince you the star is not cast against type,
even though the poster art tells you he is. But people who
walk out of *The Truman Show* or *Man on the Moon* not laugh-

ing—or *Magnolia* pissed off that Tom Cruise did not kick some serious San Fernando Valley butt—are only going to steam about it for weeks to come. Just because it's not so easy to quantify, don't think that negative word of mouth doesn't carry as strong an impact as positive. (As for why studios willingly give away the plots of movies in their own trailers—your guess is as good as mine.)

Movies as a whole are among the most conservatively advertised products currently being sold. Who says that movie trailers have to just show footage from the movie all Cuisin-arted together? Has any other product in our brief history of broadcast advertising fallen into such a rut this quickly? Look at the trailer for *The Blair Witch Project,* which tended to get overlooked in all the hoopla surrounding how successfully distributor Artisan exploited the Internet. The TV trailer starts with the printed legend from the start of the movie, has the voice-over from Heather how she's so sorry, and then shows you maybe three seconds of footage from the finished film. And everyone in America was dying to go and see it. Does anyone remember the trailer for *The Exorcist,* which showed a taxi dropping off Max von Sydow on a quiet suburban Georgetown street? No heads spinning or slashing crucifixes or projectile soup. Just the quiet promise of something much, much worse.

At a time when some movies are becoming incrementally more creative, it's time for marketing departments to follow suit. And yet where will this new bastion of creativity come from—these anointed souls who can selflessly step into the breach? Think about it for a second, and it's obvious that it should be the filmmakers themselves. Here the studios have at their unlimited disposal some of the most creative people on the planet, people who make extremely healthy livings exclusively on the strength of their imaginations, and who know the material intimately, down to the cellular level. And how are their talents utilized? They are kept in the dark at best, and treated confrontationally at worst.

Hitchcock cut most of his own trailers: *Vertigo, The Birds*—these were templates of the form. The theatrical trailer for *Psycho* is just Hitchcock himself walking around the *Psycho* set and masterfully presenting a list of clues, which you are powerless to confirm without having seen the film. "This picture has great significance in the film," he says, as he moves a painting to one side, revealing a peephole, through which we see Janet Leigh undressing. Or "An important clue was found down here," as he points down at the toilet. It does exactly what a mystery is supposed to do: It dazzles you with how plainly the answer was disguised right in front of you all along.

Go back and look at the original *Star Wars* trailer. It's a star field, you're moving along to the familiar music as a narrator intones, "This film is light-years ahead of its time. The story of a boy, a girl, and a galaxy. With thousands of creatures, spanning the universe." And you see virtually none of it; it just sets up the intrigue. Now compare that to the trailer for *The Phantom Menace.* An exquisite piece of work. Breathtaking vistas, unprecedented effects set pieces. And the most downloaded MPEG (movie file) in the history of the Internet (at least up until *The Lord of the Rings*). All with the implicit promise that it was going to recapture the speed and delight of the original. I bet if you analyzed the first-week grosses of all the films that the trailer played with, you'd find they were artificially boosted just by people coming to see the trailer and then leaving. So many people at the time said, "If this is what's in the trailer, my God, imagine what's in the movie!" It turns out, that *was* what was in the movie—all of it. You'd be hard-pressed to fault the trailer for the degree to which it presold the movie. But you can find plenty of people who walked out of the movie disappointed.

I have had lots of stories reported to me where a director will be unhappy with the trailer the studio cuts for him, takes his case directly to the marketing department, and discovers that only one out of a dozen people who worked on the campaign have actually seen the movie. Before they cut the trailer, someone goes through the film and pulls out all the money shots—climaxes, cherry effects, and the really quotable stuff—and cuts it into a highlights reel, which is then what the trailer is taken from. None of these things appear in context; it's just an abridged version of the movie, like the one-minute *Hamlet*. Rarely are the filmmakers' thoughts solicited, and rarer still are the directors who are allowed to actually design and cut their own trailer—most of whom would probably do it for free. To the contrary: Directors are generally presented with a finished marketing strategy as a fait accompli, and are labeled difficult if they request specific changes.

So from now on, let's make it optional: Let everyone who wants to, first thing out of the gate, cut their own trailer or plan their own marketing campaign. The worst case is that the studios will have something to start from. And the best case is that with this level of creativity constantly siphoned into the format, movie trailers will eventually evolve into something better.

Meanwhile, on the creative side of the studio equation, which is those people entrusted with dealing with the filmmakers, too much of the responsibility is sloughed off on whoever happens to be standing around. At the script analysis or coverage stage, it's the script readers—glorified interns paid at best $40 a pop for two-page assessments of all submitted screenplays—which then appear written in stone after the fact. With the development process, it's the small army the studio has assembled to contribute creative suggestions, exclusively so that no one person will have to be named responsible for authoring the studio's comments (by the same reasoning that sees one blank charge distributed among the members of a firing squad, so that all may claim deniability). And overall, it's part of this inverted pyramid that seems to govern Hollywood, where the real power is consistently put in the hands of those at the very bottom—assistants, development girls, phone-call rollers, mail-room workers—partly out of some sense of street-driven credibility, and partly because these are the ones who do all the real work, leaving the nominal power in the hands of those at the top, who are actually the farthest from the process. And so the least informed.

Coverage, on which all subsequent creative opinions are based, is so named because that's what it's designed to do— cover your ass. The men and women producing it are required never to be too critical, lest they alienate the agent or executive who has actually submitted the script, nor too supportive, since this may somehow appear less than rigorous. They can't really advise what should be different about the script or how it might be improved, since they are basically minimum-wage employees. Their official mandate is to simply judge whether the script is commercial or not. However, this is mainly to mask their actual role, which is to offer the supervising executive something to say when he has to justify why his company will not be pursuing the project. And the astute reader will quickly learn to calibrate his tastes to what his or her boss is looking for, and to temper his responses according to where the script originated in the vast hierarchical cosmology of the filmmaking universe.

But since the system is already swimming in material that will never be made, coverage is really meant to be the next in an endless series of stopgaps that prevent more material from entering the system. And regardless of in what context the coverage is first filed—for what executive's personal taste, in what kind of competitive environment, or with what actors or directors attached—once it exists, coverage takes on the half-life of strontium 90. Coverage filed as a confidential document anywhere in the chain of being has a way of finding itself into the private files of producers, agencies, studios, journalists, or, in several high-profile instances recently that were precluded only by threat of legal action, into online libraries accessible industrywide by subscription. It's like that mug shot taken after a hard night of pub crawling and street brawling that somehow follows you around for the rest of your natural life. It's the most inefficient system imaginable, because it is designed to keep material out of the loop. But since clearly some kind of material is going to be *in* the loop, it just rewards those who are either aggressive or dogmatic or devious or unsavory enough to push their scripts through. As if these types needed any encouragement in the first place.

Equally dysfunctional is the whole system of studio development. The more people who are entrusted with challenging a script—analyzing it, breaking it down, counting the action beats, eviscerating and autopsying it, picking it apart and performing grafts and transplants and weird genetic experiments on it—then the further off the mark the script is going to wind up. For some reason, the boatloads of film school graduates and Ivy League expatriates who routinely set their sights on the film industry tend to settle along the delta separating the actual decision-makers from the filmmakers themselves. This means that whereas it used to be a fairly simple matter for a studio to accept or reject a piece of material submitted to it, now there are almost an infinite number of checkpoints the material can be routed through, and so an infinite number of paths along which the material may drift imperceptibly further from its original impulse.

Of all the places in the film equation where the more the merrier might apply—the making of it, the selling of it—this seems the one that can least afford it. The artistic impulse, or at least the portal where unembellished bits of truth or life might inadvertently pass into dramatic being, is a strange and delicate thing; it's like a rare orchid that requires a certain hot-house environment in which to thrive. And the more people whose hands it passes through—even with the best intentions in the world—then the more likely that the rarest parts of it may wither and die.

And at its worst, development is the temptation to be God, to play with cosmic fire. It's the place where the noncreative suddenly imagine themselves possessed of divine spirit, and capable of making creative decisions on a par with designated artists, regardless of their investment in either the process or the material. That's hubris, pure and simple. No matter how appealing the impulse is, it's an addiction. If executives or independent producers genuinely feel their artistic impulses are of a caliber to compete on a professional level, then let them enter the tidal pool of their own volition—like assistant George Huang did with *Swimming with Sharks,* or October Films co-founder Jeff Lipsky did with *Childhood's End,* or exec Lance Young did with *Bliss,* or agent Steven Starr did with *Joey Breaker,* or Rysher founder Keith Samples did with *A Smile Like Yours,* or producer Lili Fini Zanuck did with *Rush.* And let history judge them accordingly.

Probably the only way the development process ever got out of control like it did in the first place was out of a general disrespect for writers. With the kind of films that have largely been made over the past twenty years, it must have been easy to forget that these were the finest talents money could buy, or exactly what they might be capable of if pushed to their natural limits. Plus the sporting abasement of writers is certainly one of the founding principles of the film industry, as well as one of its most robust parlor games. It goes back at least as far as Jack Warner labeling writers "schmucks with Underwoods," and hasn't gotten any better in the seventy-five years since. Forget that writers offered the movies a new lease on life in the '30s, as the Depression and the talkies forced literati west from the Broadway stage and the New York press, and as the tide of Nazism forced the (predominantly Jewish) leading lights of the German, Eastern European, and French film industries to relocate abroad. Or that new writers invariably accompanied the new breed of Method actors in the '50s, or the wave of auteurist directors in the '60s and '70s. This tradition of making writers the ashtrays and doormats of the industry is one it's finally time to retire.

Recent years have shown indications that writers are finally on the verge of gaining some respect. Sony made a deal with a list of thirty top writers, representing hundreds of others who meet eligibility criteria, for the first time to share in gross participation—one of the mythical hurdles separating screenwriters from everybody else in the creative mix. There are a handful of film festivals that now celebrate writers specifically, as well as numerous magazines targeting the screenwriter audience, and screenplays themselves are finally emerging as a secret literature in published form, or circulated informally or on the Internet. For the first time, the finest playwrights in the land—David Mamet, Tom Stoppard, David Hare, David Rabe, Neil LaBute maybe—are respected for their secondary work in screenwriting, and afforded the opportunity to direct their own films. And increasingly, screenwriters are being solicited to develop series material for network and cable television, to the extent that television may be where the action is in the next decade (much as it was during the era of anthology drama in the late '50s).

I've been to writers' conferences, or the Heart of Film Festival here locally that honors screenwriters, where I've come across writers whose scripts I have reviewed, not really knowing how they would feel about that. And almost without exception, they were thrilled to have their work validated. Suddenly they weren't writing for ten people around a conference table, or a hundred people around town over that first weekend, when their script either sells or it doesn't. Now there was something they could loosely, amorphously visualize as a reading public—even if it was just lowly me. And writers who feel the other way, that the work is best kept under wraps until everybody concerned is happy with it—Scott Frank (*Get Shorty, Out of Sight*), for example—all they have to do is call me up, and I'm usually happy to exempt them from that kind of scrutiny.

Something that could improve the development process immediately, toward the day when it can either be dramatically overhauled or jettisoned altogether, is that a supervising writer should always be assigned to the material, along the lines of writer-producers in television, whose business it is to monitor the emerging drafts and keep track of all the dramatic elements in a coherent manner. As it stands now, writers come and go at will, writing only what they're hired for, with no sort of gatekeeper to make sense of their contributions. That's why when you dig into the guts of most scripts these days, it's like that first great white shark they slit open in *Jaws*: You're just as likely to find an old license plate or some half-eaten groupers as you are to have the little Kintner boy spill out all over the dock.

Since original writers receive a preferred status when dispensing screen credits, in order to prevent new talent from being steamrolled over by more experienced writers who will inevitably rewrite them, each subsequent writer is no longer being paid for their professional opinion—i.e., what should and shouldn't be done to the script. Each new rewrite includes a financial incentive for a brand-new concept or take on the material, so that the writer will change at least a third of the pages, so that he'll qualify for a screen credit, hence increased royalties. This is what places writers in competition with one another, in a way that directors or actors seldom are.

But certainly the two dozen contributing writers on *Toy Story 2* didn't water down its impact any, as the baker's dozen writers on *Armageddon* were widely accused of. The difference is that it was someone's job in the former to make sure the script didn't get overwhelmed in the process.

The other thing that could improve the overall health of motion pictures is to find some way to provide an incentive for writers to contribute original spec material that they own and have cultivated over time, and to have that material protected. Most writers who remain successful eventually become script doctors, doing top-dollar rewrites or production polishes for the studios, since this is the most lucrative aspect of the business. Or they naturally evolve into writer-directors. Or writer-producers, with the nuts and bolts of writing being assigned to younger, fresher talents. With the exception of William Gold-man, who seems almost willfully perverse for refusing to di-rect, writers who remain merely writers are somehow looked down upon.

One way to change this is to experiment with the concept of copyright being retained by writers for certain works writ-ten directly for the screen on a spec basis. Such a concept may strike terror into the Producers Guild membership and around the studio commissaries, but authors of books retain copyright; playwrights retain copyright. It's time that original screenplays of a certain caliber be accorded a similar status. Screenwriters are the only writers in the world who don't au-tomatically control their own copyright. Novelists, play-wrights, journalists, songwriters, epic poets—all control their own work until they formally renounce their copyright on an individual or contractual basis. These are rights that they give up by choice or not at all. Screenwriters gave away their rights a long time ago, in exchange for the money. It's written into the standard Writers Guild contract now. Or at least that's how it's always been justified. Except that top-shelf screenplays rarely sell for more than $2 million. Top directors, by compar-ison, make generally between $2 and $10 million, and the top actors max out at around $20 million. And this is before gross participation, which, the Sony deal notwithstanding, writers virtually never see. This pay scale isn't a justification for any-thing.

Along with an increased respect for writers, there should come a renewed interest in history altogether. The film indus-try has always rewarded youth, and that's fine. Youth has vigor; youth is a source of energy. But youth can be mentored. For every King Arthur, there should be a Merlin offering his counsel and advice. The values and accomplishments of the past need to carry forward—starting with the people themselves, those emblems of the past who still pass among us. I find it almost unfathomable, for instance, that Billy Wilder still walks the earth, still sentient, and that he hasn't directed a film for over twenty years. There is no greater living resource on the fundamentals of what makes a film tick. Why didn't Orson Welles direct a film for the last twenty years of his life? Why couldn't Fellini find financing at the end of his career? Richard Gere helped secure financing for the final Kurosawa film, as did Spielberg, Lucas, Coppola, and Scorsese. Living legends are resources and should be celebrated while they still can be.

Comparably, prints of the classics need to be available for rental by campus and repertory film groups. This is how our heritage is kept alive, and each studio should do their part. Hopefully, digital technology will help meet all these needs.

One of the primary shifts that the last century has stood for is the transition from high art to popular art, or from the neoclassical to the pulp. Figures like Jack Kirby and Sam Fuller and Philip K. Dick are now being canonized in a way that once would have seemed inconceivable, in the same way that Elvis and Brando and Charlie Parker might have seemed unlikely cultural avatars at the mid-century mark. This is what makes people like Forry Ackerman historically significant; because at the beginning, they were lone voices speaking out to literally no one, and the critical mass that followed took place on their watch. Of course, this paradigm shift is often as not seen as one more tragic, trying sign of the times—one more slip in the knotted chain that suspends us above gaping chaos. But the thing about the forward roll of history is this: If you plant yourself squarely in its path, there's only going to be one possible outcome. Things tend to sort themselves out, usually in ways we can hardly imagine from the leeward side of them.

And it's the rescued treasures from the scrap heap of history that more often than not point the way.

At one point on the site, I got a letter from Jack Kirby's daughter. Jack Kirby is one of those saintlike figures buried deep in the culture; he invented all the Marvel Comics characters, worked on probably 5,000 comic books in his lifetime. He was easily one of the most influential figures in my life, and he died long before anyone like me ever had a chance to thank him. I heard roundabout that his daughter was shopping some of his properties around, trying to get them made. So I wrote up a big piece about how influential Jack Kirby was, and how underappreciated he was in the scheme of things. And she sent me a letter back, thanking me for what I'd done and telling me how much of a difference my article had made. All of a sudden, doors magically opened, people treated her with respect and received her as royalty; potential buyers started calling *her.* She was beside herself; she didn't know how to express her gratitude.

This stuff was just pouring out of her letter. And I lost it. I started blubbering like an infant. Because people like me so rarely get a measure of the difference we can make, or are able to give back to the ones who influenced us. You just pass all of that goodwill on to the ones who come after you, and hope that it makes a difference.

That's why I'm so effusive about people like Ray Bradbury and Ray Harryhausen and Harlan Ellison and Forry. Or for that matter, the unsung artists or designers or effects wizards I meet along my journeys. Because these people are still alive. It's probably all about fathers and sons. But I see history as a long, long fire brigade, and we're saving all the unsung riches of the past from the ravages of anonymity, which are always on the verge of overtaking them. The guys up on that end, who were closest when the fire began, it's their job to choose what most needs saving. But us down on this end, it's our job to make sure we put this stuff in as safe a place as possible, so that this kind of thing never happens again.

Half the people in the film business these days, even the ones in positions of power, are of a sympathetic mind. It's not like everyone at the top is stupid or evil, and that the revolution should eliminate them all from the ground up. Ask Stacey Snider, head of production at Universal, what her favorite movie is, and she'll tell you *The Way We Were.* An admirable choice: David Rayfiel, one of the great unsung screenwriters, at peak form; the best rendition of the Hollywood Ten on film; and all set against a sweeping love story that perfectly embodies the time. Ask Joe Roth, ex–production chief at Disney who now runs Revolution Studios, and has directed four movies of his own (including *America's Sweethearts*), what his favorite movie is and he'll tell you *The Loneliness of the Long-Distance Runner.* Another excellent choice. And certainly no one knows more about the anecdotal history of film than Steven Spielberg.

Half of these guys get it. And the ones that don't, it's not too late. They don't need years of film school just to keep up. All they need is the fundamentals. A curriculum. A simple instructional program, instituted by the studios or contracted on an independent basis, and augmented by a screening series, could do wonders to put everyone on a level playing field and provide a common language in discussing what it is that film is missing and where it needs to go. I think sitting down an audience of busy film executives, who long ago dispensed with the recreational joys of films, and showing them a print of *The Thief of Baghdad* or *The General,* with full orchestral accompaniment, could do wonders in demonstrating the power that film can convey. Because this stuff works on everybody, and it's impossible to argue with once you've experienced it. I heard that DreamWorks was doing this with their marketing people—screening a different vintage film every week and then studying the publicity campaign, to try and discern why people can still quote their favorite parts from it forty years later. That's a good start.

This is my modest proposal, my humble Ludovico technique. You set these people up in a projection booth, restrain them and force their eyelids open, and soon they'll be begging to change. I would bring in people like Peter Bogdanovich or Curtis Hanson—accomplished filmmakers and enthusiastic film scholars—or critics like Roger Ebert or Leonard Maltin, who already teaches a film appreciation class at USC. You could make an awful lot of headway in a concentrated month. And then there's Billy Wilder—or all the thousands of Billy Wilders still hanging around: industry resources who would like nothing better than to give back, to tell what they already know. These people are veterans; they have fought and defended our way of life. And they deserve our gratitude and respect.

And why shouldn't it work like that? We are the children of history. For the first time maybe ever, my entire generation has grown up in the shadow of one movie: *Star Wars*. I was seven when it came into being, and it rocked my world. My first coup on the Internet was reporting on footage from the *Special Edition*. Again and again, as I've set my story down here, *Star Wars* has interceded, like a benign spirit hovering over my shoulder, guiding me to Valhalla. At one point, Dad and I said, as long as Lucas makes the next three installments, at least we'll have a built-in audience. That alone would generate enough traffic to justify the site.

And *The Phantom Menace* marked its glorious return, the most anticipated film of my brief lifetime. I know there are those who feel betrayed by it, blindsided, cracked and ruined. Hallenbeck claims his heart was broken. I secretly think maybe that's why he stopped writing. For me, I had the script eight months beforehand, so I knew it was unapologetically, almost militantly, a kids' movie. I knew about Jar Jar Binks and the rest of it. And I wasn't at all sure how it would play. By the same token, I couldn't very well defend it before the fact, try and temper people's enthusiasms, when there were people lining up for it all around the globe. I would have been calling it damaged goods, and that's not what I believe.

But my views on George Lucas go beyond that. *American Graffiti* introduced more working actors into its generation than almost any film in memory. He could have kept on in that vein indefinitely. But I think Lucas had a different agenda. Partly because of his own leanings, and partly because of his point in time, he made it his mandate to do nothing less than advance the technology of cinema. And he has. His THX process and its many competitors have revolutionized sound. Industrial Light + Magic pioneered the growth industry in cinematic special effects. The number of technical breakthroughs engineered by people in his employ—among them the finest technical minds of his day—are too numerous to mention.

From a technical standpoint, the legacy that Lucas has wrought in just twenty years is for film technology what the Manhattan Project was for national defense. And it was a job that no one else was prepared to do. As film itself got shorter- and shorter-sighted, paid more and more attention to the bottom line, weekend grosses, selling off libraries and studio lots and remake or sequel rights to the highest bidder, Lucas alone was out there on some imagined vanguard, looking toward an unseen horizon for what film held in store.

In that sense, he was a one-man research and development arm for the technology of the film industry. He was his own new frontier; he single-handedly put a man on the moon. He didn't have to do that. And so every dollar he squeezed out of the *Star Wars* franchise, every dancing Ewok or plastic light saber he launched into the culture, or every *Howard the Duck* or *Captain Eo* or *Radioland Murders* he mounted to test-run some breakthrough in technology, I always saw past it to the endgame. He's like David Bowie in *The Man Who Fell to Earth,* selling off inconceivable system design patterns at astronomical prices, and then proclaiming, "It's not enough," because it can't finance his singular dream.

Hence *The Phantom Menace*: It is what it is. To fault it for what it is, or to blame it for what it isn't, is possibly a fair use of one's time, although not something I wish to engage in. But to judge it by its intentions—a suspect view of history, admittedly—it's like no film that's ever been made. Only time will reward it appropriately. As it will Lucas himself. It's easy to look back on someone like Thomas Edison and see him as an engine of capitalism: locking up the great inventions of the day in a closed shop; taking credit for them; suppressing and shutting out the true geniuses of his era like Tesla (the inventor and father of the Tesla coil). But Edison allowed the great inventions of the electrical age by establishing a laboratory where such ideas could gestate and bloom. And for what it's worth, Lucas will divide this century from the last as decisively as Edison divided the nineteenth from the twentieth.

I think the industry is largely mystified right now by the technological revolution happening all around it. The studios are fully addicted to digital technology and all the wondrous things it makes possible, and yet they must sit by and watch as effects showcase after effects showcase—*Mission to Mars, Red Planet, Supernova*—don't just crash and burn, but are ridiculed by audiences in the process. From its point of view, the industry is doing everything right, rolling the dice on million-dollar spectacle, and yet it is being resented for its trouble.

But the problem, again, is a simple one. A simple realization that, once you get it, puts everything else in perspective.

There's an old film school trick that professors use to demonstrate the power of narrative. You can show a class a cross-section of the Odessa Steps sequence from *The Battleship Potemkin,* Sergei Eisenstein's classic 1925 staging of events from the Russian Revolution, and possibly the most famous film sequence in history. Through masterful cross-cutting of the boots of faceless czarist troops and a defenseless baby carriage on the steps of the Odessa Palace, the frenetic collision of disparate images, we exit the realm of narrative entirely and enter a realm of montage, where information is conveyed through editing and the proximity of unlikely images. In its day, this constituted the state of the art of special effects, and it is still extremely arresting imagery.

Then immediately after this, you can show the same class footage from Eisenstein's later *Ivan the Terrible, Part One.* This was shot in 1945, three years before the director's death, and light-years away from the bold experimentalism of *The Battleship Potemkin* or *October, Ten Days That Shook the World.* This was after Stalin dominated Soviet politics and art, and Eisenstein was forced to renounce the revolutionary stance of montage and the vigor of his youth. Consequently, *Ivan the Terrible* is a deadly boring, stodgy, stagy melodrama, virtually a filmed play, and the opposite in every way of the earlier sequence. But then in the middle of this little experiment, you can suddenly stop the projector. And the class will physically jump. They have been pulled out of the middle of the scene; they were narratively engaged, even by this worst of all possible narratives, and when it was suddenly taken away from them, the shock produced a visceral reaction. Ask them which film sequence was the most compelling, and they will unanimously cite the former. But watch them watching the films, and it's the latter that most easily engages them.

The point is that narrative—storytelling; the recitation of dramatic events in serial fashion—is a mysterious force. One that is present in all of fiction, and one that everyone understands implicitly, but that most of us would be hard-pressed to explain. And whatever else audiences may require of their filmed entertainments, narrative is usually at the root of it. So that when special effects, for instance, suddenly become an identifiable draw for an audience, and film studios, in their zeal to please, crowd out everything else in the interest of maximizing those effects, this will only be an efficient strategy to the degree that those effects can advance the narrative. Or augment it, amplify it, and focus it. This is a limitation built into the medium. Spectacle must perform in the service of narrative.

It's like the extravaganza of musical theater—the lights, color, dance, song—and how it finally hit the wall in popular entertainment. Then Jerome Kern and Leonard Bernstein and others happened upon a way to advance the narrative through song and dance—with *Oklahoma!* and *West Side Story*—and the form became revitalized. At this late date, such innovations are so thoroughly integrated into theater as we know it that it's almost impossible to imagine their initial impact— much like Latin rhythms to the jazz of the '30s, or hip-hop rhythms to the rock of the '90s. But at the time, it was nothing short of revolutionary.

That's why *Speed* is a heady thrill ride and *Speed 2* is a crashing bore. That's why *Twister* is a perfect ninety-second trailer and taxes the senses as a ninety-minute narrative, or *The Haunting* rocks as an effects reel and sucks as a movie— to dramatize the point using the works of Jan De Bont. Because Jan De Bont is a world-class cinematographer and middling director. He is quite evidently constitutionally impatient with the requirements of narrative storytelling, and would much rather move quickly into a world where they no longer apply. Unfortunately, this is clearly not a world the rest of us would be comfortable joining him in.

But it makes more sense to look at it in the context of any technological breakthrough. F. W. Murnau's *Sunrise* in 1927 could feature a quarter-mile-long tracking shot (literally, placing the camera dolly on portable assembled track), but within five years, the advent of sound had the camera completely immobilized, trapped in one place by the giant sound hood that fit over it and blocked the noise of the motor from the ever-present microphone. Already, CGI shots from just a few years ago look clunky and amateurish. Compare *Mission: Impossible* to *Mission: Impossible 2,* or the plane crash in *Alive* to the one in *Fearless.*

It's Moore's law again: Every eighteen months, the amount of information that can be stored in a single microchip doubles. Except that now, we can see it. This is why people like *Armageddon* director Michael Bay, who just two years ago was using the technology to chronicle an asteroid on a collision course with Earth, has now used it to re-create one of the most dramatic events still present in recent memory—Pearl Harbor. This is the lesson of *Titanic*—or if you prefer, *Forrest Gump*: These are historically the films that liberated special-effects technology from exploding fireballs. And increasingly, whether it's *Gladiator*'s showbiz-allegorical re-creation of the Roman Coliseum, competing *Alexander the Great*s, or Steven Spielberg's long-rumored flirtation with *The Iliad* and a computer-generated rendition of the Peloponnesian Wars, digital technology is going to allow for historical drama. Which will in turn reinvigorate narrative filmmaking.

This is how it's always been. What we've experienced so far is little more than the birth pangs of a brand-new technology. The digital order will provide for universal access to film history: one-click shopping for all known films or broadcast material, downloaded in manageable chunks of pure memory, and materializing on your desktop without benefit of moving parts. That seems like the least they can do. As well as facilitating universal distribution for anyone with a product, regardless of whether it is studio-sanctioned or not.

People like me are living testament to the fact that there needs to be more product, not less. Whatever the means of production can handle, there is a verifiable market out there. Porno proves that. The porno market could double, even triple, and I doubt anyone would notice outside of those monitoring their profit-and-loss statements; it would all just get used in the course of business as usual. Maybe this infinite capacity for distribution will create a culture of piracy unmatched by anything in our experience, dwarfing all previous ventures into institutional crime, mobilizing international resources against it, which will then over time become legitimized and assimilated in ways we can't even begin to imagine. Who knows? But I know it's here, because I can already download *The Matrix* if I want to.

Perhaps the ubiquitous and coruscating irony that infects this tepid generation will be precluded by something as simple and wondrous as the Internet—the one communications forum designed for participants to respond in character, in managed time, and with one's personality mobilized at its glistening apex. And one that, incidentally, contains no provision for irony—the cynical reversal of stated meaning. Like I am so sure. You see? It doesn't translate. There is no way to indicate when the actual meaning is different from the literal. Just when an entire generation was in danger of barreling into a cultural tailspin, its unanticipated salvation comes from the unlikeliest of sources. Like the common cold in *The War of the Worlds.* Like seawater in *Day of the Triffids.* Or below centigrade in *The Blob.* Or the simplest of household elements in *The Wizard of Oz.* "It was beauty—beauty killed the beast."

And maybe that's why I arrived via this unlikely vehicle; maybe it's ultimately my role to play—to "discover another America," like Sergio Leone says. Because fans—geeks like me—are the one cultural antidote to these cynical times. It's always the fans who imagine it better. Who locate the things to like, the things to live for, out of the gray slag of the past. We were born under the sign of *Star Wars.* We are the R&D on optimism. We find it growing in the unlikeliest of places. We're like a rarefied, secretly evolved plant life—the Brazilian rain forest; the lungs of the world: We reinterpret and recycle and reinfuse a crucial enthusiasm into the life cycle of the planet.

It's why I part ways with most critics. Because I'd rather advocate than adjudicate. I would rather champion the worthy than punish the inadequate. Criticism is reactive and I am proactive: I prefer to argue for better films before the fact rather than after.

It's how I differ from most journalists. Because they subscribe to an objective universe, and I don't. When everything is objective, then no one argues *for* any particular morality any more than they would argue against it. In most newspaper stories, sources are quoted with scrupulous accuracy, but with a complete abdication of whether or not they are telling the truth. As long as their words are reproduced verbatim, as long as their positions are identified appropriately and their names spelled correctly, then it's seen as some sort of intrusion or bias to spell out how they're spinning the facts, or what their agenda might be. A world that is completely objective, then, is one in which anything could be true. It is a world invented by lawyers. And in law, in commerce, in art, and in our fictions, the common variable missing is honesty.

Who knows what will become of me in the months and years ahead? Maybe my time will pass naturally, as the world continues to change in ways and at geometric speeds we can't imagine. Maybe I'll fall in battle, and one of you will raise my standard and carry it forward. Maybe I'll take on the comics industry—or sports, or music, or do my own eBay of movie collectibles. (Lord knows I've got the inventory.) Or go back to politics, advance my decidedly Jeffersonian, liberal-humanist agenda with a vengeance—which ought to come as welcome respite from all the racemongers and *Generation of Vipers* millenarians out there on the hustings. Maybe I'll go really bad, destroyed by the same inexorable powers and forces I sense whizzing around me even now, in these last few vital seconds before they crush in too close.

Hope not.

But even if, it still doesn't change what I'm saying. Because what I know right now is that somewhere, floating in space, millions of times a day, in designated houses of worship, there is a wall of light, a brilliantined canvas on which I can focus these beliefs. Maybe they'll manifest themselves differently for you, or enter through different vessels than the ones enumerated here—their ways being mysterious and all. Maybe they're like Pointillism: Get too close to the image, it becomes meaningless dots; get too far, it loses its restorative and hypnagogic powers. But balanced there in the middle distance, in the dark, left to do its simple awesome bidding, this thin layer or skin or membrane; this haze or mist or pearlescent growth; this fine coating or transparent covering, acetate or emulsion, pellicle or lamina—will bring you a modicum of truth.

That's about as much as you can hope for.

Notes

Chapter 1. *The Trouble with Harry* (1955)—
Alfred Hitchcock, at the start of the decade that would mark his
most accomplished, from *Rear Window* through *Marnie*. Also
his only outright comedy (at least since the silents). The trouble with Harry is that he's a dead body in the back room that
threatens to swirl everything around him into yawning chaos.

Chapter 2. "A Boy's Best Friend Is His Mother"—*Psycho*
(1960)—Hitchcock again. Norman Bates sits surrounded by
stuffed birds in his motel anteroom; studiously bird-watching
this new specimen, Marion "Crane"; and defending his problematic mother with "She's as harmless as one of those stuffed
birds." I've always thought of this scene as foreshadowing *The
Birds* three years later, and the police psychiatrist at the end
as the spinster ornithologist in *The Birds*'s diner scene: scientific orthodoxy rendered irrelevant by the terrible spectrum of
nature. Families are difficult things.

Chapter 3. *The Abyss* (1989)—James Cameron's first folly, roundly criticized a decade before *Titanic,* and returned to glory on laserdisc. And in retrospect, a signpost telling us to stay the course. "I'm all that's standing between you and darkest night," says John Huston in *Winter Kills,* quoted elsewhere. Whether it's *Citizen Kane* or *The Elephant Man* or *Time Bandits* or *Don Juan De Marco* or *Wall Street,* this is how I negotiated the Internet because this is how I negotiate life. Through the movies. "At the signpost up ahead, next stop, it's . . ."

Chapter 4. *Wild in the Streets* (1968)—Maybe the best of the Roger Corman/AIP apocalypse operas, written by Robert Thom, the unsung genius behind Jonathan Demme's *Crazy Mama, Bloody Mama, Death Race 2000,* and the unsurpassed *Angel, Angel, Down We Go* (not to mention *The Subterraneans,* the only Kerouac ever filmed). Rock star Max Frost dumps LSD in the water supply, lowers the voting age to fourteen, and becomes president. Substitute "geeks" for "freaks."

Chapter 5. *Ace in the Hole* (1951)—Billy Wilder's cynical postmortem on the world of journalism, and, following *Sunset Boulevard,* the first film he wrote without longtime collaborator Charles Brackett. Kirk Douglas uses the trapped miner for a good story; the guy's wife uses Kirk Douglas for a payday; the miner uses a sacred Indian burial ground for some pawnable trinkets. Everybody's got an angle. Journalism can aspire to all the vaunted values it wants, but human nature is always right there behind the byline.

Chapter 6. *A Face in the Crowd* (1957)—Elia Kazan and Budd Schulberg follow up *On the Waterfront,* their "exposé" of union corruption, with the story of Lonesome Rhodes, homespun media phenomenon and lurking demagogue— played by Andy Griffith, a real-life homespun phenomenon. Remember: There's no such thing as trickle-down populism. If the powers that be stand to gain, it's either the long con or crypto-fascism. Probably both.

Chapter 7. *The Big Carnival* (1951)—When *Ace in the Hole* proved too grim for audiences (or rather, fifty years ahead of its time), Paramount re-released it under the title *The Big Carnival,* inadvertently paving the way for the term "media circus." Wilder called the Kirk Douglas character's mind "the laboratory of a potential killer." Just because it all looks like a party on the surface doesn't mean there's not darkness down below.

Chapter 8. *Lost Horizon* (1937)—Frank Capra, and the perfect antidote to "Capra-corn." A plane crash-lands in Shangri-La, a hidden city in the heart of the Himalayas, where its passengers are momentarily safe from the outside world (including World War II, which is imminent). The title says it all: The price of utopia is always isolation.

Chapter 9. "Take Your Stinking Paws Off Me, You Damn Dirty Apes!"—From the original *Planet of the Apes* (1968)— "Not Shakespeare," says Charlton Heston, "but it gets the idea across." Heston may be the poster boy for the NRA, and so square that Richard Harris once called him born from "a cubic womb." Yet not only *Touch of Evil* but also Peckinpah's *Major Dundee* never would have been made without him backing the directors. I say give him his due. He's been manhandled enough.

Chapter 10. *Sleeping with the Enemy* (1991)—Julia Roberts has a storybook marriage, except that her husband is a controlling psychopath. Like the man says in *Some Like It Hot*: "Nobody's perfect." And once you know their innermost secrets, those closest to you or the most like you will be anything but forgiving—especially if you manage to escape.

Chapter 11. "How Many of Those *Things* Are Out There?"—*Night of the Living Dead* (1968)—George Romero's indictment of the Vietnam War, racism, and Hollywood all rolled into one. There's nothing quite like flesh-eating zombies to turn the status quo ass-over-elbows.

Chapter 12. *Ocean's Eleven* (1960)—Frank Sinatra's Knights of the Craps Tables, filmed days while the Rat Pack played the Sands on the Vegas Strip by night. Best of the "stop on by" movies, as in, "Tell Jilly you're coming, we'll write a part for you." With his boys, Danny Ocean heists all the big casinos at one time by cutting the power. Without his boys, Sinatra would have been a saloon singer with an Oscar who used to be married to Ava Gardner.

Chapter 13. "Valhalla, Mr. Beale."—From *Network* (1976)—Right at the end of TV CEO Ned Beatty's speech—the one that begins, "You have interfered with the primal forces of nature, Mr. Beale!"—in which he welcomes newscaster/madman prophet Howard Beale (Peter Finch) into the pantheon, and imbues him with his new gospel. "I have seen the face of God," says Beale, in awe. "You may just be right," Beatty tells him.

Chapter 14. *Basic Instinct* (1992)—Man, Sharon Stone was so cool when she first started getting A-list pictures. In *Total Recall,* when they subdue Schwarzenegger, the would-be husband she's just betrayed, she gets in one last kick and says, "And this is for making me come back to Mars—I hate this fucking planet." But then she let the beaver come out and play, and ever since she's been a clichéd joke. Why? Because there's no one stopping her.

Chapter 15. *A Night to Remember* (1958)—The first great *Titanic* movie, done documentary-style by the Brits, whose ship it was in the first place. Of course, only 1,200 of the 2,200 aboard remember it at all, but it was a great night if you happened to live to tell.

Chapter 16. "To George Bailey, the Richest Man in Town. Hee-Haw!"—This is Sam Wainwright's telegram to the restored Jimmy Stewart at the end of *It's a Wonderful Life* (1946), after temptation, covetousness, and despair have all had their way with him, and moments after Zuzu's petals have revalidated his existence. No trial is too great to obscure the manifold blessings that await you. Go with it.

Chapter 17. *Skin Game* (1971)—James Garner and Lou Gossett are con men in the Old West who pretend to be a slaveowner and his property until the bill of sale is signed and money changes hands. "Skin game" is confidence parlance for sizing up a mark and skinning him of his valuables. Their secret is an old one, but no less effective because of it: Everybody who loses wanted to play in the first place.

Chapter 18. *Born Yesterday* (1950)—George Cukor's screen version of Garson Kanin's play in which mobster Broderick Crawford hires schoolteacher William Holden to educate his moll, Judy Holliday. In the course of Holden's wandering lectures on textbook democracy, conducted at various Washington, D.C., monuments, she manages to teach him a thing or two about politics and its practical ideals. I may be new to the game, but I wasn't born yesterday.

Appendices (next), or "You Wouldn't Put Charlie Parker in with the R&B, Would You?!"—*Diner* (1980)—Daniel Stern's outraged demand of wife Ellen Barkin when she has failed to put his LPs back in their proper order. Stern's Shrevie is the patron saint of collectors and obsessives everywhere, at least in the movies. And that includes the pedagogically despotic record-store clerks in *High Fidelity* (whose soundtrack opened on Austin homeboy Roky Erickson singing "You're Gonna Miss Me," you'll notice). All things in their proper place. That's all I'm asking.

And to make it an even twenty—this one's for free. It's from Roger Ebert's script for Russ Meyer's *Beyond the Valley of the Dolls* (1970). Ebert also wrote *Up!* and *Beneath the Valley of the Ultra-Vixens,* but, I mean, the classics speak for themselves. Phil Spector figure Z-Man Barzell, moments before the Charles Manson–inspired acid freakout in which he uses a broadsword to lop off an actor's head, stands and proclaims, "You will drink the black sperm of my vengeance!" I don't mean anything by that. It's just something I like to say.

Thanks for playing.
—Harry

Appendices, or "You Wouldn't Put Charlie Parker in with the R&B, Would You?!"

I'm Spartacus."

Every time I visit Los Angeles now, there are a handful of studio guys I always try to visit who give me the inside dope, or bring me up to speed on projects I'm tracking. Once when I was out there for a premiere, Hallenbeck and I visited one twentysomething executive (who will remain nameless) in his office on a studio lot. I noticed he had the Peter Buchman and Chris McQuarrie script for *Alexander the Great,* just then making the rounds.

So I asked the exec how the script was. And he said basically, it sucks, it'll never get made (it just sold for mid–seven figures for Scorsese to direct). Then a little bit later, this guy pulls up my Web site and studies the results of the poll on the World's Greatest Battle Scenes, and he says, "Wow! I won!" I told him, it's a poll, you can't win, and he says, "Yeah, but I picked the top three choices." They were *Saving Private Ryan, The Empire Strikes Back,* and *Braveheart.*

Well, like any self-respecting film geek, I happened to know that the best battle scene of all time actually occurred in *Spartacus.* So he kept reading down the list—*All Quiet on the Western Front,* Abel Gance's silent *Napoleon, Lawrence of Arabia*—not indicating either way whether he had seen any of these, until finally he got to *Spartacus.* Except he pronounced it "Spar-TACK-us." I said, "Whoa, wait a minute. You don't even know how to say 'Spartacus'?" He looked at me with this sheepish grin, like he probably ought to know better.

I said, "Dude! What the hell was your frame of reference for *Alexander the Great*? Have you seen *The Fall of the Roman Empire*? Do you even know who Hannibal is? Do you know anything about Alexander? What's the name of Alexander's horse?" It turns out he didn't even get all the way through the script, he just got to a point where he realized it was something that took place 2,300 years ago and it didn't interest him. Because kids don't want to see that kind of thing.

And the exec started trying to defend himself, saying, "I don't watch movies from the '60s because I don't make movies for the '60s; I make movies for today." Whatever the right thing to say might have been, this wasn't it. I practically screamed at him, "Stanley Kubrick did not make *Spartacus* as a movie for the '60s! He made *Spartacus* as a movie for all time! This is exactly the problem with you people and the ridiculous films you make now! Because they're not made for history—they're made for whatever weekend they open, and you would rather people would forget all about them as soon as possible so they wouldn't notice how shitty they are!"

Kubrick himself didn't even like *Spartacus* enough to include it in the DVD boxed set of his work. Not that it doesn't have its virtues. It broke the back of the blacklist, along with Otto Preminger's *Exodus,* when producer Kirk Douglas finally gave Dalton Trumbo the screenplay credit, allowing him to work under his own name again. It contains probably the most thinly veiled defense of sexual variety of its decade, courtesy Gore Vidal, in Laurence Olivier's "snails vs. oysters" speech to Tony Curtis (even if the scene was ultimately cut).

Tom Hanks's *That Thing You Do* inexplicably misquotes its most famous scene, when Tom Everett Scott says, "I'm *Spartacus,*" rather than "*I'm* Spartacus." Which misses the whole point: Laurence Olivier offers not to crucify the slaves if they will identify the slave rebellion leader Spartacus. But just as Kirk Douglas is about to give himself up, Tony Curtis steps forward and says, "*I'm* Spartacus." All the other slaves follow suit, until you have a chorus of voices—"*I'm* Spartacus!" "*I'm* Spartacus!"—and the real Spartacus is momentarily spared. Hanks the writer is off the hook, but Hanks the director is not.

The reason it's important is because I really *am* Spartacus. Me and every furtive emissary out there who crashes a screening, pilfers a script, files a review, or leaves a cartoon drawing of me behind where it will most strike fear into the hearts of those who would suppress us. We're *all* Spartacus. And when I hear of people who won't see films older than they are because they're boring, or they're in black-and-white, or they don't matter today, it's another Kubrick line I hear. It's Adolphe Menjou as General Broulard, addressing Kirk Douglas's Colonel Dax in *Paths of Glory*: "You're an idealist, and I pity you as I would the village idiot."

Everybody should be able to name their top 10 favorite films. Or least favorite films. Or films they'd most like to see get made. Everybody. Everybody who watches movies. That's half the fun—reliving them, putting them in new contexts, holding them up to comparison, championing them or abandoning them as circumstance requires. That's the equivalent of pouring the army men out on the floor and staging vast battles, using nothing more than your imagination and the natural terrain of the living-room carpet. It's like battlefield surgery or natural childbirth: If you don't get into it at least up to the elbows, you haven't really done your job.

And I can prove it.

Following are my lists of Top 10 Favorite Films of All Time, 10 Least Favorite Films of All Time, and the 10 Films I Would Most Like to See Made.

Appendix A: My Top 10 Favorite Films of All Time

My 10 favorite movies are not the best films I know of; in some cases, they might not even be good films at all. But they were all important to me, and each had a demonstrated impact on the way I turned out. I think choosing your favorites gets into an almost mystical realm. It may be that they choose you every bit as much as you choose them. Also, any such list can spin on a dime as soon as you commit it to paper. In *The Time Machine,* H. G. Wells returns for three books from his bookshelf to take with him into the future, for the benefit of posterity. After he's gone, Alan Young asks rhetorically, "Which three books would you have taken?" but the answer is pointedly left blank. I will attempt to approach this challenge in the same spirit. For right now, then, for better or worse, in no particular order, here are mine:

1. King Kong (1933)

Directed by Merian C. Cooper (and Ernest R. Schoedsack)

With Fay Wray, Robert Armstrong, and Bruce Cabot

King Kong is a Rorschach test. You can find almost anything in it. Hitler cited it as one of his favorite films. The Black Panthers saw it as a film about the enslavement of the black man, only to have him rise up at the first taste of power. I've seen reviews that tried to portray the entire film as the Carl Denham (Robert Armstrong) character's struggle with impotence, with Ann Darrow (Fay Wray) as the object of his affection and Kong the monster from the id, which shifts in perspective against the background in proportion to the fury of his desire. I would like to interpret it as the folly of trying to chain the creative spirit, but that would only be more conjecture on my part.

The fact is, it's a dream. That's the chief problem with the De Laurentiis remake: It loses that hazy, half-remembered feel. Even though I would be hard-pressed to match the enthusiasm of De Laurentiis himself in defending his intention: "Everybody cry when my big monkey die." I have *two* 16mm prints of *King Kong* and an original one-sheet for it. One just like it recently sold at auction for a quarter of a million dollars.

2. The Adventures of Robin Hood (1938)

Directed by Michael Curtiz (and Michael Keighley)

With Errol Flynn, Olivia de Havilland, Basil Rathbone, Claude Rains, and Alan Hale

This is the prototype for every action film from *The Dirty Dozen* to *Armageddon*. Anything with a bomber crew of reluctant heroes, this is where it comes from. It also teaches you to laugh in the face of adversity—a bit of shop lore that's worked for everyone from Cyrano de Bergerac to Indiana Jones to Chow Yun-Fat. Kevin Costner forever earned a black mark in the big book (as if his Jesus of Malibu cameo in Madonna's *Truth or Dare* documentary weren't enough) for premiering his *Robin Hood: Prince of Thieves* on network TV and making fun of how happy and lighthearted the original Merry Men were. He did the same thing with *Wyatt Earp* when he tried to ridicule Kurt Russell's rival *Tombstone.* What was he thinking? People who live in glass houses should keep their dick in their pants.

The Adventures of Robin Hood is pure joy, and Errol Flynn is the paradigm of how to go to work in the morning and face your labors. It's about the fun of danger, and vice versa. Because when you're taking on a king, when you're bamboozling the Third Reich, when you're wildcat-drilling an asteroid the size of Texas, the best thing you can be is preoccupied with the adventure. I frequently put on the soundtrack to write, because I know that when Erich Wolfgang Korngold was writing the score, he was trying to smuggle his son out of Nazi-occupied Austria, and took the job because he needed the money. And what might have been a bit of hackwork for a facile entertainment instead carries with it the intimations of epic struggle. That gives me hope.

3. The Treasure of the Sierra Madre (1948)

Directed by John Huston

With Humphrey Bogart, Walter Huston, and Tim Holt

Most of these films I discovered in childhood, and they carry the comfort of a warm blanket. Consequently, I suspect my earliest thoughts on family are also tied up in here somewhere. *The Treasure of the Sierra Madre* is John Huston's tribute to his father, Walter Huston, who had been a big star back in his day, starring in *Gabriel Over the White House* in 1933 and *Dodsworth* in 1936, but who was a largely forgotten character actor by then. And Walter won the Oscar for Best Supporting Actor two years before his death.

Plus, remember, I was raised by unrepentant hippies, and this is the classic anticapitalist parable. The longer I pan for gold in this bootstrapper's pipe dream of mine (to mix some of the more robust metaphors available to me), the more I realize its moral speaks directly to me. And the better I see that when the bandits finally come for you, stinking badges is the last thing they're going to need. Bogart is the poster child for not giving in to your paranoia, because you'll start out gruff and misanthropic like Duke Mantee in *The Petrified Forest,* chart your own plummet like the gold-feverish Fred C. Dobbs here, and wind up a crippled, dissembling psychotic like Captain Queeg in *The Caine Mutiny.* Better to laugh.

4. Casablanca (1942)

Directed by Michael Curtiz

With Humphrey Bogart, Ingrid Bergman, Paul Henreid, Claude Rains, Conrad Veidt, Peter Lorre, Sydney Greenstreet, S. Z. Sakall, and Dooley Wilson

This is the film I always watch on New Year's Eve because it's the perfect movie, pure gold, spun largely by accident—by a journeyman director, with a borrowed cast, and without the slightest inkling it would outlive its time. It was almost made starring George Raft, Ann Sheridan or Hedy Lamarr, and Ronald Reagan or Joseph Cotten in the Paul Henreid role. The script was so late in coming that it was filmed in sequence—start to finish—which is almost unheard of in a day where everything was shot on a studio backlot, one set at a time.

Its ageless appeal can't be explained by the virtues of director Michael Curtiz's *Yankee Doodle Dandy,* co-writer Howard Koch's *Sergeant York,* co-writers the Epstein Brothers' *The Man Who Came to Dinner,* or Humphrey Bogart's *The Maltese Falcon*—all made either concurrently, right before, or right after. And it's almost impossible to watch without identifying with: I gave up a girlfriend once because she belonged with someone else; I walked off into a beautiful friendship with a vast network of spies; I had secret night battles to fight that she couldn't be any part of, against the Nazi menace of bad studios and the Vichy collaborateurs of soulless self-promoters. And my experience is by no means unusual. (See Allen, Woody; *Play It Again, Sam.*) Because Ingrid Bergman is the perfect woman—the Helen of Troy figure, the one you would fight wars for, or go your whole life carrying a torch for. This is why she is barely in the picture. Women like that are ideals; they are bottled memory and brazen desire—and undiluted purity. And they inspire the highest yearnings of the human spirit.

5. All the President's Men (1976)

Directed by Alan J. Pakula

With Robert Redford, Dustin Hoffman, Jason Robards, Jack Warden, and Hal Holbrook

I've already cited this as a source of inspiration for my forays into journalism. But it's more than that. It's William Goldman at his best, probably the greatest working screenwriter, who took thousands of pages of Watergate transcripts and hundreds of spurious tell-alls jockeying for historical position and reduced it all to 138 minutes of crisp, clean dialogue. Think of how much of what we believe about Watergate comes directly from this movie. "Forget the myths the media's created about the White House. The truth is, these are not very bright guys, and things got out of hand." "You're missing the big picture: Look who they wanted to run against." "It seems thin; get another source." "Follow the money."

But for me, it's not the crusaders Woodward and Bernstein that most inspired me—even though they launched an entire generation of journalists (and could stand to launch another). It's Hal Holbrook as Deep Throat: an extremely reluctant whistle-blower, who hates the position he's in, but not as much as he hates what he sees all around him. He has to be careful what he tells them because he loves the system, and doesn't want to see it destroyed for all time. He's the ultimate patriot. I recognize this in the thousands of invisible sources I cultivate on my Web site. For the most part, these are people who love film and want to celebrate it, and they're outraged— like Tommy Lee Jones in *Jackson County Jail*—to have to sit there and watch from the next cell over, while it's being raped. Much of what goes on behind the scenes—the test-screening process foremost among it—is the film world equivalent of ratfucking: the dirty little secret no one talks about; the cancer on the presidency. And the people who fight it are the modern whistle-blowers. For my money, they're patriots as well.

6. It's a Wonderful Life (1946)

Directed by Frank Capra

With James Stewart, Donna Reed, Thomas Mitchell, and Lionel Barrymore

It's a Wonderful Life is like the *Boy Scout Manual* of optimism. No matter what tight corner you find yourself in or natural disaster you're up against—drought, starvation, snakebite, third-degree burns, financial panic, spiritual despondency—this will show you the way out of it. It's a primer on moral constancy, on why you should try and do good: because you will never know the extent of your influence. George Bailey wanted to be an adventurer; he wanted to travel the world. And when his calling came, it was duty that made him rise to the challenge. It's about getting the life you didn't know you wanted, but that you wanted all along. Because whose life ever works out according to plan? When I started the Web site, I figured someone would see my animation and hire me as an animator. Or someone would read my creative writings about my crazy life and hire me as a writer. But that's not how destiny works. Life's rewards are Zuzu's petals—the artifacts we forget we've collected, but that accidentally remind us why we're alive.

7. Pinocchio (1940)

Directed by Hamilton Luske and Ben Sharpsteen

With the voices of Dickie Jones, Christian Rub, Cliff Edwards, Evelyn Venable, Walter Catlett, and Frankie Darro

This is *The Odyssey,* with a vagabond sentient insect as the Greek chorus, for seven-year-olds of all ages. Pinocchio's only wish is to be a normal boy, and for this he is first validated with status and privilege by the Blue Fairy, then sold into slavery by feral carpetbaggers, imprisoned by the ways of the flesh on Pleasure Island, remade in the image of an ass, castigated and shamed as a liar, virtually drowned, and exiled to the digestive tract of a whale. And he returns home, prodigally, as the product of those experiences. It's a testament to self-actualization that no self-help guide can even touch. It's the best animated film ever, the best of the Disney stable, and single-handedly inspired the career of Steven Spielberg. And the best part is, as long as you have access to it, *Pinocchio* is perpetual childhood.

8. Citizen Kane (1941)

Directed by Orson Welles

With Orson Welles, Joseph Cotten, Everett Sloane, Dorothy Comingore, and Ray Collins

There are a million reasons to like *Citizen Kane*: For its technical innovations in cinematography and sound, which were largely appropriated from theater and radio, respectively. For its politics, both globally and locally—challenging a titan of public opinion, and then barely escaping the backroom deal among studio moguls that would have bonfired the negative. (George J. Schaeffer, the head of RKO studios, was offered $842,000, raised from MGM head Louis B. Mayer and the other studio heads, to burn the negative, out of fear of how newspaper publisher William Randolph Hearst might respond to this lightly fictionalized version of him. Amazingly, Schaeffer refused, even though the Hearst backlash effectively killed the film in the marketplace. It's important to note that the film's bold political stand was as much out of an adolescent distaste for authority as anything else.)

It can be championed for its clash of world views, contributed by the brash young dilettante (Welles) and the world-weary cynic (writer Herman J. Mankiewicz), and the eternal bickering between the two over which world view ultimately wins out. It can be embraced for its brazen modernism—not just the circular, crosscut structure, or the self-reflexive trickery that seems there mainly to entertain the director through every scene, but its entire attitude—the playful, endlessly inventive glee that overrides even the most morose subject matter. And of course, it's the best electric train set in the world, with the added caveat that the most fun thing you can do with an electric train set is to run the trains headlong into one another at the highest possible speed, and let someone else cart away the wreckage.

Plus, it is impossible at this late date to separate the plights of Kane and Welles—complicated by screenwriter Mankiewicz's back-alley revenge by loading it down with Welles's own biography, and Welles's bigger revenge by helplessly playing it up to encourage his own mythology. And it sends you out into the night with a moral: Never let go of your Rosebud. (The same moral as *It's a Wonderful Life*—literally.) For me, it's the house where I grew up in Austin. For you, it's something else.

Welles was wrong: Rosebud isn't just some dimebook Freud he grabbed at when he was stuck for an ending. It's the difference between pathos and bathos: the latter, you're outside looking in, protected by your clinical pity; the former, you're inside, and it's your pain as well. *Citizen Kane* is the biography of Old Man Potter. And *It's a Wonderful Life* is *Citizen Kane* if he'd gone back for his sled. The ending is the whole point. Except what no one asks is: Why did he save any of that stuff? Why did he keep the snowglobe in his room? Why did he bring a castle over brick by brick from Europe? "The loot of the world." Greed? Overcompensation? Inadequacy? I prefer to think it's because objects have power. And Kane was a collector—of stories, of people, and of things. Because things *are* their stories—just like people. That's the whole secret of being a collector. Take a look around my room.

9. Barbarella (1968)

Directed by Roger Vadim

With Jane Fonda, John Phillip Law, Anita Pallenberg, Milo O'Shea, David Hemmings, Marcel Marceau, Claude Dauphin, and Ugo Tognazzi

Not only is this adapted from a French comic book, not only is it incredibly sexy (especially to a seven-year-old), but it has all these things that have found their way into my personal mythology. Like the Matmos—that big evil thing that swallows objects. Can't find your car keys? Matmos got them. Where do your socks go in the laundry? Matmos swallows them. Or dolls with razor-sharp teeth that try to eat you.

This is the film my mother loved when she was the person I like to remember, and hated after she became somebody else. I think it was my first foreign film; although it's in English, it's by a French director, with David Hemmings from *Blow-Up* and Ugo Tognazzi from *La Cage aux Folles* and Anita Pallenberg from *Performance* and Claude Dauphin from *Is Paris Burning?* and even Marcel Marceau. It was kind of a whirlwind tour of European cinema. The score is a glorified porno soundtrack. It's the ultimate fish-out-of-water movie, except that Jane Fonda discovers orgasms and not some quaint local custom. There's a blind angel named Pygar, played by the Love Machine himself, John Phillip Law, who can't fly until after the perfect woman has had sex with him. Because he has lost his muse. As far as metaphor goes, this is incredibly powerful to a preadolescent with a burgeoning sense of curiosity.

10. Dawn of the Dead (1978)

Directed by George Romero

With David Emge, Ken Foree, Scott Reiniger, Gaylen Ross, and Tom Savini

And finally, *Dawn of the Dead,* the second of the *Living Dead* trilogy, is one of my primal drive-in memories. I first saw it as a double-feature with *Scanners,* in a folding chair we always took with us, with a cooler of generic pop and ice-cold Baby Ruth bars at my feet. It takes the farmhouse and unrelenting existential terror from *The Night of the Living Dead* and transposes it ten years later to the consumer nirvana of a shopping mall and the self-reflexive gallows humor of planned obsolescence. "What are they doing? Why do they come here?" "Some kind of instinct, memory. What they used to do. This was an important place in their lives." People who criticize gore as mindless violence are really missing the point: The guys who do this stuff—George Romero, David Cronenberg, Wes Craven, John Carpenter, Sam Raimi, Tobe Hooper— are all extremely intelligent people, as often as not making social satire. This is proof.

Appendix B: My 10 Least Favorite Films of All Time

Lists of least favorite films are also subjective, but for different reasons. Because worst in terms of sheer ineptitude is both a doomed search, seeing as how 90 percent of all films that have ever been made have physically disintegrated, as well as a pointless one, since ineptitude is probably on the lower order of sins of filmmaking, all things considered. And high-profile bad films are rarely among the worst films you can think of: *Heaven's Gate* has found its core of defenders in its long form, years after being credited with destroying United Artists. *Hudson Hawk* has a scene four-fifths of the way through, with Richard E. Grant and Sandra Bernhard as a wacked-out Borgia-style brother-sister couple who touch tongues when they get excited, that's easily worth the price of a rental. Movies like *Waterworld* or *The Postman* or *Message in a Bottle* aren't terrible movies, they're just terrible for the amount of money that was spent to make them. Some people even called *Apocalypse Now* a disaster at the time of its release. Those people would be wrong.

For me, films are bad in terms of the heartbreak they inspire. A bad film that was always going to be bad is one thing, but a bad film that had the capacity for greatness is a tragedy, and so, infinitely more important to dissect. Something like *Batman & Robin* certainly isn't one of the worst films ever made: It enjoys a level of production values and craftsmanship associated with its budget and pedigree; it was the vision of a single director and not trampled by a studio; it stars a charismatic Robin and a Batman who's at least a nice guy. But as you watch it peel off from its appointed path, chart a trajectory that the audience in good conscience cannot follow along behind, it just becomes a shame. A tragic misallocation of resources and imagination and anticipation by a built-in audience. *That's* why we should talk about it.

That said, here are my choices. I've tried to stick to modern titles, where the lessons learned are still fresh. (Or else '90s films just more naturally come to mind.)

1. Soldier (1998)

Directed by Paul Anderson
With Kurt Russell, Jason Scott Lee, Connie Nielsen, Michael Chiklis, and Gary Busey

You could make a 10 Worst list just of the movies of Jean-Claude Van Damme. Or Steven Seagal. Talentless *and* arrogant—everybody's favorite combination. But there is a place for smart action films—*Die Hard* invented it, and *Under Siege* proved it all over again. This is the reason that of all the films I've seen in the last ten years, *Soldier* has been the one to hurt the most. Because the original script (by David Webb Peoples, the secret weapon of both *Blade Runner* and *Unforgiven*) was fantastic. And Kurt Russell is a great action hero.

But then they gave it to Paul Anderson—not Paul Thomas Anderson from *Boogie Nights*; the *Mortal Kombat/Event Horizon* guy. Paul Anderson, who has now desecrated three straight films in the $70–$80 million range. Kurt Russell is the career soldier now considered obsolete who is banished to a garbage-dump planet inhabited by human scavengers. All well and good, until his buddies in the corps show up to sanitize the place, and him with it.

Yet everything about this film was trite and utterly predictable—like *Mad Max: Beyond Thunderdome,* but more fake-looking. Anderson took what was essentially *The Outlaw Josey Wales* in space—except now you couldn't pitch it as that, because nobody remembers Philip Kaufman's great script, so you'd say a younger, hipper *Unforgiven* done up *Blade Runner* style—and had it rewritten out of existence. The drafts just got blander and blander. This was going to set a new high-water mark for the post-apocalyptic Western.

When anyone talks about Michael Bay ushering in the death of movies with *Armageddon* or *The Rock* or now *Pearl Harbor,* I violently disagree, because Michael Bay manages to tell a coherent story. But I'm sympathetic, because what they mean is that MTV, flash-cut, ear-splitting style that is so much sound and fury signifying nothing. Paul Anderson is the guy they really have in mind.

2. Lost in Space (1998)

Directed by Stephen Hopkins

With William Hurt, Gary Oldman, Matt LeBlanc, Heather Graham, Mimi Rogers, and Lacey Chabert

I was a big supporter of this would-be New Line franchise at the script stage. After the finished product turned out a blended puree of half a dozen arbitrary tones, the blame naturally gravitated to Akiva Goldsman, whose scripts for *Batman Forever* and *Batman & Robin* (III and IV, chronologically) had all but toppled the biggest tentpole in modern movies (not then counting the twenty-years-after *Star Wars* revival).

The irony is that his script for this TV series update was just right—except that it was from the point of view of Will Robinson. It was the story of a boy genius who has to confront growing up with a father who's always at work, and who has to overachieve just to get anybody to pay attention to him. What happens to Mozart when no one realizes he's Mozart? Then they hired William Hurt as the father, who quickly became the center of attention, and then all the boy genius stuff fell by the wayside. Now it was Chekhov Beyond the Stars, with fine supporting players like Mimi Rogers and Gary Oldman and Heather Graham trying to stay out of Hurt's way while he "*ac-ted.*" And after the spine of it was gone, the leftover special effects were just a big windup toy that wouldn't shut up. You can't just shift points of view at will. Even thespians must know this.

3. Never Talk to Strangers (1995)

Directed by Peter Hall

With Rebecca De Mornay, Antonio Banderas, Dennis Miller, and Harry Dean Stanton

This was one of those films that Antonio Banderas made after he discovered the joys of a Hollywood paycheck, directed by a British ex–costume designer. I watched an hour and a half of it and I couldn't take it anymore, I walked out. And I hate to walk out of movies. It's a would-be sexy noir moderne in the *Body Heat* mold that stars Rebecca De Mornay. It wants desperately to be *Vertigo,* except imagine *Vertigo* if James Stewart and Kim Novak had fucked through a chain-link fence.

Rebecca De Mornay is a police psychiatrist specializing in MPD (multiple personality disorder) with no time for a love life. Until she meets Latin heartthrob Banderas, who sweeps her up on his Harley. Then all these weird stalker things start happening to her. Is it him? The movie asks this same question for two hours. So I went back and rented it, just to say I'd seen it. And you know how it ends? Here's a spoiler for you: Rebecca De Mornay is *stalking herself!* On account of she was abused as a child, and she's got a whole bunch of personalities slugging it out for control of her psyche.

What makes this movie so terrible is not that it's such a goofy premise, but that Banderas—maybe the most compelling screen presence to come along in a decade—and De Mornay, a credible, competent actress whose talent was always obscured by her beauty, are trapped inside it. And no matter how powerfully they act, there's no way out of it for them. That's what makes it tragic. I don't understand how films like this get made. Why do actors sign on to them? Is it literally the money? And yet good movies don't cost any more to make than bad ones do. And for every bad movie that someone like Anthony Hopkins or Michael Caine spends three months on— good actors who should know better—there are other, better, more redeeming movies out there that will never see the light of a projector bulb. Talent is a terrible thing to waste.

4. Blues Brothers 2000 (1998)

Directed by John Landis

With Dan Aykroyd, John Goodman, Joe Morton, and Nia Peeples

How disappointing was this? With live musical performances by B. B. King, Junior Wells and Lonnie Brooks, James Brown, Aretha Franklin, and an all-star band with Eric Clapton, Steve Winwood, and a million others, this should have been Landis back in form, after *The Stupids* and *Beverly Hills Cop III* and the Stallone "comedy" *Oscar.* But then they recast the Belushi part with John Goodman *and* Joe Morton—out of political correctness, I guess. You feel the plot creak as Aykroyd strains to carry the film all by himself. And then they moved the shoot from Chicago to Toronto—as in, "Sweet Home Toronto." Never mind that Chicago was the unspoken third Blues Brother in the original. Or that these guys had grown up there, met there, started in Second City there. And the meager second unit they shot in Chicago didn't do the trick. *The Matrix* was shot in Sydney, Australia, and still managed to get the Chicago street names and locations right. What exactly was these people's problem? And now Aretha has a BMW dealership; and now James Brown performs in a perfectly integrated church. Just everything about it seemed sanitized and compromised and politically correct. It was even rushed into the theaters in 1998, and yet it's called *Blues Brothers 2000.* I'm glad they had a good time, and I personally like Landis a lot. But they should have stopped with the House of Blues chain.

5. An American Werewolf in Paris (1997)

Directed by Anthony Waller
With Tom Everett Scott and Julie Delpy

And speaking of remaking John Landis classics: Why not just remake *An American Werewolf in London* without Landis altogether? And do it without Rick Baker, whose ground-breaking makeup special effects set the precedent for the last great era of werewolf films. And then completely abandon the conceit of the werewolf's past victims haunting him forever after. They completely deracinated it—they took all of the wildness out of the premise. Turning into a werewolf is one of the worst things that can happen to you in the movies—ask Lon Chaney Jr.: You break out in a sweat, you weep, you remember horrible things you've done that you're about to do again, and there's nothing you can do to stop it.

There are plenty of great things you can do to modernize the horror classics: You can have werewolves as New Age Malibu cultists like in John Sayles and Joe Dante's *The Howling,* werewolves as Navajo shapeshifters like in Whitley Strieber and Michael Wadleigh's *Wolfen,* werewolves as Hell's Angels like in Scott Rosenberg's spec script *Bad Moon Rising*; you can have vampires as Eurotrash like in Whitley Strieber and Tony Scott's *The Hunger,* vampires as East Village junkies like in Larry Fessenden's *Habit,* Michael Almereyda's *Nadja,* and Abel Ferrara's *The Addiction,* or vampires as the Manson Family like in Kathryn Bigelow and Eric Red's *Near Dark.* But here, turning into a werewolf is like taking a businessman's lunch. It's all computer graphics—crisp, airbrushed, streamlined. Nothing could be simpler. They've completely removed all the anxiety from it. What if Gene Kelly and Leslie Caron in

An American in Paris suddenly turned into flesh-eating feral creatures of the night? I think it would still have to be better than this tepid drivel.

6. The Last Action Hero (1993)

Directed by John McTiernan

With Arnold Schwarzenegger, F. Murray Abraham, Art Carney, Charles Dance, Frank McRae, and Tom Noonan

This is one of those films with so many cool things tossed in the mix that some of it was bound to stick: the "Hamlet Takes Out the Trash" cartoon, William Goldman's wondrous "Golden Ticket" scene, Tom Noonan's laconic Jack the Hipster–style slasher, the actors meeting their characters at the Oscars, and especially Maria Shriver manhandling Arnold past the cameras.

But it's historically seen as an unseasoned script by a couple of yahoos (Zak Penn and Adam Leff) that the Guber-Peters Sony regime bought for $2 million of someone else's money and then banked on long after they should have known better. Whereas in reality, the original script had none of the problems the film did. The studio just kept tallying up endless rewrites (from Shane Black and others), and what they were left with was an archaeological dig, with all the competing layers exposed to the elements.

But then they committed what to my mind is a cardinal sin: They set something up in the body of the film with amazing dramatic possibilities, which anyone watching could imagine, and then they failed to pay it off. After the young protagonist has landed in the world of a movie and dragged his favorite action hero back out again—*Sherlock, Jr.* or *Pur-*

ple Rose of Cairo style—Tom Noonan, as the villain, follows suit. Noonan is sitting in a modern-day restaurant in the real world, circling movie ads in the newspaper. He has *Jason and the Argonauts* circled, and *Bram Stoker's Dracula*. We know that he has the power to release these characters from the screen with a magic golden ticket, and we know that *these are all Columbia films!* Now suddenly there's the possibility of all these great movie villains coming to life, and the kid, Danny, will be the only one who will know how to defeat them. Because he's already a movie geek.

He'll know that Talos from *Jason and the Argonauts* has a spigot in his ankle, and if you turn it, all the bronze will run out of him. He'll know how to defeat Dracula, because he's seen a million vampire films. This could be brilliant! And they totally let it lie there. Instead, they bring back the same villain that Schwarzenegger has already defeated once in the movie, put him in exactly the same situation, and—surprise!—he's defeated all over again.

So I asked Zak Penn about it. He told me this wasn't in the original script, so that whoever added it was probably long gone by the time it became a possible ending. Which is exactly what happens when you commission fifty-seven rewrites. Serves them right.

7. The Client (1994)

Directed by Joel Schumacher

With Susan Sarandon, Tommy Lee Jones, Brad Renfro, Mary-Louise Parker, and Anthony La-Paglia

If you have to have John Grisham films, the best way to approach them is to hire smart actors, have them play smart characters, and try not to saddle them with "movie logic," which is where a character acts in a way that is counterintuitive just to advance the plot. There's a noise in the basement, something is down in the basement, so let's go down to the basement and see if we're right. That stuff happens constantly in movies, especially movies involving kids, and it always takes me out of the film. *The Client* is rather remarkable in that the entire first half is refreshingly free of those kind of gaffes, and then at the halfway point, all of these smart characters just turn to jelly in terms of their motivation.

It's the exact opposite of *The Silence of the Lambs,* where smart characters make smart decisions and are outwitted regardless by someone all that much smarter. Susan Sarandon and Brad Renfro and Tommy Lee Jones—these are all smart people, onscreen and off. So having them gallivanting around looking for a dead body, having Tommy Lee Jones as the press-addicted D.A. declare the movie solved once they find the body, even though he hasn't technically seen it yet, and to turn everybody into wide-eyed idiots just to make someone's job easier in moving the scenery around is a full-on travesty.

8. The Bonfire of the Vanities (1990)

Directed by Brian De Palma

With Tom Hanks, Bruce Willis, Melanie Griffith, Kim Cattrall, and Morgan Freeman

Here was a book by one of the great writers of his generation, who had waited twenty years to attempt his first novel, and one that read so fast you could barely turn the pages in time to keep up. Where there is absolutely no friction to slow you down. It had an able and agreeable cast; Bruce Willis was just starting to play against type to offset the *Die Hard* onus, and Tom Hanks has been in probably fifteen bad films and *never* given a bad performance. *Turner and Hooch,* they partner him with a dog, and still he manages some bravura monologues. And for all the heat De Palma has taken for retreading Hitchcock, he did direct *Scarface,* and he did direct *Phantom of the Paradise.* So how could the result be so miraculously unwatchable?

My opinion is that the book was described to De Palma as a comedy—as in comedy of manners, Jane Austen, the Brontës, Balzac—and he took the studios at their word. So what should be structured as an X-ray of the times is played for actual laughs. Gags, slapstick, schtick. The result is a Macy's-size gas-filled balloon that gets tangled in its guidewires on launch, causing it to blow around on the ground and bump into things helplessly. There's still all the egotism and institutional excess to be found in *The Devil's Candy, Wall Street Journal* reporter Julie Salamon's published on-set account of this accident in the making. But before that, there was this.

9. Hook (1991)

Directed by Steven Spielberg

With Dustin Hoffman, Robin Williams, Julia Roberts, Bob Hoskins, and Maggie Smith

Bad films disappoint you. If the anticipation is too great—*The Phantom Menace,* maybe; or *Eyes Wide Shut*—they may physically make you upset. But *Hook* broke my heart.

Name a subject matter and a director more perfect for each other than Steven Spielberg and Peter Pan as a grown-up. This is the stuff that dreams are made of. It's the film he was in preparation for his whole life. Except—look at every film up to *E.T.,* they're positively infused with the joy and wonder of filmmaking. But every film after *E.T.,* they're all calculating how to squeeze out one more tear, thrill, flutter of the heart. And this is the one that finally proved it.

When you watch *Raiders of the Lost Ark,* you don't see a film made for the '80s, you see a film made for all time, using the best of the '30s, '40s, '50s. But when you watch *Hook,* you see a movie made for the '90s. It appeals to skateboard culture, hip-hop culture, rap kids. The Lost Boys all have punk hairdos. It traffics in the latest fads. This is the surest way to certain death. This represents an enormous crisis of confidence. We need to see Never-Never Land and we never really did. We never got to see the Indians, any of that. And Spielberg doesn't understand that you can't kill someone in Never-Never Land. Nobody can die in Never-Never Land. It's a fantasy world.

The film was corrupt at the script level. It's what I call a "Where's Waldo?" film, where you cast celebrities for no other reason than to have a name cast, like Glenn Close as a pirate or Phil Collins as Inspector Good. Or Julia Roberts as Tinkerbell, for that matter. That was nothing but a vanity decision. And then Peter Pan as a kid suddenly becomes simpleminded. It was just a complete and utter sellout.

A story I heard, which may only be apocryphal, is that the first time Spielberg screened the film in Dallas, he realized what he had done, and he went and sat in the limo and cried. He knew there was nothing he could do. And what did he do next? He made *Jurassic Park,* then the highest-grossing film of all time, to prove he still had the magic, and then he went right into *Schindler's List,* the one film he had threatened to make for a decade and never had the courage to pull the trigger on. I truly think that was his crucible; that's when he had to face his dark night of the soul. But it doesn't lessen the pain of watching it.

10. Miscellaneous

Directed by and starring (Name Withheld by Request)

Much is made in *The Golden Turkey Awards* and elsewhere about *Plan 9 from Outer Space* or *Glen or Glenda?*, when in fact the Ed Wood films are interesting, if for no other reason than because we know his biography now. Like Trace Beaulieu from *Mystery Science Theater 3000* has claimed, "*Plan 9 from Outer Space* gets all the publicity, but I think the true connoisseur will agree that your *Creeping Horror*s, your *Manos, the Hands of Fate*s, your *The Castle of Fu Manchu*s really do go that extra distance." My contribution to this sacred list shall be threefold: *Meteor Monster, The Milpitas Monster,* and *Escape to Athena.*

In *Meteor Monster* (1957), (1) There is no meteor, and (2) There is no monster. It's about a hobo with a lot of hair who is a Peeping Tom. At this level, a film becomes pure joy, because it is nothing but a test of stamina. *Tromeo and Juliet* really wants to be *Meteor Monster,* but it simply isn't bad enough. *The Milpitas Monster* (1975) is the only film ever made by a high school that was printed in Technicolor, and features a forty-foot monster made of garbage. And *Escape to Athena* (1979), directed by George P. Cosmatos, later of *Rambo, Tombstone,* and *Leviathan* fame, is an ensemble spy film with Sonny Bono, Roger Moore, and Jim Brown, which includes a plot device where Sonny Bono has to piss in the Nazis' soup to give them dysentery so they can escape.

These films are awful, but in a gloriously awful way. A film like *Never Talk to Strangers* doesn't deserve to be watched all the way through. *Meteor Monster* is so bad, it challenges you. It slaps you in the face and says, "Watch me. I dare you. Are you still watching? I don't think you have what it takes." It's like a train wreck; you are powerless to take your eyes off it.

Of such stuff is character made.

Appendix C: The 10 Films I Would Most Like to See Made

In the world I come from—science fiction, fantasy, the pulps, comic superheroes, spectacle—there are any number of properties that would make great movies. And we are right at the dawn of the day when computer-generated technology is going to make such adaptations possible. Finally the process is being turned back over to animators instead of scientists or lab techs who understand code. And perhaps even more important, maybe the time has finally come when the classics of these genres can be approached with the respect that they and their fans deserve. We used to have John Huston around to adapt the great works of literature—*Moby Dick* (with a script by Ray Bradbury), Flannery O'Connor's *Wise Blood,* Malcolm Lowry's *Under the Volcano,* James Joyce's "The Dead." This same level of care ought to be taken with the modern classics—regardless of the genre.

Because if you screw up your latest spec script, you're the only one who knows what it might have been. But if you screw up a superhero, or a treasured novel, or someone's life story, you're screwing up people's childhood dreams. And that's not something that should be done casually, or worse yet, through criminal negligence.

In no particular order, here are the movies I'd most like to see made.

1. Argonauts

By Alan McElroy

Just when Ray Harryhausen was hitting his stride in translating classical-scale spectacle to the screen, as with *Jason and the Argonauts,* he fell out of love with filmmaking. There's currently a project over at DreamWorks, not a remake, called *Argonauts,* that's kind of a hip contemporary way of looking at the same story. It's about a team of high-tech thieves who eventually launch an assault on Mount Olympus, where they battle all the great mythical creatures we remember from Ray Harryhausen movies: sea serpents, minotaurs, harpies, a cyclops—the whole superhuman crew. It has Spielberg and Tom Cruise's names all over it, even though those two insist on making *Minority Report* instead, which is kind of a less compelling sequel to *Total Recall.*

2. The Wizard of Oz

By L. Frank Baum

Everyone's clamoring for the next *Star Wars* series of franchise spectacles, with *The Lord of the Rings* being only the most recent. But why not return to the most obvious—L. Frank Baum's Oz series. The stumbling block is always the 1939 MGM version, but that's quickly overcome if you base it on the books. The version everyone knows is a '30s Technicolor musical that found a secondary resonance in the colors and chemicals of the '60s, and added pathos in the decline of its star, making it anachronistic twice over. None of this would be relevant to a remake.

For a clue to the direction it could go in, see *Return to Oz*, the one film ever directed by *Apocalypse Now* co-editor/*Touch of Evil* restorationist/sound designer genius Walter Murch. Less a film for kids than a film for people who remember being kids, it's suitably dark and thoroughly invokes a separate world. Come at the books from this angle, and you could have a franchise that would run virtually forever.

3. Ray Gunn

By Brad Bird

&

4. The Spirit

By Will Eisner

These are two PG-or-stronger animated features Brad Bird hopes to set up on the strength of the success of *Iron Giant*.

Ray Gunn is a PG-13 private-eye comedy, where the femme fatale is named "Venus Envy." *The Spirit* is based on the Will Eisner comic from the late '40s/early '50s.

Bird calls *Iron Giant* his halfway point to animation for grown-ups. *The Simpsons* and *King of the Hill* are as sophisticated as anything around. But the studios can't see past animation as a genre yet, when in reality it's a storytelling device, and a style of filmmaking like any other. With DreamWorks in the mix now, and with Disney's animated division trying to get a little more serious in its choice of subject matter, that might change. But whereas a $60 million animated feature like *Tarzan* might be made live-action at the same price, the more fanciful or logistically complex your subject matter becomes, that price will only escalate in the real world, whereas it stays fairly consistent in the realm of animated features. This ought to make certain subject matter increasingly attractive as animated epics.

5. John Carter of Mars

By Edgar Rice Burroughs

Great speculative fiction from the author of *Tarzan of the Apes* and *The Lost Continent.* Actually, this is part of a series of eleven novels, begun in 1912, including *The Princess of Mars, The Gods of Mars, The Warlord of Mars,* and other chronicles of the culture of "Barsoom" (as Mars styles itself), and a cowboy who suddenly finds himself set down in its midst. Various versions have languished in development for years, primarily because of cost—the last of which had a really excellent script. Some characters have four, five, or six arms; or are eight-legged beasts; or are tall, green, and antennaed; or lay eggs.

And the main character can leap forty-five feet because of the lack of gravity. One potential version coalesced around Tom Cruise as John Carter and Julia Roberts as the Princess of Mars. This could be a major event film.

6. The Sargasso Ogre

&

7. The Thousand-Headed Man

By Kenneth Robeson

Doc Savage was a series of pulps from the '30s and '40s. On occasion, it makes *Raiders of the Lost Ark* look like a walk in the park. George Pal (director of *The Time Machine*; *Atlantis, The Lost Continent*; and *Tom Thumb*) wrote a horribly campy version in 1975, called *Doc Savage: The Man of Bronze,* seemingly patterned after the *Batman* TV series in tone. Also, Doc Savage was played by Ron Ely, who was the '60s TV Tarzan. Like Indiana Jones, this can easily spawn an ongoing series. Series standouts include *The Sargasso Ogre* and *The Thousand-Headed Man.* Ron Howard and Brian Grazer were contemplating remaking the Michael Curtiz submarine thriller *The Sea Wolf* with Nicolas Cage. But that's already a near-perfect film starring Edward G. Robinson, John Garfield, and Ida Lupino. Meanwhile, *The Sargasso Ogre* is set in almost the exact same universe and has never been made. *The Thousand-Headed Man* is very creepy, and has a character who is totally covered with heads.

313

8. Tarzan of the Apes

By Edgar Rice Burroughs

Despite way too many attempts of late, no one has ever captured the horror of the *Tarzan* story yet. Casper Van Dien was all looks, Christopher Lambert basically annihilated the proposed Robert Towne version (much history and anthropology research, all jettisoned when Towne had to relinquish the project in exchange for finishing funds for *Personal Best*), and Disney's cartoon apeman is a scatological goofball. Johnny Weissmuller was great as a boy's adventure hero, but the Tarzan from the books, aside from being a member of the British landed gentry, is worshipped as a vengeful god by the natives. He would do things like fashion nooses out of vines, slip them down through the jungle canopy to where a column of tribesmen was violating his forbidden jungle kingdom, slip it around the neck of the last man in line and silently haul him to his death, then keep going until he had killed the whole line. He would put a lion in a full-nelson stranglehold and snap its neck. This could be as powerful a reinvention as the brooding *Dark Knight*–style *Batman*. And the books are perfectly structured so that if you just adapt them in series, the character follows a logical arc. There are intrigues and spies and not a single elephant's graveyard. Imagine a Tarzan film without an elephant's graveyard.

9. Medea

By Euripides

Imagine a Greek tragedy at the big Hollywood level. *Medea* is basically the sequel to *Jason and the Argonauts,* after Jason has relocated to Corinth as a hero and taken up with the daughter of the king, leaving Medea abandoned to raise his children. There have been several TV versions, a Pasolini version with Maria Callas, and a slavish Lars von Trier adaptation of an aborted silent script from the Danish master Carl Theodore Dreyer, similar in impulse to how Gus Van Sant remounted *Psycho.* There has never been an American studio version. But it's one of the great classical tragedies, every bit as complex and powerful as anything that has been written in the last 3,000 years. Pitch it as *Fatal Attraction,* except Anne Archer goes crazy. Work out the toy and Taco Bell tie-ins later. I could see Spielberg mounting *Jason and the Argonauts* as a vast sweeping CGI epic, which he really wants to do, and then following it up with *Medea* as an intense psychological profile. It would be fantastic.

10. Stranger in a Strange Land

By Robert Heinlein

You think Heinlein's *Starship Troopers* was right-wing fascist propaganda? Then you'll think *Stranger in a Strange Land* is a brilliant left-wing allegory. This story of Michael Valentine Smith, descendant of the first manned mission to Mars, who was raised by Martians and returns to Earth as a New Age messiah, virtually screams out for Robert Zemeckis to direct with Tom Hanks in the lead. And he actually has the rights. It's not even all that much science fiction—more like *The Man Who Fell to Earth,* but with a *Forrest Gump*–like savant at the center. It's one of the great unmade films, and as such, it belongs to the world. It's there for any working filmmaker to figure out how to solve.

But wait—that's not all.

The Crowded Room is a fantastic Todd Graff script about a guy with thirty-seven distinct personalities that was once intended for James Cameron and John Cusack. Probably too smart to ever get made . . . The *Houdini* script is really good. It's written by Stephen J. Rivele and Christopher Wilkinson, the guys who wrote *Nixon* for Oliver Stone, but then it was abandoned by Paul Verhoeven so he could make *The Hollow Man,* his invisible rapist movie . . . *The List of Seven* is a fantastic script from Guillermo del Toro, adapted from a Mark Frost novel about Sherlock Holmes author Arthur Conan Doyle and a secret satanic cabal modeled on the nineteenth-century London-based Hellfire Club . . . Danny Elfman has a musical called *Little Demons,* about three kids who kill people in a carnival so their souls can serve as handmaidens to their mother in heaven. His brother's *Forbidden Zone* (for which he wrote the music and starred as Satan) is still one of the great overlooked shoestring independents . . . *My Life As a Girl* is a really wonderful script, kind of an interior-perspective *Ally McBeal,* only more grounded, with really cool male supporting characters like a Ben Kingsley-as-Gandhi worshipper, a high school hard-on, and a pre-op transsexual. It's by Kim Krizan, who co-wrote *Before Sunrise* . . . *Needle in a Time Stack,* an original by George Huang, who did *Swimming with Sharks,* could be the single best time-travel story ever written . . . *Plastic Man* was written by *The Matrix*'s Wachowski Brothers from the DC comic. Every few years, either this or *Stretch Armstrong,* his rival rubber-limbed crusader, pulls ahead in the production schedules, and the other one gets tabled until the deal collapses. This script is really good, but it's set in a really heavy '40s noir, and I think too many of those *Dark City*–style movies bombed for this to get made . . . *Puppet Love and Mirth* is a script nobody's ever heard of, written by a fan up in New York, but I really loved it. A guy named Giuseppe Umberto Lovero, who writes under the name Joe Lovero. It's about this weird band of three outsiders who have to team up on a quest . . . And although I was griping about Ron Howard's *Sea Wolf* remake, the David Koepp script is really stellar . . . *Shadow Over Innsmith* has been a pet Stuart Gordon project for the last ten years or so, from an H. P. Lovecraft novel about a gothic New England town descended from fish people. A man follows his missing bride to a strange island. Horror ensues. The designs are amazing . . . *The Untitled Wolfgang Peterson Project* is really good—a true story of a ship that becomes ice-locked in the Arctic Circle, man against the elements, including all these unlikely threats like walrus attacks. Kind of *The Red Tent* without the European cofinancing . . . One of the things people always talk about is Terry Gilliam's *Watchmen* project, from the Alan Moore graphic novel. But there's little chance you could ever get it into two hours; it would have to be a $140 million miniseries . . . *WWIII* is a fantastic script over at Fox, a what-if by Jason Hightman, but maybe too realistic to make them comfortable with it . . . And for that matter, why can't we see Orson Welles's *Don Quixote*? Seven years ago, there was something billed as a finished version at the San Sebastian film festival. But then the Oja Kodar camp (his mistress) and the

Beatrice Welles camp (his daughter) started slinging injunctions at each other. Declare a truce, starting now. All monies are to be split down the middle. Make your peace, and I'll give you a million readers a day to tout whatever collaboration you want to announce. Let's see this one first, and then the first half of *The Deep,* with Laurence Harvey and Jeanne Moreau (from the same novel as *Dead Calm,* but all the stuff that happened back on the boat), and *The Dreamer* from Isaak Dinesen's *Seven Gothic Tales* and Welles's lost *Lear* and *Merchant of Venice* and *Filming Othello.* And then let's gear up to release *The Other Side of the Wind.* Beatrice Welles doesn't think anyone can approximate her father's editing style? I for one was glad they finally accorded *Touch of Evil* the respect it deserved, not to mention *Apocalypse Now Redux.* Let's give Walter Murch a call. We can make him final arbiter . . . And last, Michael Douglas is developing an unproduced Preston Sturges script (*Mr. Big in Littleville* aka *Nothing Doing,* written for Clark Gable); Stephen Frears made an unproduced pet Peckinpah project (*The Hi-Lo Country,* by *Wild Bunch* scripter Walon Green); and Charlie Matthau is reviving an unproduced story editor's favorite, *Tweedledum and Tweedledee,* from *Vertigo* scribe Alec Coppel (an unemployed actor lookalike sets out to ruin the actor's life because he can't get work).

Let's send an army of interns and readers into the archives and dig out all the undetected jewels still half-buried there. The raw material for the online broadband broadcast revolution is going to come from somewhere—if and when it finally happens. Let's shake out the libraries and clear the development slates—we've got a century of backlog to choose from. Then we'll all meet back here, fresh and relaxed, for the work ahead.

Deal?

About the Authors

HARRY KNOWLES is the CEO, editor in chief, and Head Geek of Ain't It Cool, Inc., a Web site dedicated to the world of film. Harry has been seen on television, featured in magazines, and heard on the radio for the past seven years talking about the movies. His favorite seat is third row center. He doesn't eat popcorn or slurp on a drink while watching movies. Contrary to popular belief, he is not a virgin—or so he professes. Harry is first and foremost a fan.

PAUL CULLUM is a writer for *L.A. Weekly* in Los Angeles and numerous other obscure publications throughout the world. He was managing editor of the late, lamented *Film Threat* magazine during its final print incarnation under the Larry Flynt aegis. Like Harry, he originally hails from Austin, Texas.

Award-winning investigative journalist MARK EBNER has covered Hollywood for dozens of publications, including *Spy, Details, Premiere,* and *New Times.* He lives in Venice, California, with his loving pit bulls, Roxie and Poorboy.